Books by Quintus Curtius

Translations:

Cornelius Nepos's Lives of the Great Commanders
Cicero's On Moral Ends
Cicero's On Duties
Sallust's Conspiracy of Catiline and War of Jugurtha

Essay Collections:

Digest
Thirty-Seven
Pantheon
Pathways

ABOUT THE AUTHOR

Quintus Curtius is the pen name of writer and translator George Thomas. He graduated from MIT in 1990 and served on active duty for a number of years as a US Marine Corps officer, with deployed service worldwide. After leaving active duty, he enrolled in law school and began to practice law after graduating in 1998. He resides in Overland Park, Kansas and travels frequently. He can be found at www.qcurtius.com.

TUSCULAN DISPUTATIONS

by
Marcus Tullius Cicero

A New Translation by Quintus Curtius

Tusculan Disputations

Cover art by James Seehafer

Printed in Charleston, South Carolina, USA

Published by Fortress of the Mind Publications

www.qcurtius.com

ISBN: 978-0-578-96804-9

View of Arpino (Arpinum), Cicero's hometown
(Courtesy of Gianni Di Poce)

Two busts of Cicero

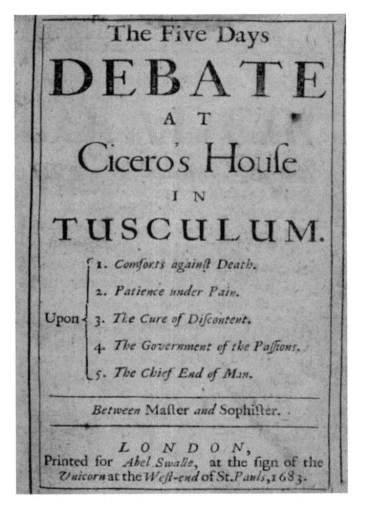

The Five Days

DEBATE

A T

Cicero's Houſe

I N

TUSCULUM.

Upon
1. *Comforts againſt Death.*
2. *Patience under Pain.*
3. *The Cure of Diſcontent.*
4. *The Government of the Paſſions.*
5. *The Chief End of Man.*

Between Maſter *and* Sophiſter.

L O N D O N,
Printed for *Abel Swalle,* at the ſign of the
Unicorn at the *Weſt-end* of St. *Pauls,* 1 6 8 3.

Title page of a 1683 English translation of Tusculan Disputations

Let man then contemplate the whole of nature in its lofty and full majesty, and let him avert his view from the lowly objects around him. Let him behold that brilliant light set like an eternal lamp to illuminate the universe. Let the earth seem to him like a point in comparison with the vast orbit described by that star.

Blaise Pascal, *Pensées*

TABLE OF CONTENTS

FOREWORD

Late in his life, the novelist Herman Melville posted a quote by Friedrich Schiller on the wall beside his heavy mahogany desk. It said, "Keep true to the dreams of thy youth."[1] Cicero in his later years would have approved of this sentiment. For by the time he began to write the *Tusculan Disputations* in 45 B.C., his youthful dreams were among his few remaining consolations.

Cicero's world lay in ruins, and his list of heartaches was long. The republican institutions he had worked all his life to support were wrecked beyond repair, having long since been dashed against the jagged rocks of factionalism and civil war. His worst fear—the rise of a charismatic authoritarian leader—had now materialized in the form of the victorious and popular Caesar. Historical events had overwhelmed him, and he found it difficult to adapt to the tenor of the times. Cicero's personal life had also devolved into a succession of crippling sorrows. His marriages to Terentia and the much younger Publilia had been failures. When his beloved daughter Tullia died unexpectedly in 45 B.C., the old consul was so grief-stricken that he nearly suffered a mental breakdown.

He was in his early sixties, and he was exhausted. The closing words of the *Tusculans*[2] make no effort to hide the author's state of mind: "I cannot easily judge how useful my efforts will be to others. Nevertheless, for the grim sufferings and various adversities that surround me completely, no other source of relief could have been devised."[3] Philosophy, which he had studied in Greece as a young man and had continued to love all his life, came to his rescue. It

---

[1] Laurie Robertson-Lorant, *Melville: A Biography*, New York: Clarkson Potter (1996), p. 565.
[2] This is the shortened name (*Tusculanae*) used by the ancient writers (Priscian, Nonius, Tertullian's *Apol.* 50, etc.).
[3] V.41.

soothed his restless temperament, gave him strength of purpose, and provided unyielding support in his hour of need.

In all probability Cicero began composing the *Tusculans* in the latter half of 45 B.C. (after completing *On Moral Ends*) and finished it early in the following year.[4] Comments in his other works point to this conclusion.[5] We may speculate that it was completed before the assassination of Caesar in 44 B.C. Cicero's text makes no mention of Caesar's death, and it is unlikely he would have passed over without comment an event of such importance. The work was intended for the general public. It is structured as a series of expository dialogues that take place during five days at Cicero's villa at Tusculum (now the town of Frascati near Rome). Cicero dedicated the composition to his friend Marcus Junius Brutus, the same Brutus to whom he had inscribed *On Moral Ends* and several other works. Tutored by his maternal uncle Cato, Brutus had long been a student of philosophical studies.

One of the goals Cicero had for the *Tusculans* was to give the average Roman an acquaintance with the beauty and profound significance of moral philosophy. "For if I have been useful to my fellow citizens during my political career," he announces, "my hope is that I may likewise prove useful to them, if possible, in my retirement."[6] The five books of the *Tusculans* deal with questions that are just as essential in the modern era as they were in Cicero's day. The first book discusses the fear of death; the second, enduring pain; the third, the management of anxiety and distress; the fourth, the various other disorders of the mind; and the fifth, whether virtue alone is sufficient for leading a happy life. What questions in life could be more important than these?

The *Tusculans* is a less technical work than *On Moral Ends*, and covers a much broader range of topics than *On Duties*. Although there is a subtle unity and organization to the treatise, Cicero does not feel bound to follow a rigid set of didactic formulas. The tone is relaxed, intimate, and yet commanding. Someone suggests a topic for discussion and offers his view; Cicero then attempts to rebut that view.

---

[4] A comment in V.11 of the *Tusculans* indicates that *On Moral Ends* was finished.
[5] *Academica* II.2, *On Moral Ends* V.11, and *On Divination* II.1.
[6] I.3.

We do not know the identities of the interlocutors in the dialogues, but they do not seem to be Cicero's peers, as were the speakers in *On Moral Ends*. As an older man with considerable experience in politics and law, Cicero enjoyed being surrounded by young men of good character whom he could instruct in philosophy. It seems he held at his villa what we might today call "private seminars" for select students. In the mornings the attendees received instruction in rhetoric, then later in the day spent time at the *academia* where philosophical questions were discussed.[7]

Although each of the five books of the *Tusculans* deals with a discrete topic, there is a common theme pulsing through the work, centered on the question of how to live a happy life. What principles form the basis of the happy life? How should we go about acquiring and implementing these principles? The fact that Cicero was able to focus his mind on such profound human questions while mired in extreme personal grief says a great deal about his character and intellect. The reader of the *Tusculan Disputations* is carried along not just by the nobility of the ideas, but by the striking grandeur and loftiness of the language. It remains one of the greatest and most accessible works of Western philosophy; and, in raw honesty, depth of sentiment, and stylistic power, it would find no prose rival in Europe until the advent of Montaigne, Bacon, and Descartes.

For all of its compelling merits, the *Tusculans* has been relatively neglected by scholars in the modern era. As far as I can tell, the only complete English translation in print is that of J.E. King for the Loeb Series, which dates to 1927. Now almost a hundred years old, however, it is unavoidably dated; its language and syntax make it nearly inaccessible for the contemporary reader or student. There have been several partial translations of the *Tusculans* in recent decades, but the fact remains that until now no complete, annotated, modern translation of the text designed for the general reader has been available. This situation encouraged me to conclude early in 2020 that the time was ripe for a new and fully annotated translation of this neglected classic.

Why has the *Tusculan Disputations* been relatively overlooked? The answer, I think, has something to do with our modern era's discomfiture with what is termed "moral philosophy." I suspect many uninitiated readers are likely to wince at hearing the phrase.

---

[7] II.3.

Moral philosophy—so they think—smacks of preachiness, of stodgy rules and restrictions, of intimidating old men in marble statutes with wrinkled visages, wagging their fingers scoldingly at onlookers down the centuries. Perhaps we moderns have also grown too confident in the ability of our medical science and technology to alleviate the kind of existential distress that Cicero discusses. What can the wisdom of the ancients teach us about pain, fear, anxiety, and sorrow, when we can simply reach for another bottle of pills, anesthetize ourselves with more food and drink, or submerge our anxieties in mindless entertainments and frivolous distractions?

If those who hold these views were actually to open and read the *Tusculans*, they would quickly discover how mistaken they are. The book is an agonizingly honest personal testament written by a suffering man who was groping in the dark for answers that might save his sanity and his soul. What predicament could be more "modern" than this? Who among us is not looking for ways to alleviate the fear of death, to deal with pain, and to cope with anxiety and grief? Who among us has not wondered if virtue was truly necessary for living a happy life?

Moral philosophy, it turns out, has nothing to do with being lectured or scolded. It is, rather, a courageous attempt to make sense of the human condition, and to find techniques of coping with the world's heartless cruelties and injustices. After many generations of neglect, our era is rediscovering that Cicero's ideas on moral philosophy offer a fresh, relevant perspective on timeless problems, and provide a soothing antidote to the toxic stresses, pressures, and anxieties that modern consumerist society generates.

Let us say a few words on the art of translation. In his essay *On Translation*, the poet and scholar John Dryden suggested that translations fall into three general types. The first kind he called metaphrase, by which he meant a literal rendering of a work in a word-for-word equivalence. The second kind he called paraphrase, where "the author is kept in view by the translator, so as never to be lost, but his words are not so strictly followed as his sense." The third type he called "imitation," where the translator takes his own liberties with the text as he sees fit.

I reject out of hand Dryden's third category as not qualifying as a translation at all. True translations inevitably fall somewhere between the poles of metaphrase and paraphrase; and it is the translator's art to decide when and where to gravitate towards one pole or the other. The brilliant Wilhelm von Humboldt, in the introduction to his translation of Aeschylus's *Agamemnon*, offered these astute observations:

> The inability to attain the peculiar beauty of the original easily entices one to embellish [a translation] with foreign decoration, which as a rule simply produces a false coloring and a different tone…A translation cannot and should not be a commentary…Never expect that what is sublime, immense, and extraordinary in the original language will be easily and immediately comprehensible in the translation. Ease and clarity always remain virtues that a translator attains only with the utmost difficulty, and never though mere hard work and revision: they are due for the most part to fortuitous inspiration…[8]

His points are well taken. My own goal has always been to remain as faithful as possible to the words and ideas in Cicero's text, while at the same time being mindful of my responsibility to convey these words and ideas in an English idiom that is modern, accurate, and seasoned with Ciceronian flavorings. Judgment calls must inevitably be made. Not every complex Ciceronian sentence, for example, should be mechanically reproduced in a single English sentence if the result would sound absurd or clumsy. Perhaps Dryden said it best when he noted, "He [the translator] ought to possess himself entirely and perfectly comprehend the genius and sense of his author, the nature of the subject, and the terms of the art or subject treated of. And then he will express himself as justly, and with as much life, as if he wrote an original: whereas he who copies word for word loses all the spirit in the tedious transfusion."[9]

Textual presentation and formatting are underappreciated arts. In formatting the dialogues, I have opted for modern conventions

---

[8] Schulte, R. & Biguenet, J. (*ed.*) *Theories of Translation*, Chicago: Univ. of Chicago Press (1992), p. 59.
[9] *Id.* at 31.

in which each statement by a speaker begins with its own separate indented paragraph. This was the method used in my translation of *On Moral Ends* and the result proved to be very satisfactory. The reader can see who is saying what to whom, and can easily track the flow of discourse.

The footnotes in the text are designed to assist readers by identifying unfamiliar names, places, and terms. References to passages in the *Tusculans* are given by book (Roman numeral) and chapter (Arabic numeral). I have added a title page and frontispiece written in Latin so that readers might see the language used in a contemporary context. Illustrations have been included to provide visual refreshment, and to augment enjoyment of the text. They have been reproduced from several older reference works.[10]

The Latin text used was Tischer and Sorof's excellent 1884 critical edition (Tischer, G. & Sorof, G., *M. Tulii Ciceronis Tusculanarum Disputationum Ad M. Brutum Libri Quinque*, Berlin: Weidmannsche Buchhandlung (1884)). For the first book of the *Tusculans*, I also consulted Rockwood, F.E. (*ed.*), *M. Tulii Ciceronis Tusculanarum Disputationum Liber Primus Et Somnium Scipionis*, New York: Ginn and Company (1903).

Finally I would especially like to thank Dr. Michael Fontaine of Cornell University, who was an enthusiastic supporter of the project from the beginning. His unmatched erudition, patience, and irrepressible sense of humor for the past year and a half have been greatly appreciated. Gratitude is also owed to my friend Gianni Di Poce, who kindly allowed me to include several of his photographs of Arpino, Cicero's hometown. James Seehafer, as always, lent his artistic skills in the preparation of the cover art and was a consistent supporter from beginning to end.

I am also indebted to the many readers of my earlier translations for their helpful comments and recommendations, all of which I found insightful. A characteristic of any noble enterprise is the maximum effort that it demands; and I have taken to heart the poet Lucan's counsel when he said:

---

[10] These are: Baumeister, A. (*ed.*) *Denkmäler des Klassischen Alterums*, Munich: Druck & Verlag Von R. Oldenbourg (1889); J.C. Ridpath, *Cyclopedia of Universal History*, New York: Hunt & Eaton (1885); C.F. Horne (*ed.*), *Great Men and Famous Women*, New York: Selmar Hess (1894); Allen, J.R. (*ed.*), *The Reliquary and Illustrated Archaeologist, Vol. X*, London: Bemrose & Sons Ltd. (1904).

I beg you, do not hold back on what is needed;
Give to things their names and places,
And furnish a voice through which
Fate may speak to me.[11]

Quintus Curtius
(George Thomas)
Overland Park, Kansas
June 2021

---

[11] *Pharsalia* VI.773.

INTRODUCTION

1. Cicero And His Philosophy

Cicero cultivated an interest in philosophy from an early age. He was exposed to the teachings of Phaedrus the Epicurean and Philo of Larissa (a scholarch of the Platonic Academy) at Rome when he was nineteen. Later in life he spent time at Athens listening to the lectures of Zeno the Epicurean and Antiochus of Ascalon, who influenced him greatly. On the island of Rhodes he attended the lectures of Posidonius the Stoic. He even arranged for the Stoic philosopher Diodotus to take up residence in his own home as a personal tutor, an arrangement that lasted until the old sage's death in 59 B.C. These experiences were of course supplemented with a large amount of intensive reading, writing, and discussion.

The four major philosophical schools in Cicero's day were the Stoic, Epicurean, Peripatetic (Aristotelian), and Academic (Platonic). As we have noted in some of Cicero's other works, he had few good things to say about Epicureanism. He considered it corrupting and unsuitable for a serious man of affairs. He was offended by its materialism, its rejection of the eternity of the soul, and its insistence on naming "pleasure" as the highest good. His attitude towards the Peripatetics was more neutral, although this may be due to his relative unfamiliarity with their doctrines. Cicero has a great deal to say about the Stoics, however. While he disliked their pedantic logical formulations and rigid unwillingness to recognize different degrees of virtue, he generally held their ethics in high regard.

The Academic school he found most congenial to his tastes. In Cicero's day the school had changed significantly enough since Plato to be called the "New Academy," but there was still enough of the old Platonic spirit to retain his adherence. He shared the Academic belief in the permanence of the soul, the importance of virtue, and the necessity of Socratic discussion and debate. As a lawyer Cicero liked to argue ideas and weigh their relative merits; he saw no reason why he could not adopt or discard them eclectically as he saw fit. Skepticism seemed to him reasonable and practical. An honest investigator should, after considering the different possibilities, adopt the view that seemed most probable under the circumstances.

One of Cicero's greatest legacies was his understanding of the need to introduce Greek philosophy to a Latin-speaking audience. Because Greek philosophy is familiar to us today, it is perhaps difficult to appreciate the significance of this achievement. Before him there existed only rudimentary summaries of Greek philosophical ideas; he had to engineer new words, new ideas, and new ways of presenting unfamiliar concepts with intellectual rigor. He succeeded brilliantly, and his innovations provided the foundation for medieval philosophy's lexicon. Some unsympathetic critics have charged him with not being an "original" writer, in the sense that he is conveying the doctrines of others; but in composition, style, and presentation, his writings are marked by an extraordinary degree of originality. No one writes, argues, and presents ideas in the way Cicero does. Montaigne was correct in his assessment that Cicero will probably never be surpassed in eloquence.

His literary legacy is his enduring triumph, and we owe him a profound debt of gratitude. He genuinely believed in the sanctity of the institutions he spent his life serving; he possessed unshakeable faith in philosophy's power to train young minds, alleviate distress, and provide solace in old age; and he took seriously the obligation to transmit his knowledge to future generations. He was the last and the greatest of the old republic's idealists.

2. The Composition Of The *Tusculans*

Cicero is quite frank about his motives for composing the *Tusculans*. During his political career, he tells us at the beginning of book I, he had little time to devote to philosophical writing. Now that he was in forced retirement, he could concentrate his efforts on the subject he had loved all his life. His professional and personal bereavements had convinced him of the need to discuss, in an extended way, the most fundamental questions of human life: death, the immortality of the soul, pain and how to endure it, and whether virtue really was sufficient for leading a happy life. As we work our way through the flow of conversation in the *Tusculans*, we sense that the fundamental theme running through all five books is this: *how does one go about living a happy life?*

As stated in the Foreword, the premise of the book is simple. Cicero, along with a small group of friends or students, intends to spend five days discussing a variety of topics. A member of the group proposes a subject, gives his own view, and then surrenders the floor to Cicero, who states his own ideas at length. The letters *A* and *M* in the text mark the different interlocutors. The consensus among scholars is that *A* stands for *auditor* (listener), and *M* stands for *magister* (teacher). Cicero probably did not insert these markers himself; they seem to have been added by later copyists.

A much-debated question has been Cicero's original sources for the dialogues. Definitive answers will probably never be forthcoming. The text refers by name to a large number of philosophers, as well as to poetic and dramatic works of Greek and Latin literature. Cicero was an ardent bibliophile; he had not only his own books, but access to the collections of his wealthy friends. He was well-read in Greek and Latin literature, and apparently could recall a great deal of it from memory. It would not have been difficult for him to have by his side the works of nearly every name he mentions in the *Tusculans*.

3. Summary Of Book I: On Despising Death

The remainder of this introduction will review the subject matter of the five books of the *Tusculans*. A general acquaintance with the contents of each book will assist the reader in following the arguments in the text.

The first book is a well-constructed dialogue that sets the tone for the remaining four books. Cicero begins by explaining why he resumed his philosophical studies. The field of philosophy gives him a chance, he says, to render a worthwhile service to his countrymen. While the Greeks may have bested the Romans in literature, music, and art, the Romans have demonstrated their superiority in the masculine virtues.

It has been said that death is an evil, but this is not correct. The stories found in literature about the underworld are not based on fact. Death is not only *not* an evil, it is actually a blessing. If the soul dies with the body, then death is the end of all, and there is no suffering; but if the soul is immortal, then it returns to the original source from

21

where it came. The authorities of tradition and custom tell us that the soul is in fact immortal and returns to a higher region where it dwells forever: "And without doubt, things of much greater purity and clarity will be understood when the soul is freed from the body, and arrives at the destination to which it is transported by nature."[12] Even if the doctrines of Plato on the immortality of the soul happen to be mistaken, they are still greater and nobler than the demeaning materialism of the Epicureans. The greatness and power of the soul is also proved by man's intellectual achievements. It cannot be doubted that it possesses divine attributes. It is indivisible and therefore indestructible. Furthermore, anyone observing the workings of nature will not doubt that some supreme being oversees its operation.

The Stoics believe that the soul has a long life; but they do not believe it to be immortal. Yet even if the soul is mortal, death should not be seen as an evil, for all suffering would end in death. While death brings life's pleasures to an end, we often forget that it brings life's sufferings to an end, too. We should not pity those who die early or die young. Life is a blessing that may be revoked at any time. No one has any right to life with a guaranteed duration: "The hour will come. And whether you distance yourself from this fact, or whether you look forward to it, the time will come quickly. For time indeed flies by."[13] For this reason we must practice every virtue, for only virtue and greatness of soul can dignify our mortal existence.

Burial customs and funerary rites have no effect on the dead. Those who are wise and good will meet death with courage and dignity. A worthy life prepares the mind for this task. We should take note of the examples of those who faced death with fortitude: "Yet death may be confronted with the serenest state of mind when a waning life can find consolation in the glory it has gained for itself. Anyone who has fully performed the obligation of perfect virtue has not lived too briefly."[14]

In this sense, the wise and the good even welcome death. Death is therefore not an evil; this is true whether the soul is mortal or immortal. We should look upon death as a final refuge to be entered at the end of a journey. Indeed, it is something we should be grateful for: "Let us reflect that we have been released from prison, and unshackled from our chains, so that we may either return to the eternal

---

[12] I.20.
[13] I.31.
[14] I.45.

abode which clearly belongs to us, or be liberated from all sensation and worldly difficulties."[15] In all, the first book of the *Tusculans* is a persuasively crafted masterpiece of logic and argumentation. It could easily stand alone as a separate treatise.

4. Book II: On Bearing Pain

The subject discussed in the second book is pain. Is pain the greatest evil? After a brief introduction, Cicero begins his analysis of this question. The successors of Aristippus (i.e., the Cyrenaic philosophers) and the Epicureans have made it clear that they believe pain is the greatest evil. Cicero recoils from this idea, as pain is an unavoidable part of life. Learning to endure it is something every seeker of virtue must accept: "We must not ask whether pain is an evil; rather, we must fortify the soul in order to bear pain's burdens. The Stoics weave their petty syllogisms to explain why pain is not an evil, as if the issue can be clarified with verbal artifices instead of looking at the nature of the subject."[16]

On the other hand, Cicero also rejects the Stoic position, which occupies the opposite extreme. They believe pain should not be considered an evil at all. Clearly, this position is absurd and cannot be rationally defended. The Peripatetics have taken the most reasonable stance. Pain must be counted an evil, they say, but there are other evils that are worse than pain. We can train our minds and bodies to endure pain if we adopt the right techniques. Spartan youths, Roman soldiers, and others have trained their bodies to endure pain. These techniques include the study of wisdom, the practice of virtue, and the imitation of great men who were forced to bear sufferings. Many examples from history and literature point to the conclusion that even if pain is an evil, it is not the worst evil.

5. Book III: On The Unburdening Of Sorrow

The subject of the third book is the unburdening of sorrow, that is, the alleviation of mental distress. Two frequently encountered words in the *Tusculans* are *aegritudo* and *animus*. These words have multiple meanings, and context must determine which meaning is

---

[15] I.49.
[16] II.12.

most suitable. *Aegritudo* can mean sickness, anguish, mental distress, grief, sorrow, or anxiety. *Animus* can mean either soul or mind. We must remember that when Cicero uses the phrase *aegritudo animi* (anguish of mind), it can embrace a wider scope of mental distresses than its English translation might suggest. The oppressive emotions we call grief, anxiety, sorrow, distress, and anguish all fall under the same rich Latin word *aegritudo*.

Book III begins with eloquent observations on the origins of sicknesses of the soul, and on the nature of false glory. Philosophy is the medicine of the soul, and can be used to cure its ailments: "There surely exists a medicine for the soul—it is philosophy. We must seek its help not from the outside, as we do with bodily ailments. We must exert ourselves intensely, deploying all our efforts and powers, so that we can act as our *own* healers."[17] But is it the wise man's fate to suffer from mental distress? What exactly is *aegritudo*? Mental distress appears to be a disorder of the mind. The Stoics take the position that courage and mental anguish are not consistent with each other.

The wise man is not affected by such sorrow. Certain harmful emotions like anger and envy are forms of distress; somewhat incongruously, pity is a form of distress as well. Anxiety is the worst type of disorder of the mind. When we truly examine the question of anxiety, we find that anxiety is based on our own views and judgments. In other words, it is we who determine whether we feel anxiety. By anticipating the arrival of bad events, or by forming preconceived views about things, we create and nurture our own mental distresses. Cicero's discussion of anxiety and sorrow leads him to many astute psychological insights: "And just as pity is anxiety generated by someone else's adversities, so jealousy is anxiety provoked by someone else's good fortune. Therefore, he who is inclined to pity others is equally inclined to envy others."[18]

The Epicureans claim that the alleviation of anxiety can be found in shifting our attention to other matters. The Cyrenaics hold that the anticipation of the unknown (i.e., dread) is a cause of anxiety. The passage of time gradually reduces the oppressive burden of anxiety. The ultimate source of mental distress is found in the human mind, that is, in our own imagination. Our minds have a tendency to imagine unexpected problems are worse than they are: "Yet when you

---

[17] III.3.
[18] III.10. Many of Cicero's suggestions for the treatment of anxiety, sorrow, and melancholy have an unexpectedly modern tone.

carefully consider the true nature of unexpected events, you will discover without exception that all such events appear greater than they really are."[19] We voluntarily shoulder the burdens of anxiety and distress by our mistaken ways of thinking. Our own erroneous beliefs and judgments create and sustain anxieties. Some people believe they ought to feel distress, but the emotion serves no useful purpose. We should not get used to it as something natural.

6. Book IV: On The Other Disorders Of The Mind

The fourth book of the *Tusculans* continues and elaborates on the points presented in the third book. It contains many terms and definitions, which may seem to slow down the flow of the discussion. But pointing out the names and definitions of different emotional states helps us to think about nuances we may never have considered. Cicero begins by making the remarkable assertion that the philosophy of Pythagoras was influential in Rome's formative period. He then begins an examination of *perturbationes* (perturbations or disturbances) of the mind. The question to be refuted is: *the wise man does not appear to be free from all perturbations of the mind.*

But what are these mental perturbations? There are four of them: *aegritudo* (anxiety), *laetitia* (joy), *metus* (fear), and *libido* (desire). The basis of mental disorder is our own bad judgment, which is against nature and reason. Perturbation of the mind is essentially desire or hostility. There are differences between disorders of the body and disorders of the mind. Afflictions of the mind originate in our rejection of reason.

The wise man will not fall victim to such perturbations. This is because his mastery of virtue gives him the use of reason, and mental distress cannot flourish when reason is in control. The Peripatetics take the view that perturbations of the mind are expected and natural. The emotions of anger, lust, competitiveness, envy, and pity are examined. A man cannot be considered virtuous, according to the Stoics, unless he has freed himself from mental perturbations *and* the beliefs that produced such distresses.

But since these perturbations of the mind are powerful, how can they be eradicated? We can try to use reason to explain how the source of the disorder is not what it appears to be. Another way is to

---

[19] III.22.

explain the general futility of allowing oneself to be hounded by distresses. These suggestions may be difficult to implement in practice, since perturbations are emotional, not rational, and an afflicted person is unlikely to be convinced by appeals to reason. Love and anger are discussed. The ultimate conclusion is the same as what was pointed out in the third book: perturbations of the mind are matters of *choice*. We *allow* ourselves to be afflicted by them. And we do so because of our mistakes in properly judging things. Philosophy is the way to remove disorders of the mind.

7. Book V: On Whether Virtue Is Sufficient For Living A Happy Life

The fifth book unifies the topics raised in the preceding books. Like the first book, it is rich enough to form a separate treatise in its own right. The thesis to be disproven is this: "It does not seem to me that virtue is sufficient for living a happy life (*Non mihi videtur ad beate vivendum satis posse virtutem*)." Philosophy offers us a precious resource, but we often do not recognize its value or have faith in its conclusions. We are surrounded by confusion and error. "Sometimes," Cicero writes with a heavy heart, "I even begin to feel dismayed at the vulnerability and fragility of human beings."[20] Pythagoras compares a philosopher with someone who acts as a spectator at the Greek games. The earliest type of philosophy was natural philosophy. Before Socrates, philosophy confined itself to questions about the universe; Socrates's contribution was to bring it down from the clouds, and make it relevant to everyday life.

Antiochus says that virtue can make a man happy, but not completely happy. The Peripatetics under Theophrastus proceed from incorrect assumptions. The Epicureans are inconsistent: they make pleasure the chief good, but at the same time advocate temperance. Every living being, plant and animal, is designed to reach its highest natural state. Because man is gifted with the power of reason, he occupies the highest position. Whoever lacks nothing can be said to be happy. A truly happy man must not fear the loss of something, and courage that is mixed with fear is not true courage.

Grief and fear come from evils conjured up by the mind, while desire and pleasure come from goods conjured up by the mind. Moral

---

[20] V.1.

rectitude alone is good, and provides happiness. An external good cannot really be called a true good. The happy life must be dependent on virtue, and all analysis points to this conclusion. In fact, the happy life concentrates and congeals the virtues: "Yet this is impossible under any circumstance: the virtues cannot adhere together without a happy life, nor can a happy life be in harmony without the virtues."[21] Since vice makes life miserable, virtue clearly makes it happy. Some examples are provided of good and bad leaders.

Happiness is possible even in the midst of the most terrible sufferings. The wise man can be happy even if he lives in obscurity, is underappreciated, or finds himself exiled. Neither blindness nor deafness can prevent the wise man from being happy. We can choose to be miserable, or we can choose to seek a happy life. In the end, all of us must make a conscious decision between these alternatives. "As I see it, in life we should keep to the guiding principle that the Greeks apply at their dinner parties. It says, 'Let him either drink, or leave.'"[22] If the Epicureans believe that the wise man is always happy, the other schools should do the same. Clearly it is true that virtue itself is sufficient for living a happy life. Cicero closes book V by stating that philosophy has been a way for him to deal with his own sufferings.

This concludes our brief review of the five books of the *Tusculan Disputations*.

---

[21] V.28.
[22] V.41.

M. Tulii Ciceronis
Tusculanarum Disputationum
Ad Marcum Brutum
Libri Quinque

Ad Usum Scholae Accommodati

Continens argumenta philosophica quod dividuntur hoc modo:
Liber primus, qui est de contemnenda morte;
Liber secundus, qui est de tolerando dolore;
Liber tertius, qui est de lenienda aegritudine;
Liber quartus, qui est de reliquis animi perturbationibus;
Liber quintus, quo perdocetur virtutem se ipsa esse contentam
ad beate vivendum.
Additae sunt notae doctissimae, animadversiones, imagines,
et rerum nominumque index.
Quintus Curtius recensuit, ordinavit, et Anglice convertit.

EDITIO PRIMA

Carolopoli:
Anno 2021

Excudebat *Castellum Mentis* Typographus

Studiosis philosophiae et litterarum
hoc opusculum, gratissimi animi signum,
offert ac inscribit
auctor devinctissimus.

Ad rem iudicandam animis mentibusque nostris ducimur.

BOOK I

ON DESPISING DEATH

BOOK I

1. Now that I have finally been freed, or at least substantially freed, from the labors of legal defense work[23] and my responsibilities in the senate, I have once again turned my attention—mostly at your insistence, Brutus—back to those intellectual interests which, although ever-present in my mind, had at times been displaced by other priorities. After a long period of inactivity, I have now rekindled these studies. And since the rules and principles of all the arts that pertain to right living are found in the study of wisdom, which is called philosophy, it seemed to me appropriate to explain them in Latin.

I say this not because philosophy cannot be learned from Greek writers and instructors. But I have always believed that, in those fields they thought were worthy of sustained exertion, our people[24] have everywhere shown themselves to be wiser than the Greeks, either in discovering things for themselves, or in bettering what was received from Greek culture. We certainly uphold personal conduct, principles of life, and domestic and family matters better than they do, and with more refinement—and without doubt our ancestors established our republic with better institutions and laws.

What can I say about military affairs? In this field our countrymen have distinguished themselves in bravery, and even more so in discipline. With regard to things attained by nature, and not through books, neither the Greeks nor any other nation can be compared to our people. Where do we see in any other nation the kind of seriousness, constancy, greatness of soul, honesty, loyalty, and exceptional virtue in every field, that would merit a comparison with our ancestors?

In every branch of literature, Greek erudition outdistanced us: since there was no real challenge, winning was not difficult for them. While the oldest literary category among the Greeks is poetry—as Homer[25] and Hesiod[26] certainly lived before Rome was founded and

---

[23] Cicero preferred defense to prosecutorial work, seeing it as more challenging (*On Duties* II.49).

[24] I.e., the Romans.

[25] Homer's period of activity is contested, but he and Hesiod are generally considered Greece's oldest poets. Herodotus (II.53), writing around 440 B.C., says that his generation "is separated by no more than four hundred years from that of Homer and Hesiod." If so, this would place the poets roughly at 800 B.C.

[26] Hesiod of Ascra probably flourished between 750 B.C. and 650 B.C.

Archilochus[27] flourished during Romulus's reign—we began our poetic activity much later. Around five hundred and ten years after Rome's founding, Livius[28] produced a play on the Roman stage during the consulship of Caius Claudius (the son of Caecus) and Marcus Tuditanus in the year before Ennius's birth. And Ennius[29] was older than Plautus[30] and Naevius.[31]

2. After a good deal of time had passed, however, poets were either acknowledged or given a favorable reception by our people. Although the *Origines* claims that guests at dinner parties used to sing about the virtues of great men as a flutist played, a speech of Cato's makes it clear that this type of activity did not engender much respect. For in this speech he disapproves of Marcus Nobilior's[32] conduct in bringing poets into his province. (As is well-known, when Nobilior was consul he had taken the poet Ennius to Aetolia). Thus the less respect the poets received, the less effort was devoted to composing verses.

Nevertheless, those who distinguished themselves with superior talent in this literary form could compete with the poetic glory of the Greeks. Or should we think that if Fabius Pictor[33]—that noblest of men—had been given some positive recognition for his paintings, we would not have produced many artists like Polyclitus[34] and Parrhasius[35]? Recognition nurtures the arts, and everyone is roused to productive effort by the prospect of glory—but those endeavors tinged with public disfavor will inevitably remain uncultivated.

The Greeks believed that the highest learning could be found in the music of stringed instruments and the human voice. Thus Epaminondas,[36] in my view Greece's most significant figure, is said to

---

[27] Archilochus of Paros is supposed to have invented iambic verse. He flourished during the reign of Tullus Hostilius (673 B.C.—641 B.C.), according to Aulus Gellius (*Noct. Att.* XVII.21, citing Cornelius Nepos).

[28] Livius Andronicus (284 B.C.—c. 205 B.C.) was born at Tarentum and is said to have translated Homer's *Odyssey* into Latin. This and his play (produced around 240 B.C.) make him one of the first names in Latin literature.

[29] Ennius (239 B.C.—169 B.C.) is considered the father of Latin poetry.

[30] Titus Maccius Plautus (c. 254 B.C.—184 B.C.) is the earliest Latin dramatist whose works have survived.

[31] Gnaeus Naevius (c. 270 B.C.—c. 201 B.C.), and early Latin dramatist. His first play appeared around 235 B.C.

[32] Marcus Fulvius Nobilior was consul in 189 B.C, and appointed censor in 179 B.C.

[33] Caius Fabius Pictor ("The Painter") painted the Temple of Salus in 303 B.C.

[34] A sculptor from Argos in the Age of Pericles.

[35] A painter from Ephesus active in Athens around 400 B.C.

[36] The famous Theban general and statesman.

have been an admirable harpist, while Themistocles, many years before him, was considered poorly educated when he declined to play the lyre at formal dinners. Musicians consequently thrived in Greece, and everyone learned music; those untrained in the art were seen as poorly educated. With them the study of geometry carried tremendous prestige, and thus no one was accorded more respect than the mathematicians; but we ourselves have confined this discipline within the utilitarian boundaries of measuring and calculating.

3. We readily embraced the orator, however: not at first the educated type of orator, but the kind who was willing and ready. Only later was the refined orator accepted. It is said that Galba,[37] Africanus,[38] and Laelius[39] were learned men; and Cato, who predated them, was eager to grow his knowledge. Lepidus,[40] Carbo,[41] and the Gracchi[42] followed. Then came our own time, and with it the advent of such brilliant public speakers that little or no prestige was ceded to the Greeks. Until the present era, philosophy has been ignored: Latin letters have made no effort to reveal its secrets. Philosophy must be explored and raised to prominence by us. For if I have been useful to my fellow citizens during my political career, my hope is that I may likewise prove useful to them, if possible, in my retirement.

In this regard I must make even greater efforts, for it seems that there exists a good number of slapdash Latin books which—although composed by outstanding men—are products of uninformed pens.[43] It is possible for someone to think correctly, and yet be unable to convey such sentiments eloquently; but he who is incapable of organizing and explaining his thoughts in written form, and unable to engage the reader with a bit of allure, is someone who egregiously wastes both his spare time and his words. These authors read their

---

[37] Servius Sulpicius Galba was consul in 144 B.C.

[38] Scipio Africanus the Younger.

[39] Caius Laelius Sapiens (c. 188 B.C.—?) was consul in 140 B.C., and was a friend of Scipio's.

[40] Marcus Aemilius Lepidus was consul in 137 B.C.

[41] Caius Papirius Carbo was consul in 120 B.C.

[42] The Gracchus brothers, Tiberius and Caius, who both served as tribunes of the plebs before being assassinated by the conservative faction.

[43] Cicero does not name these authors, but some scholars believe he is referring to several popularizers of Epicureanism, specifically Caius Amafinius, Rabirius, and Caius Catius. He also criticizes these writers in his *Academics* (I.2). Their writings have not survived, so we cannot evaluate Cicero's views.

own books with their followers, and never manage to reach any outsiders except those who themselves want to be granted this same entitlement to write. So if I have earned acclaim in oratory through my past efforts, I will now, with even more diligence, reveal the nourishing wellsprings of philosophy, from which also flowed the inspiration for my public career.

4. Yet just as Aristotle (a man of unchallenged intellectual power, knowledge, and capabilities), who, when influenced by the fame of Isocrates's rhetoric, began like him to instruct the youth on how to speak and how to fuse wisdom and eloquence, so it is my intention not to give up my original dedication to the study of oratory, but to use it to advance the cause of this greater and richer art form. I have always believed that mature philosophical expression can handle the most crucial questions with eloquence and grace. And I dedicated myself with such intensity to this cause that I even tried to instruct others, as the Greeks do. Since I had some close friends staying with me recently in Tusculum after you had left, I made an effort to conduct this type of philosophical discussion. For just as I was occupied with professional declamation[44] earlier in my life—a job that no one else did for a longer time—so this is now for me an elderly declamation.[45]

I asked those present to propose any topic they wanted to hear debated. And I did indeed discuss whatever subject was raised, either while sitting or as I was walking around. I have collected in five books these expositions[46] (as the Greeks call them) that were the fruit of an equivalent number of days. The discussions were conducted in this way: when someone wanting a dialogue stated his position, I would then suggest a contrary view.

As you know, this is the time-honored Socratic method, where one adopts an opposing stance on some given position. Socrates believed that this form of discussion could reveal the likely truth in the most efficient way. To show our disputations in a more helpful fashion, I will relate them here not in descriptive form, but rather as a dialogue. Introductory remarks thus began as follows.

---

[44] Professional speech-making (*declamatio*) before the courts and in politics.

[45] *Sic haec mihi nunc senilis est declamatio.* The humor here is well-placed, and helps to soften the effect of Cicero's self-praise.

[46] I.e., philosophical disquisitions (*scholae*) by a teacher.

5. A.[47] Death seems to me an evil.

M. Do you mean for those who are already dead, or for those who have to die?

A. For both categories.

M. Since it is an evil, it is thus utter misfortune.[48]

A. Without doubt.

M. Then those who have already died, and those who are about to die, are both utterly miserable.

A. It seems so to me.

M. Everyone, then, is in a state of utter misery.

A. Absolutely everyone.

M. And indeed, if you want to be consistent in your position: everyone who has been born, or will be born, is not only in a state of misery, but will *always be* in a state of misery. For if you meant that the only miserable ones were those who had to die, you wouldn't exclude anyone living, since everyone must eventually die. Death would still bring an end to this state of misery. However, *since the dead are also miserable*, we are born into a condition of permanent wretchedness. The inevitable conclusion is that those who died a hundred thousand years ago are miserable—or, to say it another way, every person who has been born!

A. I believe exactly that.

M. So answer me this. Do these things terrify you: the three-headed Cerberus[49] of the Underworld, the menacing rumble of Cocytus,[50] Acheron's crossing,[51] and "Tantalus,[52] fatigued with thirst, his chin touching the water's surface"? And what about this ghastly image:

---

[47] As stated in the Introduction, the letter *A* stands for *auditor* (listener), and *M* for *magister* (teacher).

[48] *Est miserum igitur, quoniam malum.* There are other ways of rendering *miserum* here: utter misfortune, wretchedness, or misery are possibilities.

[49] The monstrous dog that stood watch at the gates of the Underworld (Hades). See *Aeneid* VI.417.

[50] One of the rivers surrounding Hades.

[51] A river in Epirus in northern Greece, and also considered one of the rivers of the Underworld. Dead souls were ferried across the Acheron by Charon. See *Aeneid* VI.323.

[52] King of Sipylus; for revealing the secrets of the gods, he was punished by being condemned to endure eternal hunger and thirst in Hades.

Sisyphus,[53] sweating in his labors, rolls his stone,
And yet makes no progress.

Or perhaps you are somewhat unsettled by the thought of those implacable judges, Minos and Rhadamanthus?[54] Before them neither Lucius Crassus[55] nor Marcus Antonius[56] will speak on your behalf. And because the hearing will be conducted before Greek justices, you cannot retain Demosthenes as counsel, either. You will have to argue your case in person before a great assembly. Perhaps you dread the thought of these images, and so conclude that death is a permanent evil.

6. A. Do you think I'm so deluded as to believe in these things?

M. You don't believe there is any truth to them?

A. Of course not.

M. I'm surprised! What a shame.

A. Why do you say so?

M. Because if I had argued against these legends, I could have been very persuasive.

A. Who couldn't be, when dealing with this type of subject? Or what real achievement is it to expose these figments of poets and painters?

M. And yet there are a great number of books in which philosophers have rejected these myths.

A. I find that pointless. Who is so deluded as to be convinced by these stories?

M. Then if the miserable are not in the underworld, there are no people at all in the underworld.

A. That's exactly what I think.

M. Then where are all these people whom you say are utterly miserable? Or what region do they inhabit? For if they indeed exist, they cannot be nowhere.

---

[53] King of Ephyra; for his hubris and dishonesty, he was condemned to make unending efforts in rolling a boulder uphill.

[54] Minos was king of Crete, and Rhadamanthus was his brother. Tradition held them to be firm but wise justices in their lifetimes; this supposedly made them (along with Aeacus, king of Aegina) fit for adjudications in Hades.

[55] Lucius Licinius Crassus (140 B.C.—91 B.C.), a famous orator of the generation before Cicero. Served as consul in 95 B.C.

[56] Marcus Antonius (143 B.C.—87 B.C.), another noted Roman orator, elected consul in 99 B.C.

A. I really do think they *are* nowhere.

M. So, then, you believe they don't exist?

A. That's entirely correct. I still consider them miserable, for the reason that they have no existence.

M. I would have preferred you to fear Cerberus, instead of tossing out such careless words.

A. What do you mean?

M. You declare the existence of that which you say does not exist. Where is your common sense? When you say a non-existent thing is miserable, you are essentially saying that it *does* exist.

A. I'm not so stupid as to say something like that.

M. Then what are you saying?

A. That Marcus Crassus,[57] for example, who lost a fortune when he perished, is miserable. And that Cnaeus Pompeius,[58] who was deprived of his honor, is miserable. In the end, everyone deprived of daylight is miserable.

M. You keep returning to the same point. If they are miserable, they must exist. But you are denying that the dead exist. If they do not exist at all, they cannot be anything. Thus they are not miserable.

A. Perhaps I am not clearly stating my true feelings. I believe this: not to exist, when you have once existed, is something truly miserable.

M. What? More miserable than never having existed at all? By that logic, those not yet born are miserable now, because they don't exist, and we—if we are to be miserable after death—have been miserable before we were born. Yet I don't recall being miserable before I was born. If you have a better memory, I want to know what you remember about yourself then.

7. A. You're mocking me, as if I were saying that those *who are not born* are miserable, instead of saying that those *who are dead* are miserable.

M. So you concede that they exist.

A. No, I'm not saying that. I'm saying that they are miserable because they don't exist, after they have previously existed.

---

[57] Marcus Licinius Crassus (115 B.C.—53 B.C.) was considered one of Rome's richest men He was killed during a disastrous expedition against the Parthians in 53 B.C. According to legend, the Parthians poured molten gold into his mouth to mock him in death. *See* Dio Cassius XL.27.

[58] Julius Caesar's civil war adversary Pompey, who was treacherously murdered in Egypt in 48 B.C. after having been defeated by Caesar.

M. Don't you see that your opinions are in opposition with each other? What could be so illogical as to say that a nonexistent person is not only miserable, but is anything at all? When you pass through the Porta Capena[59] and lay eyes on the tombs[60] of Calatinus,[61] the Scipios,[62] the Servilii,[63] and the Metelli,[64] do you think they're miserable?

A. Because you're pressing me with your words, from now on I won't say they "are miserable." I will just use the word "miserable" for the plain fact that they don't exist.

M. So you are not saying "Marcus Crassus is miserable," but instead "Miserable Marcus Crassus."

A. That's right.

M. As if it weren't mandatory for anything presented in this way either *to be* or *not to be*! Haven't you been given basic lessons in dialectics?[65] This is completely straightforward. Every logical proposition—this is the word I now think is right to convey the meaning of *axioma*,[66] and later I'll use a different one if I can find something better—is a proposition that is either true or false.[67] Thus when you say, "Miserable Marcus Crassus," you are either saying, "Marcus Crassus is miserable" (so that one can judge whether it is true or false), or you say nothing at all.

A. I'll concede now that the dead are not miserable. You've wrung a confession from me that those who didn't exist at all certainly can't be miserable. But so what? Aren't we—the living—miserable, since we must eventually die? What charm can there be in

---

[59] A gate in Rome's Servian Wall, through which the Via Appia passed.
[60] Tombs were often constructed on the sides of Roman roads. *See* Parker, J.H., *Tombs In Or Near Rome*, Oxford: James Parker & Co. (1877).
[61] Aulus Atilius Calatinus, consul during the First Punic War in 258 B.C. and 254 B.C., and dictator in 249 B.C.
[62] The location of the Tomb of the Scipios (*Sepulcrum Scipionum* or *Hypogaeum Scipionum*) was discovered in a vineyard in 1614, then lost, and rediscovered again in 1780. *See* Lanciani, Rodolfo, *Ruins and Excavations of Ancient Rome*, New York: Houghton Mifflin & Co. (1897), p. 321.
[63] Meaning Cnaeus Servilius Caepio (consul in 169 B.C.), and Quintus Servilius Caepio (consul 106 B.C.).
[64] Notable members of this family were Lucius Caecilius Metellus (consul in 251 B.C. and 247 B.C.), Quintus Caecilius Metellus Macedonicus (consul in 143 B.C.), Quintus Caecilius Metellus Numidicus (consul 109 B.C.).
[65] I.e., logic.
[66] The Greek ἀξίωμα.
[67] This sentence is poorly composed in the original, but the meaning is clear.

this life when, day and night, we have to think about the fact that sooner or later we have to die?

8. M. Do you know how much oppressive evil you've lifted from the human condition?

A. In what way?

M. Well, if death were utter misery even for those who've died, we would be immersed in infinite and eternal evil during life. I now see an ending-point of this life. And when it has been reached, there is nothing left to fear. But I think you'd endorse the view of Epicharmus,[68] a sharp man who, like a typical Sicilian, was anything but naïve.

A. What view? I don't know what you're referring to.

M. I'll say it in Latin, if I can. Of course you know I'm no more used to speaking Greek in a Latin conversation than I'm used to speaking Latin in a Greek one.

A. Definitely true. But what is this saying of Epicharmus?

M. "I do not desire death, but I attach no importance actually to being dead."[69]

A. I recognize the Greek now. But because you forced me to concede that the dead are not miserable, keep talking—if you can—to convince me that having to die is also not utter misery.

M. Certainly that would be no major task. I'm planning more important objectives.

A. Why is it not a major task? Or what are these "important objectives" you're trying to reach?

M. I mean: since after death there is no evil, death is also not an evil. Because you have conceded that there is no evil in the time that comes after death. Thus, having to die is not an evil either, for this is simply having to arrive at a destination that we admit is not an evil.

A. Please expand on that. The words you just said are so thorny that they force me to admit them before I approve them. But what are these more important objectives you are working towards?

M. I wish to demonstrate, if I can, that death is not only *not an evil*, but is actually a *good*.

A. I certainly don't hope for that, but I'd still love to hear you. Although you might not accomplish what you want, you'll certainly

---

[68] Epicharmus of Cos (550 B.C.?—460 B.C.?), a Pythagorean alleged to have been the inventor of comedy. *See* Diog. Laert. III.9. He is said to have lived until his nineties.

[69] *Emori nolo, sed me esse mortuum nihili aestimo.* A literal translation of this saying would not be the best choice here.

be able to demonstrate that death is not an evil. But I won't stop you from speaking. I'd like to hear an unbroken presentation.

M. What? If I ask you something, won't you respond?

A. That would be rude. But unless it's really necessary, I'd rather you didn't ask questions.

9. M. I'll follow your guidance and reveal what you want, as far as I'm able. But I won't do it like the Pythian Apollo,[70] where I issue rigid and absolute pronouncements. I will do it as one average man out of the multitude, following the path of probable propositions. I can't progress beyond that which I think approximates the truth. Let "the truth" be spoken by those who say these things can be absolutely known, and who call themselves wise.

A. Proceed as you wish. I'm certainly ready to listen.

M. We must first discover what death—something apparently familiar to everyone—really is. Some believe death is the departure of the soul from the body. Some hold that there is no such departure, but that body and soul die as one, and that the soul is extinguished along with the body's physical form. Of those who think that the soul leaves the body at death, some say the soul is dissipated immediately upon death. Others say it persists for some time; and others that it lingers for eternity. There is also much debate about what the soul is, where it resides in the body, and where it originally comes from. For some, the soul is considered the heart itself. The words *excordes*, *vecordes*, and *concordes* are derived from this view.[71] Nasica,[72] who served twice as consul, was given the name *Corculum*,[73] and

A man of remarkable heart, the wise Aelius Sextus.[74]

---

[70] The Delphic Oracle. The Pythia was the priestess of the Temple of Apollo at Delphi.

[71] The etymology is clear in Latin, but requires explanation in English. The word *cor* means "heart." The three Latin words listed here are constructed from *cor*: *excors* (*excordes*) means silly or stupid [*ex* + *cors*]; *vecors* (*vecordes*) means mad or insane [*ve* + *cors*]; and *concors* (*concordes*) means peaceful or harmonious [*con* + *cors*]. The idea is that the "conditions" of the heart determine mental states.

[72] Publius Cornelius Scipio Nasica, consul in 162 B.C. and 155 B.C. His wisdom earned him the surname Corculum ("wise").

[73] Wise or prudent, a word also incorporating *cor*.

[74] Sextus Aelius Paetus Catus, consul in 198 B.C. and a noted jurist. "Catus" is the Latin word for wise; the surname was attached to him on account of his prudence.

Empedocles[75] says that the soul is blood overspreading the heart. Some others believed that a certain part of the brain held the chief position of soul. Still others think neither the heart nor a certain part of the brain are the soul.

But some have claimed that the local seat of the soul is found in the heart, while others find it in the brain. Some, however, associate soul and breath[76] as we ourselves[77] do in a colloquial sense when using expressions like "drawing his last breath," "exhalation of the spirit," "animated" people, "spirited" people, and "soul-felt conviction." Even the Latin word for "soul"[78] is derived from the word for "breath."[79] And Zeno[80] the Stoic identified the soul with fire.

10. But these explanations I've talked about—heart, brain, spirit, fire—are common explanations of the soul's nature. The remaining opinions are mostly held by specific persons, just as old philosophers did many years ago. One such thinker very close in time to our own era is Aristoxenus,[81] who was both a musician and a philosopher. He held that the soul was a kind of "vibratory spasm"[82] of the body, similar to what is called harmony in song or instrumental music. Various oscillations are generated, he thought, from the nature and disposition of the entire human body, just as sounds are produced by song. Aristoxenus has not stepped beyond the boundaries of his specialized knowledge. But he has still enunciated something important that was stated and explained by Plato long ago.[83]

Xenocrates[84] did not believe that the soul had any form[85] or material component.[86] His position was that soul is number, and the

---

[75] Empedocles of Agrigentum (c. 494 B.C.—c. 434 B.C.), an eclectic Greek philosopher. He is said to have been the first to propose the four "classical elements" (earth, air, fire, water).

[76] *Animus* is soul or mind; *anima* can mean breathing, air, or soul.

[77] Meaning, we Romans.

[78] *Animus.*

[79] *Anima.*

[80] Zeno of Citium (c. 334 B.C.—c. 262 B.C.), founder of the Stoic school of philosophy.

[81] Aristoxenus of Tarentum (fl. 330 B.C.), a philosopher and musician, and pupil of Aristotle. Part of his treatise on music has survived.

[82] The word used is *intentio*, literally meaning stretch, tension, spasm, or straining. "Vibratory spasm" best suits the context.

[83] See *Phaedo* 92.

[84] Xenocrates of Chalcedon (400 B.C.—316 B.C.), pupil of Plato and head of the Platonic Academy from about 339 to 314 B.C.

[85] *Figura.*

[86] *Corpus.*

power of number was greatest in nature: a conclusion that Pythagoras[87] had reached long before him. His instructor Plato imagined a tripartite soul. In the head, as the controlling part, he placed reason as a kind of fortress; he wanted the other two parts, anger and desire, to be subordinate to reason. He placed anger within the human chest, and desire below the lower part of the chest.[88]

Dicaearchus,[89] however—in a dialogue sited in Corinth and composed in three books—features in the first book a number of educated speakers who participated in the debate. In the other two books he offers one Pherecrates, an old man from Phthia,[90] whom he says is a descendant of Deucalion.[91] Pherecrates takes the position that there is no soul at all, the very name "soul" being absurd. The words *animalia* and *animantes*[92] are also meaningless; soul exists in neither man nor animal. All of our ability to do things or to experience sensation is distributed equally in every living body, and cannot be separated from the body. There is nothing, he says, except the one single body, configured in a way that its naturally balanced constitution allows it to use its senses and to thrive.

Aristotle, who stands ahead of everyone—besides Plato, of course—in brilliance and productivity, once he understood the widely-accepted theory of the four elements which comprise all things, believed there was a fifth nature that produced mind. Mind thinks, plans ahead, learns, teaches, innovates, remembers, and does many other things besides. It loves, hates, desires, fears, and experiences trauma and happiness. Aristotle believes these things exist in none of the first four categories. He creates a fifth category with no identifying name, and so uses a new word for the soul, *endelecheia*.[93] This term expresses a kind of continuous and perpetual motion.

---

[87] Pythagoras of Samos (c. 570 B.C.—c. 495 B.C.), influential founder of the Pythagorean school, which stressed the primacy of numbers as an underlying principle of nature.

[88] *Subter praecordia*, or below the midriff.

[89] Dicaearchus of Messina (c. 350 B.C.—c. 285 B.C.), a historian, philosopher, and pupil of Aristotle.

[90] In Thessaly.

[91] Legendary king of Phthia, and son of Prometheus, who according to myth survived the deluge with his wife Pyrrha.

[92] I.e., living organisms animated by soul. *Animalia* are living beings; *animantes* is a plural present participle meaning "living" or "having life."

[93] ἐνδελέχεια. This Greek word means "continuity" or "persistence" and has often been confused with ἐντελέχεια, "perfection."

43

11. Unless some others have escaped me, these are just about all the opinions regarding the soul. Let us here omit Democritus,[94] who was certainly a great thinker, since for him the soul was smooth, round bodies interacting in random conjunctions with each other;[95] for the adherents of his school, anything can be created by the agitations of atomic particles.

Only a god would know which of these views about the soul is the true one. Which theory most approximates the truth is a question of vital importance. Do we want to decide among these theories, or would we rather return to our original topic?[96]

A. I'd like to deal with both of them, if possible, but it's difficult to mix them together. So if we can free ourselves from the fear of death, without talking about these other subjects, then we should do this. But if this can't be done without first resolving the problem of the soul, then it seems we should deal with that now, and after that the earlier question.

M. What I think you're asking for is more suitable. Reason will show that, no matter which of the different opinions I've offered is true, death is either *not* an evil, or is an actual good. For if the soul is heart, blood, or brain, then because it is a physical substance, it will certainly die with the rest of the body. If it is breath, it will probably diffuse into the air; if it is fire, it will be extinguished; if it is the harmony of Aristoxenus, it will simply dissolve. Why should I even mention Dicaearchus, who claims that soul is nothing at all?

Nothing has any relevance to us after death, these theories say. As life passes away, so also do we lose our powers of sense. And when sensation is absent, nothing is of much importance. The views of the remaining philosophers hold out the hope, if this prospect comforts you, that souls travel to a kind of final home in heaven once they depart the body.

A. This idea does indeed make me feel happy, and of course I want it to be so. Even if it is not true, I would still like to be convinced of it through argument.

M. In what way, then, can our assistance be of use to you? When it comes to eloquence, can we do better than Plato? Carefully unroll[97] this book, which deals with the soul, and you will want nothing more than this.

---

[94] Democritus of Abdera (c. 460 B.C.—c. 370 B.C.), originator of atomic theory.
[95] Referring to Democritus's atomic theory. Cicero criticized it in his *On Moral Ends* (e.g., I.19)
[96] I.e., the question about the meaning of death in I.9.
[97] Because books in Cicero's day were scrolls. F.E. Rockwood suggests that the Platonic treatise referred to here is the *Phaedo*.

A. By Hercules, I have read it, and quite often! I'm not sure why, but I nod in approval when reading it. Yet when I set the book down and begin to think about the immortality of the soul, all of this agreement evaporates.

M. What do you mean? Do you agree that our souls either persist after death, or they expire at the time of death?

A. Yes, I concede this.

M. So, what if they continue to exist?

A. Then I concede that they are happy.

M. And what if they cease to exist?

A. Then they are not miserable, since they will not even exist. We conceded this fact just a little while ago, through the strength of your logic.

M. Then in what way, or why, do you say that you see death as an evil? For either it makes us happy, if our souls persist after death—or it removes our misery, if death terminates all sensation.

12. A. Unless it's hopelessly tiresome, convince me first—if you can—that souls persist after death. Then, if you can't do this—for it's certainly not easy to do—you should demonstrate that death is free from all evil. What I'm apprehensive about is that death *might* be an evil. I'm not talking about the loss of sensation, but rather *having to face* this unavoidable, eventual deprivation.[98]

M. With regard to the writers who advocate the viewpoint you want proved, we can make use of the very best. This is a fact that ought to be, and is, worth a great deal. Indeed, we can avail ourselves of all antiquity which, perhaps, better grasped the truth of these matters since it was closer to its origin and divine heritage. It was an accepted article of faith among our predecessors—those whom Ennius called "the ancients"[99]—that sensation still exists at death, and that the departure of life does not bring such an end to man that he is utterly destroyed.

One may infer this from pontifical law and funerary ceremonies, along with other examples. These rituals would not have been honored by distinguished historical figures, nor would disrespect of these rites have been outlawed by inexpiable religious prohibitions, unless

---

[98] I.e., the anxiety of thinking about death's finality.

[99] The word used is *cascus*, meaning ancient or primitive. According to the Ox. Lat. Dict., it is an Oscan word related to *casnar* (old man) and *canus* (white). Varro (*De Lingua Latina* VII.28) claims *cascus* is of Sabine origin.

a sincere belief was fixed in their minds that death did not destroy and eradicate everything, but instead functioned as a kind of *migration* and *commutation* of life. This life served as a "pilot"[100] to heaven for distinguished men and women. For other people, it was limited to this earth, but in such a way that it still endured.[101]

We can see how from this that—as the Roman people saw it— "Romulus dwells in heaven with the gods for eternity," as Ennius wrote according to the customary belief. The Greeks believe that Hercules is a great and providential god, a tradition that we inherited from them, and which now extends as far as the ocean. Thus was born the worship of Liber,[102] son of Semele, who was given the same divine status. The same notoriety is attached to the legend of the two brothers,[103] the sons of Tyndareus, who have not only helped guide the Roman people to victory in battle, but are also supposed to have been messengers of favorable news. Don't you agree? Isn't Ino, the daughter of Cadmus, called Leucothea by the Greeks and worshipped by us under the name Matuta?[104] Do I need to offer more examples,

---

[100] *Dux*, as in a guide.

[101] This sentence is problematic both grammatically and conceptually. Cicero leads the reader to believe that its subject is *migratio commutatioque vitae* from the preceding sentence, when in fact its subject is intended to be *vita*. We must also be aware of Roman beliefs about the afterlife and the spirit world (e.g., the categories of spirits known as *Manes* and *Lemures*). For distinguished individuals, life served as a "road to heaven," and the souls of such people were elevated there upon death. Cicero makes this clear in his essay *Dream of Scipio*, the final book of his treatise *De Republica*. See p. 92 of my translation of Cicero's *Stoic Paradoxes* (Charleston: Fortress of the Mind Publications, 2015), i.e., *Dream of Scipio* §16. The spirits of bodies that were properly disposed of (i.e., according to sacred rites) entered the underworld and were known as *di inferi* (lit., "the gods below"). The spirit of an improperly buried corpse, it was feared, might return to haunt the living as a *Lemure* (in modern terms, a poltergeist). *Manes* were ancestral spirits of family members, and belonged to the general category of *di inferi*. Specific Roman festivals centered around honoring those who had passed away.

[102] An ancient Italic god often equated with the Greek god Bacchus.

[103] Referring to Castor and Pollux (the Dioscuri). Conflicting information is given by Homer and Hesiod about their parentage. They were generally regarded as helpers of humanity, and their assistance was often invoked by travelers, athletes, and sailors. A temple to Castor and Pollux was erected on the Roman Forum.

[104] Ino was the daughter of Cadmus, the legendary founder of Thebes. Matuta was an old Italic goddess of the dawn. In this perceptive paragraph, Cicero shows that he recognizes cultural diffusion and, perhaps, would be receptive to the study of comparative religion.

or can't we just say that nearly all of heaven is filled with divinities of human creation?

13. In fact, if I were to research the old traditions, and select from them what Greek writers have asserted, we would see that even what are considered "original gods" were taken to heaven by this same pathway. Ask whose tombs are singled out for attention in Greece. And since you have been initiated, remember what things are taught in the mysteries. You will then appreciate the true extent of this notion. Those who had not yet acquired a knowledge of natural philosophy (which only began to be studied many years later) only knew as much as what they could glean from nature's hints. They did not understand the underlying principles and rational causes of things. They were persuaded by visions, usually experienced at night, to believe that those who had left this mortal life were still alive.

The most convincing evidence offered to support our belief in the existence of gods is generally this: that there is no people so savage, and no person so brutish, that his mind is unable to form a notion of supernatural deities. Many have debased conceptions about gods, since this is the expected consequence of dissolute morals. All, nevertheless, subscribe to the idea that a divine nature and power is a reality. This belief was not formed by human design or agreement, and was not implanted by legislation or decree. But the consensus of every nation in the world on this point must be reckoned as a law of nature.

Who, then, does not mourn the loss of those dear to him, because he thinks they have been denied life's pleasures? If you remove this view, you will remove grief.[105] No one mourns because of something he himself has suffered. Perhaps people feel pain, and are distressed. But that truly anguished lamentation and doleful weeping are traceable to the belief that our loved one has been denied life's enjoyments, and senses this deprivation. The hand of nature is what guides this feeling in us; it is not a consequence of rational thought or learned teachings.

14. Indeed the most convincing argument is that nature herself offers a quiet verdict in favor of the immortality of souls, because everyone is interested—deeply interested, in fact—about what may lie in store for them after death:

---

[105] *Tolle hanc opinionem, luctum sustuleris.*

> One plants trees that will be enjoyed by future
> ages,

as the poet Statius says in his *Synephebi*.[106] And what is his purpose in saying this, except that future ages are his concern? Should a diligent farmer plant trees, the fruit of which he will never live to see, and a great man not plant the seeds of laws, institutions, and the infrastructure of a republic? The procreation of children, the propagation of a family name, the adoption of sons, the careful drafting of wills, the erection of sepulchral monuments and the inscriptions carved on them—of what significance are they, except that *our mindfulness of the future is what motivates us to do them*? What do you think of this? Do you doubt that it's right to construct an ideal human nature from the very best natures that can be found?

What better kind of nature can we find in human beings than the nature of those who consider themselves born to help, protect, and preserve their fellow men? Hercules left this mortal life to be with the gods. He would never have arrived at this glorious destination unless, through his own labors, he had constructed this divine road while he lived among men. These ideas are very old, and are consecrated by the sanctity of all religions.

15. And in this country, what do we think was going through the minds of so many men—and such great men—who were killed in defense of this republic? Were they thinking that their names would be rigidly confined to the boundaries of their mortal lives? No one would ever risk death for the sake of his country without a prevailing anticipation of immortality. Themistocles[107] might have lived at ease, and Epaminondas[108] might have lived at ease, too. And not to cite more historical examples from foreign countries, so also might have I myself. I do not know how it happens, but there is a kind of premonition of future ages embedded in our minds: and this instinct is

---

[106] Caecilius Statius (c. 219 B.C.—c. 166 B.C.), Roman comedic dramatist. According to tradition he was a Gaul brought to Rome as a slave; once freed, he became a playwright. His *Synephebi* was based on a Greek play by Menander. His work is mostly lost; a large fragment of about 400—500 lines was recently unearthed at Herculaneum.

[107] Themistocles (c. 524 B.C.—c. 460 B.C.), a brilliant Athenian general and statesman.

[108] Epaminondas of Thebes (?—362 B.C.), Theban general and statesman.

48

most powerful, and manifests itself most clearly, in men of the most sublime genius and noble spirit. If this conviction were absent, who would be so delusional as to fritter away his life in unremitting labors and dangers?

I am here talking about rulers. But what about poets? Don't they also want to achieve renown after death? How would you interpret this passage, then?

> Look, citizens, upon the image of old Ennius's countenance:
> He composed verses on the immortal deeds of your forefathers.[109]

He solicits a reward of glory from those whose fathers he had enshrined in glory. The same poet tells us:

> Let no one adorn me with tears, or sob at my funeral rites.
> Why do this?
> I float, still living, from the mouths of men, one to the other.

But why talk only about the poets? Artists also seek enduring fame after death. For what reason did Phidias put his image on Minerva's shield, when he was not allowed to write his name on it?[110] What about our philosophers? Don't they write their own names on the very books they compose about despising fame?

If a general consensus is the voice of nature, and everyone, no matter where they are, agrees that there is something applicable to those who have departed from life, then we should also believe the same thing. If we believe that those with superior ability or virtue

---

[109] Verses supposed to have been composed by Ennius to be placed with his funerary bust in the tomb of the Scipios in Rome.
[110] A legend about the great Greek sculptor Phidias (c. 480 B.C.—430 B.C.). He supposedly had his own image embossed on the goddess Minerva's shield, an act of arrogance and impiety. This led to his imprisonment and death. *See* Valerius Maximus VIII.14.6.

perceive nature's power with the most clarity—because they represent nature's best—then it is probably true that, since the best men serve posterity most effectively, there is something they will sense after death.

16. Just as nature enables us to accept the existence of gods, and the operation of reason allows us to discover their qualities, so do we believe, by the common consent of all nations, that our souls survive after death. Where these souls reside, and what their distinct properties may be, are questions that must be answered by rational thought.

Disregard of this question is what led to the creation of the Lower World, and of those terrors which you seem to disdain, not without reason. Bodies are deposited into the ground and then covered with earth—this is the origin of the Latin verb "to be buried."[111] People concluded that the afterlife was lived underground. And from this supposition many false conclusions followed, which the poets propagated. A theater's packed assembly, lined with fatuous women and children, is roused to delight at hearing the inspiring lines:

> By a steep and arduous road, I come and appear
> only just from Acheron,[112]
> Through caves formed with jagged, hanging rocks,
> A sight to behold, where the mist of Hades hovers
> stern and thick.[113]

So influential was the error, which to me now appears to be removed, that even though people knew corpses were cremated, they still believed certain things transpired in the Lower World that can neither happen nor be comprehensible without physical bodies. They were unable to comprehend the idea of souls living for themselves alone, and sought out an acceptable form and shape for them. This is

---

[111] Connecting the words "to be buried" (*humari*) and "soil" (*humus*) with their common origin.
[112] The Acheron is a river located in Epirus in northern Greece. It was also considered one of the five rivers of the Underworld.
[113] The author of these lines is unknown.

where Homer's *nekyia*[114] comes from, and the source of the *nekro-manteia*[115] which my friend Appius[116] practiced. It is also the origin of the idea that Lake Avernus,[117] which is near where we live,

Where souls are raised up in the dark shade from the opened gateway
Of Acheron's depths by the simulated blood[118] of man,
The apparitions of those from whom life has departed.[119]

Nevertheless, they want these ghosts to speak, something that is not possible without a tongue or palate, or without an existing and functional throat, chest, and lungs. They could picture nothing with their unaided minds; everything depended on what their eyes told them. It is a characteristic of great mental ability to remove the mind from the realm of the senses, and separate one's thoughts from habitual custom.

I think there were many such people in previous centuries. But according to what the written record tells us, Pherecydes of Syros[120] was the first to teach that human souls were immortal. He was a very ancient philosopher, and lived during the reign of my old kinsman. His pupil Pythagoras very much concurred with this view. He arrived in Italy when Tarquinius Superbus[121] was on the throne, and became

---

[114] The Greek word is νέκυια, the rite of summoning the ghosts of the dead (a ritual in the art of necromancy). The reference is to *Odyssey* XI, which describes Odysseus's sojourn to Hades.

[115] Greek νεκρομαντεία; Latin *necromantia*, or necromancy.

[116] Appius Claudius Pulcher (97 B.C.—49 B.C.), consul in 54 B.C. Like Cicero, he also served as an augur.

[117] Near the town of Cumae. The grotto of the Sibyl was believed to be an entrance to the Underworld.

[118] "Simulated blood" (*falso sanguine*), in the sense that the blood of sacrificed animals was used in place of human blood.

[119] These verses are of unknown authorship.

[120] Pherecydes of Syros (c. 600 B.C.—c. 550 B.C.), Greek philosopher from the Aegean island of Syros, considered one of the first Greek prose writers.

[121] Lucius Tarquinius Superbus (?—495 B.C.), the last Roman king.

51

powerfully influential in the Magna Graecia[122] area through the prestige of his teachings as well as his charisma. Even many centuries later, Pythagoras's name was surrounded by such a mystique that no non-Pythagoreans were considered learned.

17. But let us return to the ancients. They usually did not bother to provide a comprehensive rationale for their views beyond what could be explained by numbers or geometric proofs. We are told that Plato traveled to Italy and absorbed everything that Pythagoreanism had to offer. He not only grasped the sect's doctrine of the eternity of souls, but was also the first thinker to offer a cogent proof. Unless you object, let us pass over this proof, and give up this whole hope of immortality.

A. So you're now going to let me down, after having built up my expectation to the maximum! By Hercules, I'd rather make mistakes with Plato—whom I know you greatly respect, and whom I admire just from hearing you talk about him—than be right with those other thinkers.

M. Bravo, and well said![123] I myself could not voluntarily go wrong with this same philosopher as a guide. Do we have any doubts as we do in many other things (although there is little doubt on *this* issue, since the mathematicians tell us how it is), that the earth is located at the center of the universe, comprising a kind of point which they call *kentron*,[124] and is surrounded by the entire sky?

We also have no doubt that the nature of the four elements that produce all things is such that—as if their principles of movement were reciprocally divided and allocated—the earthy and the humid are brought at equal angles[125] to land and sea by their own weight and inclination. In contrast, the remaining two parts (one being fiery, the other vaporous) rise upward by straight lines into the celestial region, just as the first two are carried to the center of the world because of their mass and weight. Fire and air behave this way either because some propensity in their nature directs them to seek higher regions, or because lighter bodies are naturally repelled by heavier ones.

Since these things are evident, it ought to follow that, whether they are vaporous (i.e., like the air) or fiery, souls are carried high

---

[122] Magna Graecia was the collective name given to the Greek colonies in southern Italy.

[123] The idiomatic expression is *macte virtute*.

[124] Greek κέντρον, and Latin *centrum*, meaning "center."

[125] *Ad pares angulos*, or in a perpendicular fashion.

into the air after leaving the physical body. But if the soul is some number (something said with more ambiguity than lucidity), or if it is that fifth nature (something that is more without a name than something not understood), then there are entities of such purity and unity that they carry themselves a tremendous distance from the earth. The soul is thus something of this sort. And we should not believe that the dynamic mind lies submerged in the heart or the brain, or in the blood, as Empedocles teaches.

18. Although they were learned men, let us omit Dicaearchus as well as his peer and schoolmate Aristoxenus. One of these philosophers did not believe he had a soul, and never seems to have grieved over this. The other is so delighted with his own songs that he tries to insert them into discussions on these subjects. We can detect harmony from the intervals between musical sounds; the varying sequence of such sounds forms additional harmonies. Yet I do not see how, if a soul is absent, the arrangement of the limbs and the body's figure can generate harmony. Although he certainly was an erudite man, he should leave such questions to his master Aristotle, and stick to teaching singing. The following Greek proverb admirably counsels us:

> May each person practice that art which he best comprehends.[126]

We should also completely disregard the idea of a soul composed of smooth, round particles that collide randomly with each other—even though Democritus assures us that it is warm and gaseous (i.e., airy).

However, if soul is associated with the four types of elements said to comprise all things, then it is made of agitated air, as I believe is the view Panaetius[127] finds most acceptable. This type of soul must seek out the elevated areas. The two classes of air and fire are not inclined to move in a downward direction: they always seek the

---

[126] A similar adage is found in Pliny (*Hist. Nat.* XXXV.85): *Ne supra crepidam sutor*, or "a shoemaker should not go beyond the sandal."
[127] Panaetius of Rhodes (c. 180 B.C.—c. 110 B.C.), a Stoic philosopher active in Athens and Rome. His treatise *On Duties* has been lost, but much influenced Cicero.

higher regions. Thus if souls are dissipated, this happens at some distance from the earth. If they endure and retain their particular properties, they must be carried to heaven, and this thick, condensed air closest to the earth is breached and divided by them. The soul is warmer—or perhaps we should say "more heated"—than the air I just now called thick and condensed. We know this to be true because our bodies, formed from the terrestrial category of elements, are warmed by the soul's incandescence.

19. We should also note that the soul departs more easily from this earthly air (which I have identified several times now) and passes through it, because nothing is faster than the soul. There is no quickness that can contend with the soul's velocity. If it remains pure and unsullied in essence, it must be transported with such speed that it penetrates and breaks through our entire sky, where clouds, rains, and winds gather, and which is humid and misty due to the earth's exhalations.[128]

When the soul leaves this region, and then discovers and learns about a nature similar to itself, it pauses at fires composed of thin air and subdued heat from the sun. From here it does not attempt to travel any higher. Once it has achieved a lightness and heat similar to its own, it no longer moves, being now balanced by equal weights: and here, at last, is its natural seat, where it has arrived at something resembling itself. Here the soul desires nothing more. It may be nourished and sustained by the same nutrients that nourish and sustain the stars.

Since we are accustomed to being incited by the body's covetous fires to nearly every physical craving—and these fires burn hotter when we try to emulate those who have what we want most ardently—we will without doubt be happy when we have liberated ourselves from this physical body, and can shed the burdens of this constant desire and rivalry. And what we do now—when we investigate and examine things after setting aside our burdens—we will be able to do more freely.

We will devote ourselves entirely to contemplation and study. For nature has placed in our minds an unrelenting desire to lay eyes on the truth. The shore of this heavenly region we will have reached, which gives us the ability to comprehend celestial matters more easily, will itself augment our appetite for knowledge. Even in our

---

[128] The phrase used is *exhalationes terrae*, the "breathing" effect produced by the evaporations and condensations of the earth's water cycle.

earthly abode, this beauty produced that "communal and ancestral" philosophy (as Theophrastus[129] calls it) which was first inspired by a desire for knowledge. They will especially cherish this notion who, when only denizens of this world and surrounded by terrestrial gloom, still desired to probe into the nature of things with their mind's eye.

20. Now if men think they have accomplished something, who have seen Pontus and the straits[130] that were penetrated by the ship named

> *Argo*, since her well-chosen Argive men
> Did once sail to find the ram's golden fleece,[131]

or those who have seen the narrows of Ocean,[132]

> Where the raging wave divides Europe and Libya,[133]

then what sort of awe-inspiring scene do we think it will be when our vision takes in the entire earth, with its orientation, form, and outline, and those terrestrial regions that are habitable, as well as those that remain uncultivated due to the forbidding influence of cold or heat?

It is not with our eyes that we perceive the things we observe, for the body has no senses. Not only natural philosophers, but also physicians—who have seen these things exposed and confirmed—teach us that there are certain perforated conduits[134] from the seat of the soul to the eyes, ears, and nose. Often, therefore, we neither see nor hear, being obstructed by thinking or the effect of some sickness,

---

[129] Theophrastus of Lesbos (c. 371 B.C.—c. 287 B.C.), a prolific Peripatetic philosopher who succeeded Aristotle.
[130] Referring to the narrows of the Hellespont and the Bosporus.
[131] Lines apparently from *Medea Exsul*, a play of Ennius.
[132] The Straits of Gibraltar.
[133] A line probably from Ennius's *Annales*.
[134] *Viae perforatae*, meaning bored channels or apertures. The reference is to the body's arteries, and can be found in Cicero's *De Nat. Deorum* III.9 and in Pliny (*Hist. Nat.* XI.146).

even though our eyes and ears are open and working properly. It can easily be understood that *the soul* is what sees and hears, and not those parts of us that function as windows to the soul. Yet the mind can comprehend nothing through them, unless it takes action and is present.

What do you think of the fact that with the same mind, we comprehend such dissimilar things as color, taste, heat, smells, and sound? The soul would never have learned about these things from its five messengers, unless everything was referred back to soul and it remained the only judge of everything. And without doubt, things of much greater purity and clarity will be understood when the soul is freed from the body, and arrives at the destination to which it is transported by nature. Although these perforated conduits which now lead from the body to the soul have been created by nature with consummate artistry, they are still in some way blocked by dense, earthly particles; but when there will be nothing but soul, then no obstruction will interfere with our understanding of the true quality and nature of things.

21. Indeed, if the need arose, we could say a great deal on the number, variety, and degree of the astonishing scenes that the soul will experience in these celestial locations. Indeed as I think about these things, I usually become amazed at the haughtiness of many philosophers who are infatuated with knowledge about nature and, overflowing with emotion, give effusive thanks to its architect and designer, venerating him as a god.

They claim that through him they have been liberated from oppressive masters, permanent terror, and anxiety that haunts them day and night. But what terror is this? And what anxiety? What old woman is so irrational as to fear those things that you clearly would have feared, if you hadn't learned something about natural philosophy? "The tall Acherunsian temples of Orcus, the pale realm of the dead, a domain cloaked in darkness."[135]

Shouldn't a philosopher be ashamed to brag about not fearing these things, and about knowing they are bogus? From this one can appreciate the natural sharpness of those who, without formal training, would lend credibility to such things. What an amazing discovery they have made, to learn that when their time to die finally arrives, they will be utterly annihilated! And if this really is true—I

---

[135] A quote (not in verse form) supposedly from Ennius's *Andromache*.

am not now contradicting it—what could be cheerful or glorious about it? Yet I can't think of any legitimate reason why the views of Pythagoras and Plato would be wrong. Although Plato offered no explicit proof (and remember how much I respect him), he would demolish me with his prestige. He put forward so many reasons that it seems he wanted to persuade others. He certainly appears to have persuaded himself.

22. Yet many philosophers dispute this view, and condemn souls to death as if they were doling out capital punishment. They have no reason to view the soul's immortality as something unbelievable, except for the fact that they cannot understand and appreciate the soul's nature in the absence of the body. As if they actually understood the soul's nature, constitution, size, and location while in the body! But if everything now concealed in a living man were open for inspection, would it be true that the soul is visible to our eyes? Or would it be of such tenuity that it eludes visual detection?

Those who say they cannot comprehend the soul without the body should ponder these things. And then they will see what they understand about soul when it is in the body. When I think about the soul's nature, it seems to me that the question of the soul's specific quality *while in the body* (which is really its foreign home), is a much more problematic and obscure issue than the question of what happens to the soul when it leaves the body and reaches the free heavens, which we can think of as the soul's home. Unless it is impossible to understand the nature of something we have never seen, we can certainly form an idea of God, and of a divine soul that has been liberated from the body.

Indeed, since it was difficult to gain information about the soul's nature and characteristics, Dicaearchus and Aristoxenus taught that there was no such thing as soul at all. It is indeed a critical thing to perceive the soul by using the same soul; and without doubt this was the thrust of Apollo's saying when he counseled that every person should know himself.[136] I don't think the meaning of his advice is that we should know our limbs, stature, or form. We are not just bodies; and when I speak to you now, I am not talking to your physical form. So when Apollo says, "*Know thyself*," he is really saying, "*Know thy soul.*" For the body is a kind of vessel, or a receptacle, for

---

[136] The first clause of this sentence is opaque, and not entirely satisfactory, but the meaning can be generally discerned.

the soul: and whatever is done by the soul, is also done by you. This saying, which describes a very sagacious soul, would never have been attributed to a god unless knowing one's soul was seen as a divine thing.

But if the soul itself does not understand the nature of soul, then I'd ask you to tell me this: does it know that it exists at all? And is it aware of its own movement? The origin of this idea is traceable to Plato, which is explained by Socrates in the dialogue *Phaedrus*. I also included it in the sixth book of my treatise *De Re Publica*.

23. "That which is in perpetual motion is eternal. But that which causes something else to move, and is itself caused to move by an external force, must stop living when its motion ends. That which moves itself is the only thing that never stops moving, because it is always concerned with itself. This is the source and the original cause of movement for all things that move. But a foundational principle has no birth: everything arises from a foundational principle, and this formative cause cannot be born from anything else. That which is produced by something else is not a foundational principle. Now if it is never born, it also never dies. A formative principle that has been extinguished will not be reborn from anything else. Neither will it create anything from itself, if indeed everything must be generated from a foundational principle.

It follows from this that *the foundational principle of motion is traceable to that which moves itself*. It cannot be born, and it cannot perish. Otherwise the whole sky must fall, and all nature must come to a shuddering halt, and receive no force by which it might first be made to move. Since it is obvious that whatever moves itself is eternal, who will deny that this nature should also be attributed to souls? That which is caused to move by an external force is without soul. What has soul, however, is roused by movement that is internal and uniquely its own. For this is the original nature and power of soul which—if it really is that unique thing that actually moves itself—has definitely not been born, and is truly eternal."

Even if all the run-of-the-mill philosophers (so I think we should call those who dissent from Plato, Socrates and the rest of their school) confer with each other, not only will they never explain anything so artfully, but they will be incapable of understanding how subtle this conclusion is. The soul, therefore, senses that it moves itself. Because it senses this, it knows that it moves by its own force, and is not moved by some external force. It can never happen that the soul deserts itself. *And these statements demonstrate the soul's eternity*—unless you can offer something to refute this.

A. It is very easy for me not to allow anything to enter my mind that contradicts you. I agree with your conclusions.

24. M. Let me ask you this. What about the arguments that say the human soul has divine properties? Do you think they are less persuasive? If I could understand how such divine properties were created, I could also see how they might cease to exist. For I think I can say from what the blood, bile, phlegm, bones, tendons, and veins—indeed all the limbs and the whole body—were made and constituted. If there were nothing to the soul except that it grants us life,[137] I would believe the life of man to be sustained by the workings of nature, just as a vine or a tree. For we say that these things live. If a man's soul had no motivating impulse except acquiring or avoiding things, it would also have this in common with the wild beasts.

Let us first note that the soul has memory: an infinite memory of things beyond our capacity to count. Plato represents this as being the memory of a past life. In his dialogue *Meno*, Socrates asks a youth certain geometric questions about the measurement of a square; and the youth responds as a boy might be expected to respond. Although the questions are not difficult, the boy—by answering in a logical, step-by-step manner—arrives at the same destination as if he had known geometry. Socrates cites this as evidence of his view that learning is nothing more than recalling. He explains this point with greater precision in that dialogue held on the day he died.

Socrates teaches that anyone, even someone who seems to be uneducated, demonstrates in response to proper inquiry that he is not learning something new, but rather recalling what was already contained in memory. In no other way could we, from the time we were children, have such a quantity of notions (those both preexisting and in a way imprinted on our souls, and which the Greeks call *ennoiai*) unless the soul had been hungrily absorbed in learning things before it entered the body. It had no existence, as Plato is constantly reminding us. For Plato believes nothing that is born or perishes exists. For him, the only existing thing is that which has a perpetual and unchangeable essence that he calls *idea*[138] and we call *species*.[139]

---

[137] Literally, "we live through it" (*per eum viveremus*).

[138] The Greek word ιδέα. In this sentence and the previous two sentences, Cicero is referring to Plato's theory of ideas. Plato believed that the "idea" alone had real existence, and that material objects did not, since they were impermanent.

[139] The Latin word *species* is used, meaning a specific nature, form, or character. *See* Cicero's *De Orat.* III.34; *see also* Lucretius II.665.

Trapped in the body, the soul was unable to become aware of these ideas. Yet it brought along what it already knew. Our sense of astonishment at knowing so many different things is thus lessened. When the soul suddenly migrates into such an unfamiliar and confused domicile,[140] it does not clearly see ideas; but when it has gathered itself together and revived itself, it becomes aware of them by recollection.

Memory, in many ways, amazes me even more. Through what process does the memory operate? What potential does it have, and how was it created? I am not investigating the ability for recollection that Simonides[141] is said to have had, or the ability of Theodectes,[142] or that of Cineas,[143] who was sent by Pyrrhus to the senate as an envoy. Neither am I referring to the more recent capabilities of Charmadas,[144] nor to those of Metrodorus of Scepsis[145] (who died not too long ago), nor to those of our Hortensius.[146] I am talking about the common memory of the human race, and mainly the memories of those individuals occupied in some advanced study or artistic pursuit. Since these types of people remember a great deal, the dimensions of their mental powers are not always easy to evaluate.

25. So what is the point of my argument? I think you must know what this power is and where it comes from. It definitely does not come from the heart, blood, brain, or atomic particles. I don't know if it belongs to air or fire. Unlike those other men, I'm not afraid to

---

[140] I.e., the human body. For Plato, knowledge was the soul's "remembering" or recalling what it knew in its former state.

[141] Simonides of Ceos (556 B.C.—467 B.C.), a Greek lyric poet said to have been proficient in the art of memory. *See* Quintilian XI.2.11 and Pliny (*Hist. Nat.*) VII.89. The cited names that follow were all famous for their powers of memory.

[142] Theodectes (fl. 350 B.C.), a poet from Lycia in Anatolia. *See* Quint. XI.2.51.

[143] Cineas of Thessalia, sent by King Pyrrhus to Rome as envoy after the Battle of Heraclea (280 B.C.).

[144] Charmadas (c. 168 B.C.—c. 100 B.C.), Academic philosopher and pupil of Carneades in Athens.

[145] Metrodorus of Scepsis (c. 145 B.C.—c. 70 B.C.), a philosopher said to have had a prodigious memory.

[146] Quintus Hortensius (114 B.C.—50 B.C.), Roman orator noted for his memory and persuasive delivery. (This sentence and the previous one are a single brilliant period in the original; it makes masterful use of repetitive clauses beginning with the word *quanta*: *Non quaero quanta memoria Simonides fuisse dicatur, quanta Theodectes, quanta is, qui a Pyrrho legatus ad senatum est missus, Cineas, quanta nuper Charmadas, quanta, qui modo fuit, Scepsius Metrodorus, quanta noster Hortensius.*).

60

admit that I don't know something when I don't know it. *But if I were to offer an opinion on such an enigmatic subject, I would swear that, whether the soul is air or fire, it is divine.*

What do you think? I would ask this: does it seem to you that the formidable power of memory arose or was constituted on earth, with its foggy and gloomy skies? If you don't see what this is, you still see the kind of thing it is. If you don't even see this, you certainly can sense its magnitude. So what do you think? Do we think that there is some sort of hollow space in the soul, into which we can pour the things we remember, as if filling some receptacle? Something like that is absurd.

What can be perceived as the foundation or form of such a soul, or what kind of capacity can it even have? Do we see the soul as something that is imprinted, as if it were made of wax, and that memory is the remnant of things stamped in the mind? What are the vestiges of words and of physical things themselves, and what sort of overwhelming greatness could even depict so many things?

What, finally, is that power which tries to find what is hidden—what is called discovery and rational thought? Does that man appear to you to be created from this terrestrial, impermanent, and destructible material, who first devised names for everything, a feat that Pythagoras saw as the pinnacle of wisdom? Or the man who first gathered together human beings who had been widely dispersed, and unified them in social organization? Or the man who marked the limits of the human voice—which had once seemed an infinite quantity—with a few lettered characters? Or the man who recorded the processions of moving celestial bodies, their courses through the heavens, and their arrangements? All of them were great. Before them were those who discovered the cultivation of crops, garments, methods of building shelter, the improvement of living standards, and methods of protection from wild beasts—men of civilized character and bold innovation with whose assistance we meandered from the arts of necessity to those of leisured refinement.

A great deal of pleasure has been devised for our ears through the ordered variety of contrasting types of sounds. We have gazed up at the stars, both those that are fixed in certain places, and those that are not (but which are incorrectly called "wandering"[147]). He who has observed their revolutions, and all of their motions, shows that his

---

[147] Cicero disapproves of labeling the planets Mercury, Venus, Mars, Jupiter, and Saturn as "wandering" since their motion followed regular, and not random, orbits.

soul has taken on the attributes of the divine power that created these celestial bodies. For when Archimedes attached to a sphere the courses of the moon, sun, and the five wandering stars, he constructed his model (just as the Platonic God of the *Timaeus* did when he built the world) so that one rotation of the sphere would indicate starry paths that moved quickly or slowly in different degrees.[148] If events cannot happen in this world without a God, then neither could Archimedes have duplicated these celestial motions on a sphere without divine ability.

26. To me it seems that not even the more noted and distinguished disciplines are lacking in divine influence. No poet, I think, pours out his intense and exuberant verses without some divine incentive acting on his consciousness; eloquence does not flow abundantly in sonorous words and fecund thoughts without the action of a higher power. Consider philosophy, the mother of all the arts. What else is it except the "gift of the gods" (as Plato calls it), or as I call it, the discovery of the gods? This pointed us first towards a reverence for the gods, then to a cultivation of human law, which is an outgrowth of human social organization. It finally taught us modesty and greatness of soul. It cleared away the foggy haze from the "mind's eyes," so to speak, so that we could see everything above, below, first, last, and in the middle.

In my view, a power that can produce wonders of such number and magnitude is entirely divine. Indeed, what is the memory of things, and the memory of words? And what is invention? Certainly nothing can be understood, even in God, that is more important than this. I do not think the gods are enchanted by ambrosia or nectar, nor by Juventas's filling up their drinking-cups.[149] Neither do I accept the word of Homer, who says Ganymede was abducted by the gods on account of his enticing form in order to serve drinks to Zeus. There was no justifiable reason why Laomedon[150] was subjected to such injury.

---

[148] The great scientist Archimedes of Syracuse (287 B.C.—212 B.C.) was said (see Cicero's *De Republica* I.14) to have built a model displaying the orbits of the planets (in Cicero's day called "wandering stars") Mercury, Venus, Mars, Jupiter, and Saturn. Also referenced here is Plato's *Timaeus* 38.

[149] Juventas (Hebe in Greek mythology), the goddess of youth. She was the daughter of Zeus and Hera, and the cupbearer to the gods.

[150] A Trojan king, the son of Ilus, and nephew of Ganymede. The injury Cicero refers to is the punishment that was visited on Laomedon. He was forced to sacrifice his daughter Hesione to a monster after he breached a promise to the gods. Heracles offered to save the girl if Laomedon would give him certain horses that had been gifts from Zeus; the king agreed, then broke his word to Heracles. In a rage, Heracles then killed Laomedon and all his sons except Priam.

Homer painted these scenes and ascribed human motivations to the gods—but I would have preferred him to ascribe divine motivations to us. But what are these divine characteristics? To be vigorous, to comprehend, to discover, and to remember. Therefore, the soul is divine, as I say; as Euripides dares to say, it is God. And if God is either air or fire, so also is the human soul. For just as this heavenly nature is untainted by earth or dampness, so also is the human soul uncontaminated by these things. If, however, there is some sort of "fifth nature," as Aristotle first proposed,[151] this is the nature of gods and men.

27. I have expressed this position and elaborated it with these words from my book the *Consolation*[152]: "No souls have their origin on earth. In souls, there is nothing that seems blended or mixed, and nothing apparently born of the earth, or molded from the earth. Nor is there a trace of anything humid, airy, or fiery. There is nothing in these natures that has the power of memory, reason, and thought. There is nothing that can preserve the past, predict the future, and embrace the present moment. These qualities are exclusively divine: *and they will never reach man from any other origin except from God.*

"The soul possesses a certain singular quality and power that is unconnected to these common and obvious natures. Thus whatever is capable of sensation, whatever understands, whatever lives, and whatever thrives, must be transcendent and divine, and therefore eternal. God Himself, who is understood by us, cannot be understood in any other way except as a divine mind that is unbound and unencumbered. It is separate from all transitory material substance, aware of everything and setting everything in motion, and it is gifted with eternal motion." The human mind possesses this same attribute, and shares this same nature.

Then where is this mind, and what sort of mind is it? Where is *yours*, and what kind is it? Are you able to say? Or, if I don't have

---

See *Iliad* V.265, 640; Smith, William, *Dictionary of Greek and Roman Biography and Mythology*, London: John Murray (1880), p. 719.
[151] The adding of a "fifth" element to the four earthly elements was suggested by Aristotle in his cosmological work *De Caelo* (*On the Heavens*). Some scholars believe the idea was also raised in his lost treatise *De Philosophia* (*On Philosophy*).
[152] *De Consolatione* is a lost treatise of Cicero's that he composed after the death of his daughter Tullia in 45 B.C.

everything needed for understanding that I would like to have, won't you let me use what I *do* have? The soul does not have the capacity to see itself. But like the eye, the soul perceives other things, even while not seeing itself. The soul does not see its own form (which is something of minimal importance). Yet it may be able to do this too, although for now we will set that question aside. Certainly the soul sees its power, sagacity, memory, and quick motion. These things are transcendent; these things are divine; these things are truly eternal. What the soul's appearance may be, and where it may dwell, are certainly questions that should not be asked.

28. Just as when we see the sky's splendor and radiance, and the drama of its speed of revolution that we cannot comprehend; then the alternation of days and nights and the progression of the four seasons to nurture the growth of crops and the physical development of organisms; and the sun, the master and leader of all of them; and the moon, with its advancing and receding luminescence, noting and displaying the progress of days[153] as a kind of calendar; then the five stars[154] traveling in the same twelve-part sphere,[155] adhering unceasingly to fixed paths that are different for each starry wanderer;[156] and the night sky festooned with stars as far as sight extends; then the orb of the earth towering over the sea,[157] fixed in the center of the universe, habitable and cultivated in two different regions, with the region we inhabit being

> Under the axis positioned towards the seven stars
> Where the freezing, howling north wind
> Sets the icy snows in motion,[158]

and the other being the southern hemisphere, which is unknown to us and called *antichthon*[159] by the Greeks (the other parts remain uncultivated, because they are either frigid wastelands or roasting in

---

[153] The degree of illumination of the lunar surface as seen from Earth varies throughout the month (the "phases" of the moon).

[154] The five known planets.

[155] Referring to the twelve "parts" (i.e., constellations) of the zodiac.

[156] In Cicero's day, planets were called "wandering stars."

[157] The meaning of this phrase is obscure.

[158] A quote from Accius's *Philoctetes*.

[159] The Greek word used is ἀντίχθων. This arcane term means "counter-earth."

heat); yet here where we live, reliably appearing in their own special moments, are

> Skies beginning to glow and trees starting to sprout leaves,
> Luxuriant vines maturing with vine-shoots,
> Branches of berries bending with abundance,
> Crop-fields bountifully laden with grain, garnished everywhere with blossoms,
> Springs bubbling, and grasses overspreading the meadows;[160]

then the multitude of domesticated animals used in part for our consumption, in part for cultivation of the fields, in part for carrying loads, in part to make human clothing; and man himself, created almost to contemplate the heavens and till the land; and then the fields and seas conforming to human commands—and so, when we see all these things and myriad others like them, can we doubt that some divine agent or maker presides over them, if these things have a known origin (as Plato says), or, if they have always existed (as Aristotle maintains), that a controller of such an awe-inspiring work and spectacle directs them?[161]

It is the same with the mind of man, even though you do not actually see it. *Just as you do not see God, but know him from his works, so will you know the divine power of mind from its capacity for memory, discovery, speed of movement, and all the transcendent beauty of virtue.*

29. Then where is its location? I personally believe that it is located in the head. I can offer my arguments explaining why I believe this. But the location of the soul is an issue we need not discuss now. There is a soul undoubtedly within you. What is its nature? I think it

---

To the Pythagoreans, it was a companion planet of the earth that protected it from the universe's fires. But Cicero here seems to use it as a general term for the southern hemisphere.

[160] F.E. Rockwood, in his edition of the Latin text, speculates that this quote is from Ennius's play *Eumenides*.

[161] To convey this poetic sentence's full power in English, I judged it necessary to preserve its original extended length.

has its own specific nature. But if you think it is fiery or airy—that is not relevant to what we are now discussing. You should understand this: just as you know God, even though you are unaware of his location and appearance, so should your soul be known to you, even if you do not know its location and form.

When investigating the soul, we cannot doubt—unless we are clearly fools in natural philosophy—that in souls there is nothing mixed, nothing blended, nothing joined or connected with something else, and nothing duplicate.[162] Since this is its nature, it is absolutely impossible for the soul to be separated, divided, fractured, or ripped apart. It is also impossible for it to die. For dying is like the partition, division, and shattering of those parts which, before death, were held together in a kind of coherent whole.

Guided by these rationales and others like them, Socrates neither desired anyone to defend him during his capital trial, nor prostrated himself before his judges. He manifested a dignified defiance that came from greatness of soul, rather than pride. On the last day of his life, he talked a great deal about this very thing. A few days before his death, he turned down an offer[163] to be delivered out of custody. And when the hour drew near for holding the poisonous cup in his hands, he spoke to his followers in a way that made him appear not as a man driven to death, but as a man ascending to heaven.[164]

30. His belief system, and the ideas he discussed, were these. There are two roads, two possible paths for souls at the moment they leave the body. Those who contaminated themselves with human vices and surrendered entirely to their baser passions—those who, once blinded by these things, debased themselves either with private vices or infamies, or perpetrated unforgivable offenses with public scandals—had a very particular path assigned to them, a path far removed from association with the gods. But those who maintained their uprightness and moral integrity, had minimal contact with the

---

[162] I.e., nothing that is two-fold (*duplex*).

[163] One of Socrates's pupils, an Athenian named Crito, offered to arrange an escape. Socrates turned down the offer, preferring to remain in prison and allow his death sentence to be carried out. See Plato's *Crito*.

[164] These comments refer to the trial and execution of Socrates in Athens in 399 B.C. Plato's *Apologia* depicts the trial of Socrates. The *Phaedo* describes the dialogue (discussing the immortality of the soul) that took place before Socrates consumed the lethal hemlock.

body and always detached themselves from it, and while in the human body, imitated the life of the gods: these people had extended before them an easy return journey to those they had once left.

Plato says that just as swans—which for good reason are sacred to Apollo because like him they seem able to predict future events, and sense the good that may exist in death—die with a song of euphoria, so must all who are good and learned follow this example.[165] No one could have any doubt about this, unless when thinking intensely about the soul we suffer the same injury that happens to those who spend too much time looking at the setting sun (that is, losing one's sight completely). In the same way, the mind's eye occasionally grows feeble when scrutinizing itself closely. For this reason we decrease the intensity of rumination. Thus our reasoning—doubting, observing, hesitating, and plagued by many obstacles—is carried along in the same way as a ship in the limitless ocean.

But these are things that belong to the past, and to the heritage of the Greeks. Cato left this life in a mental state where he was happy to have found a reason for dying.[166] The God who commands our lives does not permit us to leave it without his approval. Yet when God himself supplies a valid justification, as he did anciently with Socrates and modernly in the case of Cato (and often to many others), then most definitely, the wise man will be happy to depart this land of shadows and enter the realm of light. He will not break the chains of his prison, as the law will not allow it. Nevertheless, just as if he were following the order of a judge or some other legitimate authority, he will leave, called forth and sent out by God.[167] For as Plato says, *the entire life of a philosopher is a meditation on death.*[168]

31. For what else are we doing, then, when we separate the soul from physical pleasure, that is, from the body? Or when we separate it from our personal possessions, which are the body's servants and attendants? Or when we separate it from public life, or any other kind of work? What are we doing, I want to know, except calling the soul before itself, forcing it to be with itself, and guiding it away from the

---

[165] *See* Pliny, *Hist. Nat.* X.63.

[166] Cato took his own life after learning of Caesar's victory at the Battle of Thapsus in 46 B.C.

[167] Meaning that the wise man will not "break out" of his mortal prison until God allows him to do so.

[168] The phrase is *commentatio mortis*, which may also be translated as "preparation for death."

body? Is the separation of the soul from the body anything other than learning how to come to terms with death? So believe me: let us make ourselves ready for this. Let us unlink ourselves from our bodies— *that is, let us become accustomed to the inevitability of our own deaths.*

This will be similar to the life of heaven, while we are here on earth. And at the time when we are brought out of our earthly shackles here, the soul's journey will be less hindered. For those who have always been restricted by the chains of the body will make much slower progress, even after they have been released from these fetters, just as it is with those who have been wearing irons for many years. When we come to our final destination, we will then finally live. For indeed this mortal life is death—and I could lament it, if I chose to do so.

A. You have mourned this life enough in your *Consolation*. When I read it, I prefer nothing more than to depart this mortal life. And when I hear you explain these things as you did, I long for it even more.

M. The hour will come. And whether you distance yourself from this fact, or whether you look forward to it, the time will come quickly. For time indeed flies by.[169] But death is very far from being an "evil" to man—an idea you yourself believed just a little while ago. I tend to think that there is nothing else for mankind that is *not* an evil. If we are either to be gods ourselves, or we are to walk with the gods, then certainly there is no other good that is preferable to death.

A. How is this important?

M. There are some here who don't approve of these ideas. But in this discussion, I will never let you walk away with the chance that, under the influence of some argument, you might conclude that death is an evil.

A. Since I've accepted your ideas, how could that happen?

M. Are you asking me how it's possible? A good number of naysayers are going to attack these ideas. They will be not only Epicureans, against whom I feel no antagonism. I'm not sure why, but the most learned thinkers look down on the Epicureans. My valued friend Dicaearchus has articulated a quite compelling case against the immortality of the soul. He composed three books under the title

---

[169] *Volat enim aetas.*

Lesbiacs,[170] since the dialogue took place at Mytilene, and his objective is to demonstrate that the soul is indeed perishable. The Stoics, however, indulge us with a generous amount of time to enjoy ourselves, as if we were old crows:[171] they say that the soul can last for a long time, but deny its immortality.

32. So do you want to hear the reason why—even if our argument is correct—that death should still not be considered an evil?

A. Say what is on your mind. But no one will force me to give up the idea of immortality.

M. I commend you for that, but we should not be too self-assured in these matters. Often we are swayed by some opinion that has been artfully constructed. We hesitate and change our views even on things that are obvious. It is like that for this topic, too, for there is a degree of ambiguity about it. If that situation comes about, let us approach it sufficiently well-equipped.

A. Of course. But I will take precautions to make sure it doesn't happen.

M. So is there any reason why we shouldn't part ways with our friends the Stoics? I'm talking about those who say that souls persist for some time after leaving the body, but do not last for an indefinite amount of time.

A. We certainly should dismiss them. They believe that the soul can exist outside of the body, which is the most problematic issue in this question. But then they prune away something that not only should be easy to believe, but that also follows naturally if we accept their point: this is the idea *that when the soul lasts for a long time, it does not die.*

M. You quite rightly find fault with them, and that is how things are at present. Should we put our trust in Panaetius when his views diverge from those of his master Plato? At every opportunity he calls Plato divine, the wisest, the most sanctified, and "the Homer of the philosophers." And yet he does not endorse this one doctrine of Plato's about the immortality of souls. He advocates what no one denies: that whatever is born will also die. He says that souls are born, and that this is evident from observing the similarities that offspring have to those who produced them—not only physically, but also in behavioral characteristics. Another argument he offers is this

---

[170] I.e., one work consisting of three books. The title is derived from the Greek island of Lesbos. The capital of Lesbos is Mytilene.

[171] According to folklore, crows were supposed to live for many years. See, e.g., Pliny's *Hist. Nat.* VII.153.

one: there is nothing that feels pain, that cannot also be vulnerable to sickness. And what may be vulnerable to sickness, will also die. Souls feel pain—and therefore, they must die.

33. These views can be rebutted. He is not aware that when something is said about the immortality of souls, it is said about the mind, and the mind is always free of confused instinct. It is not said about those bodily parts that are agitated by sickness, anger, and sexual passion. Plato—the ultimate target of his criticisms—taught that these things were distant and detached from the mind. The similarity is more apparent in wild beasts whose souls are deficient in reason. Similarity in man, however, exists more in the form of the body; the type of body in which souls are placed matters a great deal.

For there are many factors that can act to improve the mind, and many that can act to impair it. In fact Aristotle says that all accomplished men suffer from melancholy—an observation that allows me to feel less embarrassed at my own foolishness.[172] He articulates many examples; and as if it all were neatly certain, he offers reasons why things are that way. For if the things that arise in the body have such control over the mind's habit (whatever they are, these things are what cause the similarity), similarity indicates no decisive reason why souls are born. I will omit situations where there are no similarities.

I wish Panaetius were here, for he lived with Africanus.[173] I would have asked him which family member Africanus's great-nephew looked like.[174] His face was similar to his father's face, but the life he led was just like the life of every dissolute man—yet he was easily the most dissolute. I would also have asked whom the grandson[175] of Publius Crassus (a wise, well-spoken, and distinguished man) resembled, as well as the sons and grandsons of many other notables we need not bother mentioning. But what are doing? Has it slipped our minds that our discussion topic (after we had satisfactorily talked about eternity) was that death was not an evil, even if the soul had only a finite life?

---

[172] Seneca also makes this observation in his *De Tranquilitate Animi* 15.16.

[173] Panaetius was the teacher of Africanus the Younger.

[174] The individual referred to is Quintus Fabius Maximus, grandson of Quintus Fabius Maximus Aemilianus. He was well-known as a dissolute character; *see* Val. Max. III.5.2.

[175] Publius Licinius Crassus was consul in 97 B.C., and also had a son with the name Publius Crassus. The son of this son is the person Cicero is referring to here. *See* Val. Max. VI.9.12.

A. I certainly remember what our topic was. But I easily tolerated your straying from the topic when you were discoursing about eternity.

34. M. I see that your vision is directed skyward, and your desire is to journey to heaven. I hope it is true that this destiny awaits us. But imagine that souls do not survive after death, as some of these philosophers teach. If this is true, I think we are robbed of the prospect of a happier life. What sort of evil does this view bring? Let us say that the soul dies just like the body. Is there any pain, or any kind of sense-perception, in the body after death? No one takes this position, although Epicurus alleges that Democritus does.[176] The students of Democritus deny the accusation. No sensation remains in the soul either, since the soul is nowhere.

Since there is no third thing,[177] then where is the evil? Is it because the flight of the soul from the body does not happen without pain? I ought to believe this, but what an unimportant thing it is! But I think it is false. Often the soul's flight occurs without sensation, and even at times with enjoyment. No matter how it happens, the whole matter is of minor importance, since this removal of the soul takes place in an instant of time. What truly vexes us—or rather what torments us—is the separation from all the things that are good in life. But consider that it might more properly be said: *the separating from all of life's evils.*

Why should I now feel sorrow when reflecting on the life of man? I could bemoan it truly and justly. But why is this necessary, when I am arguing that we should not think ourselves miserable after death, thereby making life more miserable by continuous grieving? We already did that in a book in which we comforted ourselves as much as we could. Therefore, if we want to know the truth: *death takes us away from evils, not from goods.*

Indeed this point was so eloquently argued by Hegesias the Cyrenaic that they say he was ordered by King Ptolemy[178] to stop teaching it, since some of his listeners had decided to take their own lives. There is an epigram of Callimachus[179] about Cleombrotus of

---

[176] Rockwood here cites Pseudo-Plutarch's *Placita Philosophorum* (*Doctrines of the Philosophers*) at IV.4 as evidence that Democritus believed the body's atoms retained some degree of sensation even after death.

[177] Meaning that "there are only these two things, the physical body and the soul, and nothing else."

[178] Ptolemy II Philadelphus (c. 308 B.C.—c. 246 B.C.), Ptolemaic king of Egypt.

[179] Callimachus of Cyrene (c. 310 B.C.—c. 240 B.C.), poet and scholar of the Alexandrian Library.

Ambracia[180] who, Callimachus says, threw himself from the city walls into the sea after reading a book of Plato's, even though he had not experienced a reversal of his personal fortunes.

Hegesias of Cyrene,[181] of whom I have already spoken, authored a book called *Apokarteron*.[182] In this book, a man committing suicide by starving himself is enticed by his friends to abandon this enterprise; he responds by enumerating the odious aspects of human life. I could do the same thing myself, though to a lesser extent than Hegesias does, who thinks that living brings no one any kind of benefit. I ignore others: is it expedient *for me* to live? If I had died before losing the sustaining power of my own family[183] and the comforting honors of my public career, death would have removed me from life's evils, not from life's goods.

35. Suppose, then, there is someone afflicted by no evil, someone who has experienced no wound from fortune. The well-known Metellus[184] had four sons who had public honors conferred on them; but Priam had fifty,[185] of which seventeen were born of his legal wife. Fortune had the same power in both of these cases, but used it on only one of them. Many sons, daughters, grandsons, and granddaughters laid Metellus on his funeral pyre. But Priam, deprived of his many offspring when he retreated to the altar, was killed by the hand of an enemy. If he had died here with his sons alive and his kingdom intact,

The barbarous resources standing near,
And carved ceilings, adorned with panels,[186]

---

[180] Cleombrotus of Ambracia (in Epirus), an Academic philosopher and follower of Plato about whom little is known. He is mentioned in Plato's *Phaedo* as being absent from Socrates's deathbed.

[181] A Cyrenaic philosopher (fl. 290 B.C.) who followed the teachings of Aristippus. He was essentially a pessimist.

[182] ἀποκαρτερῶν, or "The Man Who Starves Himself." This work has not survived.

[183] Cicero here is referring to the death of his daughter Tullia.

[184] Quintus Caecilius Metellus Macedonicus (c. 210 B.C.—c. 116 B.C.), consul in 143 B.C., was the Roman conqueror of Macedonia. All four of his sons eventually became consuls (three during his life, one after his death).

[185] Homer (*Iliad* XXIV.496) says that Priam and Hecuba had nineteen sons.

[186] These verses, and the ones in the following paragraph, are from Ennius's *Andromache*.

would he have been taken away from good things, or from evil things? At that time it certainly seems that he was being taken away from the good. Without doubt it would have turned out better for him, and they would not have sung these lines so mournfully:

> I saw all these things consumed by fire,
> Priam forcefully deprived of life,
> The altar of Jove reddened with gore.

As if anything better could have happened to him at that time, while this sort of brutality was taking place. If he had died before this, he would have entirely avoided this outcome. But due to the timing of his death, he evaded awareness of the evils that threatened him. Our friend Pompey, when he fell seriously ill at Naples, eventually recovered. The Neapolitans decorated their heads with wreaths, and certainly the people of Puteoli did likewise. Community messages of support came in from the towns. It may have been a frivolous display—the kind of thing you might expect from the Greeks—but it still confirms his good fortune.

If he had died at that time, would he have avoided good things, or bad things? Without doubt, he would have avoided miseries. He would not have waged war against his father-in-law,[187] would not have taken up arms when untrained for conflict, would not have left his home, would not have fled Italy, and would not have been intercepted by hostile slaves after losing his army. His hapless children and his entire fortune would not have fallen into the hands of those who defeated him. If he had died at that time, his life would have ended while his fortunes were at their greatest extent. Yet because of the lengthening of his life, what shockingly severe and pervasive calamities he later had to swallow!

36. These terrible events are avoided by the intervention of death. Although they have not yet happened, they very well *could* happen—yet men do not believe that these kinds of disasters can happen to themselves. Each person expects the good fortune of Metellus, acting as if more people were lucky than unlucky, or that human affairs are consistently predictable, or as if it were more prudent to rely on hope instead of vigilance.

---

[187] Meaning Julius Caesar. Pompey was married to Julia, the daughter of Caesar.

But one may concede the fact that men are deprived of good things by death. Does it follow that the dead yearn for life's enjoyments, and that this is something miserable? That is definitely what they have to say. Can someone who does not exist "yearn for" anything? The verb "yearn for" itself has a sad ring to it, because it reinforces the idea of *he had, he does not have, he longs for, he requires, he needs*. I think these are the inconveniences of those who "yearn for" something: he yearns for eyes, since blindness is odious; he yearns for children, since childlessness is odious. This is true for living persons. But as for the dead, a deceased person does not regret the loss of life's amenities, for the deceased does not feel the loss of life itself.[188]

I am talking about the dead, meaning those who do not exist. But do we, who are alive, "miss" horns or feathers? Would anyone at all say this? Certainly no one would. But why? Because when you lack something that is unfit for you either by earned merit or nature, you do not yearn for it, even if you are aware that you lack it. This point must be pressed regularly once we have proven the argument that (if souls are mortal) no one can doubt: *the annihilation of death is so final that not even the slightest residue of sense-perception can remain.* Once this truth is laid down and firmly fixed, the real meaning of "to yearn for" must be investigated so that it is clearly understood, and no error might result from the use of this verb.

The verb "to yearn for" carries this meaning: to lack something that you would like to have. For the idea of wanting is embedded in the verb "to yearn for," except when this verb is used in an entirely different way, such as when we say that someone is "lacking a fever." The expression "to yearn for" is used in a very divergent sense when you don't have something, and you are aware that you don't have it, even if you can easily tolerate the fact that you don't have it. We do not use "to yearn for" when talking about evil, nor is the act of yearning always tragic. The correct way to say it is, "to yearn for a good," and that is an evil.

Yet even a living man does not yearn for a good, if he does not feel the need for it. But for a living man it can still make sense to say that you yearn for a kingdom. In your situation, however, that cannot properly be said; but it could have been said about Tarquin when he

---

[188] Meaning that the dead cannot possibly miss life's pleasures, because the dead have no sense-perception and can feel nothing.

was expelled from his kingdom. But when we are talking about the dead, it does not make any sense. "To yearn for" is an expression reserved for those who can still feel—and the dead feel nothing. With regard to the dead, therefore, there is no "yearning" for anything.

37. But why do we need to philosophize about this topic, when we can see that it doesn't much need philosophy? How many times have our commanders, as well as entire armies, engaged in battles where death was guaranteed from the outset? If this truly is what they were afraid of, Lucius Brutus[189] would not have died in battle while trying to prevent the return of the tyrant he had previously expelled. Decius (the father), struggling with the Latins, his son in battle with the Etruscans, and his grandson at war with Pyrrhus, would not have hurled themselves against the enemy's spears.[190]

Spain would not have witnessed the Scipios[191] dying in battle for their country in one war. Paulus and Geminus[192] would not have sacrificed themselves at Cannae, Marcellus would not have fallen at Venusia, nor Albinus at Litana, and not Gracchus at Lucania.[193] Are any of these men "miserable" today? They were not even "miserable" at the moment life departed their bodies; for when sense-perception has been extinguished, no one can be miserable.

Someone may claim that it is odious to be without sensation. If by "odious" one means "yearning for" something, then it is odious. But since it is clear that there is nothing remaining in a person who does not exist, how can there be anything "odious" when the person

---

[189] Lucius Junius Brutus (?—509 B.C.), one of the first Roman consuls. He is credited with overthrowing the monarchy and founding the republic. He died fighting the son (Arruns Tarquinius) of the last Roman king, Tarquinius Superbus.

[190] Publius Decius Mus (consul in 340 B.C.) sacrificed himself to secure victory (a ritual called *devotio*) during the Battle of Vesuvius against the Latins in 340 B.C. His son followed this example at the Battle of Sentinum in 295 B.C. against the Samnites and Etruscans. The grandson apparently did the same at the Battle of Asculum in 279 B.C. in combat against King Pyrrhus.

[191] Referring to Publius Cornelius Scipio and Cnaeus Cornelius Scipio, who both died in Spain during the Second Punic War in 212 B.C.

[192] Lucius Aemilius Paulus and Cnaeus Servilius Geminus both perished while fighting Hannibal at Cannae in 216 B.C.

[193] Marcus Claudius Marcellus (c. 268 B.C.—208 B.C.) died fighting the Carthaginians at Venusia in 208 B.C. The consul Lucius Postumius Albinus died fighting the Boii in Cisalpine Gaul (at the forest of Litana, south of Mutina) in 215 B.C. Tiberius Sempronius Gracchus (consul in 215 B.C. and 213 B.C.) was killed fighting the Carthaginians at Lucania in 212 B.C.

neither yearns for anything, nor senses anything? This may have been stated too often, but this is because here is where we find everything that makes the soul morose from the fear of death.

He who has the vision to see what is clearer than daylight—that when body and soul come to an end, when all life force has been extinguished, and when total destruction has occurred, then the living organism that once existed has now become nothing—will clearly understand that there is no difference between a hippocentaur[194] (a creature that never existed) and King Agamemnon.[195]

Such a person will also realize that Marcus Camillus[196] worries no more about our current civil war than I worry about the sacking of Rome that happened when he was alive. Why, then, would Camillus grieve, if he knew we would experience civil war three hundred and fifty years after his own time? And why should I myself grieve, if I thought that ten thousand years from now some foreign people would take over Rome? Because love of country is so deep that it is judged not by our personal feeling, but by the well-being of our country itself.

38. Thus death does not discourage the wise man. Life's uncertain fortunes mean that death hovers about us on a daily basis; and the brevity of mortal life places death never too far distant. The wise man attends to his public and domestic responsibilities at all times, conscious of his duty to safeguard the interests of those future generations that he will never directly know. He who believes the soul to be mortal may strive to achieve things that last for all time, not from a desire for glory—of which he will have no awareness—but for the sake of virtue, which necessarily achieves glory even if this is not one's goal.

Nature decrees that, just as our moment of birth announces the start of all things, so does the arrival of death bring an end to all things. And just as nothing concerned us before we were born, so nothing will concern us after death. When death troubles neither the living nor the dead, what evil can there be in this? The living are not touched by it, and the dead do not exist. Those who devalue the significance of death try to equate it with sleeping—as if someone

---

[194] Another word for centaur.

[195] The Mycenaean king who led the Greek expedition to Troy.

[196] Marcus Furius Camillus (c. 446 B.C.—365 B.C.), Roman statesman who freed Rome after it had been captured by the Gauls in 390 B.C. He is said to have stated, *Non auro, sed ferro, recuperanda est patria* ("Not with gold, but with iron, must a nation be recovered").

would want to live until the age of ninety provided he spent the first sixty years living, and then slept for the remaining thirty years. Not only would any person reject this, but even his relatives would not want it.

If we want to hear fables, recall that Endymion supposedly once fell asleep on Latmus, a mountain in Caria—and I don't believe he has ever awakened.[197] Do you think he is bothered at the fact that the Moon has problems, even though she is said to have put him to sleep in order to kiss him? Indeed, why would someone worry if he does not even feel anything? You have sleep, the imitation of death, and this is something you dress yourself in every day. And you doubt that there is no feeling in death, even though you can see that there is no feeling in its imitation?

39. Let us banish from our minds, therefore, ideas such as "it is a miserable thing to die before one's time," which are mostly the nonsense of old women. What "time" are you talking about? Nature's time? But nature has only lent us life, just as she might lend us money with no agreed day of repayment. Why would you complain, then, if she asked for repayment at a time of her own choosing? You accepted the loan under this condition. These same people believe that if a small child dies, the emotional burden must be carried by the family with quiet resignation. And if the child is still in the cradle, they think there should be no complaint at all. Yet in this situation nature demanded back what she had given with greater harshness.

"The child had not yet tasted the sweetness of life," they say. "But the other had begun to form hopes of happiness, and he had started to enjoy them." In other things, it is thought better to get a part of something, instead of nothing. Why should it be any different when we talk about life? Callimachus certainly was not wrong when he commented that "Priam cried much more often than Troilus."[198] Yet the fate of those who die at an advanced age is considered praiseworthy. Why is this? I don't suppose that anyone would find a longer life to be more enjoyable, if it were given to him.

For without doubt nothing is sweeter to a man than prudence; and although old age robs us of everything else, it certainly grants us this. But what age is "long," or what is "long" for a person at all? Doesn't old age

---

[197] According to myth, Endymion was a handsome shepherd on Mt. Latmos. Zeus gave him immortality in the form of permanent sleep at the request of Selene, the goddess of the Moon, who had fallen in love with him.

[198] Troilus, a son of Priam, was killed by Achilles in the Trojan War.

First the children, then the youths,
Following in the race one after the other,
Pass them by without their knowledge?[199]

Yet since nothing is beyond old age, we call this "long." All
things are said to be long or short in conformity with the *pro rata*
share of the whole that has been given to them. Along the Hypanis
River,[200] which flows from a part of Europe into the Pontus, Aristotle
says[201] certain little animals are born that live for only one day. One
of these animals that dies in the eighth hour has expired in old age.
One that dies at sunset is practically ancient—even more so if the
death occurs on the day of the summer solstice.[202] Compare the age
of the oldest person with eternity: we will discover that our existence
is governed by the same brevity that applies to the lives of these small
animals.

40. So let us treat all foolishness with contempt. What softer
name could I give to such insignificant things? Let us place the entire
essence of correct living in fortitude and greatness of soul, in aver-
sion and contempt for all fluctuations in human affairs, and in the
exercise of every virtue. For indeed we are made so effeminate these
days by such flaccid thoughts that, if death happens to come to us
before the predictions of the Chaldeans[203] have come to pass, we see
ourselves as having been forsaken, swindled, and robbed of tremendous benefits. But if our minds are made to dangle in the torment and
heartache of expectation and desire—then, immortal gods! Then how
joyous will the migration be that brings no more troubles when it is
complete, and no apprehension about the future! How Theramenes[204]
pleases me, and how sublime is his spirit!

Although we weep when we read, a great man still does not die

---

[199] The author of these verses is unknown.
[200] The Bug River in southwest Russia.
[201] The reference is to Aristotle's *Hist. Animals* V.19.
[202] Meaning midsummer, the time (occurring twice per year) when one of the
Earth's poles is most inclined towards the Sun.
[203] In Cicero's day, this (*Chaldaei*) was a generic term given to astrologers or
fortune-tellers.
[204] Theramenes of Athens (?—404 B.C.) was an Athenian statesman chosen to
serve as one of the so-called "Thirty Tyrants." One of his colleagues (Critias)
denounced him for treason, and he was forced to drink hemlock.

miserably. When he was thrown in prison by order of the thirty tyrants, he eagerly gulped down poison, then shook out the rest of it from the cup, so that the liquid made an audible sound.[205] Laughing at the noise this gesture made, he said, "I drink to the health of the handsome Critias" (a man who had grievously wronged him). During their dinner parties, the Greeks are accustomed to naming the person whom they intend to give the drinking cup. This great man bantered amiably as he ended his life. When he ingested the fatal potion, he correctly predicted the death of the man he had toasted as he drank the poison. And death did indeed soon come to Critias.[206]

What person who believed death was an evil would praise this steadfastness of a great soul in the face of death? Socrates found himself a few years later in the same prison, presented with the same goblet, and facing the same injustice from his judges as that which the thirty tyrants had doled out to Theramenes. What was the speech that Plato alleges Socrates delivered before his judges when they had sentenced him to death?[207]

41. "Gentlemen of the jury," he said, "I have great hope that it is good for me to be sentenced to death. For then it is certain that one of two things will happen: either death takes away all sensation entirely, or in death one is removed from this location to some other place. So if sense-perception is extinguished, and death is similar to that sleep which sometimes brings the most placid tranquility without the mental images of dreams—then, good gods! What a benefit is dying! How many days can be found that are worth more than this kind of night? And if this night of slumber will be similar to a perpetual, uninterrupted length of time, then who would be more pleased than I?

"But if what people say is true—that death is a migration to shores populated by those no longer living—then I would certainly be even more pleased. Know that, when you have escaped from those who want to be *counted* as judges, and arrive before those who *truly*

---

[205] A reference to the Greek dinner party game of *cottabus* (κότταβος). A drinker would shake the last few drops of wine from his cup at some target or into a metal receptacle; if the drops hit with a ringing noise, the event was interpreted as sign of good luck. There were other variations of the game.

[206] He died in 403 B.C. in a battle between the Thirty Tyrants and a force led by Thrasybulus.

[207] See Plato's *Apology* 40c.

can be called judges—Minos, Rhadamanthus, Aeacus, and Triptolemus[208]—you will meet men who have lived justly and ethically. Can this sojourn look to you like an ordinary journey? To think that one may actually speak with Orpheus, Musaeus,[209] Homer, and Hesiod—what sort of value can we attach to a journey that provides this? Indeed, I would want to die multiple times, so that I could be allowed to discover for myself these things I'm describing.

"It would arouse such joy in me to meet Palamedes, Ajax,[210] and others victimized by unjust sentences! I might be able to question the great king who led his forces to Troy, and evaluate the prudence of Ulysses and Sisyphus,[211] without having to face the death penalty for quizzing *them* just as I was doing here. Indeed, those of you judges who said I was not guilty should not fear death, either. For no evil can come to a good man in life or in death; his affairs will not be ignored by the immortal gods. What has happened to *me* did not occur by chance. Nor in truth do I hold any resentment against those who have accused me or condemned me, except for the fact that they thought they were harming me."

In this way did he speak before the judges. But nothing could surpass his final words. "It is now time" he stated, "for me to proceed to my death, and for you to continue with your lives. Only the immortal gods know which of these two paths is better. For I believe that no mortal man knows."

42. I would rather have the soul of Socrates than the fortunes of all the men who served as judges in his case. Yet he knows the very thing that he says no one knows except the gods—that is, which of the two choices is better. For he had earlier said that he knew which was better. But right up to the bitter end, he stays true to his principle

---

[208] See I.5, above. Triptolemus (also known as Buzyges) was the eldest son of King Celeus of Eleusis. He is linked to the Roman goddess of agriculture, Ceres, and the Eleusinian Mysteries. He was said to be connected with the three judges of the underworld.

[209] Orpheus and Musaeus of Athens were early mythic Greek musicians and poets.

[210] Palamedes was the son of Nauplius, king of Euboea, and Clymene. He was falsely accused of treason and stoned to death by Odysseus and Diomedes. Ajax was the son of King Telemon and Periboea; he committed suicide after losing a competition to possess the armor of Achilles.

[211] Sisyphus was a mythical king of Ephyra (Corinth) who was killed by Theseus. He was condemned to spend eternity in futile labor by rolling a heavy stone up a hill, only to see it roll back down again.

of not explicitly stating his own position. Let us, however, hold firmly our own ethic: *we consider nothing to be an evil that nature has given to us all, and we understand that if death is an evil, then it is an eternal evil.* For death appears to be the end of a miserable life. If death is something miserable, then there can be no end to its misery.[212]

But why do I point out Socrates and Theramenes, men distinguished by the renown of their virtue and wisdom? There was once a Lacedaemonian—his name has not come down to us—who had such contempt for death that, when the Spartan ephors[213] pronounced his death sentence, a buoyant and enthusiastic expression appeared on his face. An opponent snarled at him, "Are you mocking the laws of Lycurgus?" His response was, "I certainly am grateful to him for imposing a punishment that I can satisfy without accepting help from someone else, and without having to take out another loan to pay it off."[214] Here was a man worthy of Sparta! He displayed such a great spirit, in fact, that it seems to me they condemned an innocent man.

Our own country has turned out a large number of such men. But why should I name military commanders and leaders, when Cato writes that legions often went eagerly to a place where they did not think they would return? The Lacedaemonians who died at Thermopylae[215] were imbued with the same spirit. About them Simonides says,

> Visitor, tell the Spartans that you have seen us
> Here in death's repose,
> While we dutifully obeyed our country's sacred laws.[216]

---

[212] *Mors si est misera, finis esse nullus potest.* Cicero's wording could have been clearer here.

[213] Ephors were the highest Spartan judicial council. There were five of them, and they were elected annually.

[214] The phrase "accepting help from someone else" is *mutatione*, or contractual borrowing of money; the "having to take out another loan to pay it off" is *versura*, or the taking out of a loan from a third party creditor to pay off an original loan.

[215] The famous Battle of Thermopylae in 480 B.C., where Leonidas and the Spartan "three hundred" died fighting the Persians.

[216] *See* Herodotus VII.228.

In a dialogue with one of these Spartans, a Persian opponent braggingly taunted, "You won't even see the sun due to the number of javelins and arrows we will fire at you." The Spartan said in response, "Then we will fight in the dark of the shadow."[217] I am mentioning great men; but what about the character of the Spartan woman? When one Spartan mother[218] sent her son off to battle and received the news of his death, she said, "Thus did I bring him into the world: that he would be the kind of man who was always prepared to die for his country."

43. Let it be so, you strong and stern Spartans: the discipline of a republic has a formidable power. Well, what? Don't we marvel at Theodorus of Cyrene,[219] a very respectable philosopher? When King Lysimachus[220] threatened to crucify him, he said, "I ask you to direct those terrible threats to your attendants in purple garments. It does not matter to Theodorus whether he decomposes in the soil or in the open air." This quote reminds me that I should mention burial and entombment. This is not difficult, especially once we have understood the things just recently stated about the lack of sense-perception. Socrates's views on this issue are made clear in that book which gives an account of his death, which we have already discussed at length.

Once Socrates had finished debating the immortality of souls, and the hour of his death was drawing near, he was asked by Crito in what manner he wanted to be buried. "My friends," he said, "I have truly exerted much effort in vain. For I have not persuaded our friend Crito that I will remove myself from here and leave nothing behind. Yet despite this, Crito, if you can catch me, or if anywhere you happen to stumble upon me, feel free to bury me as you please. But believe me, none of you will catch up with me once I have left this place."

Indeed Socrates expresses himself wonderfully: he allowed his friend to act as he saw fit, and made it clear that burial concerns of

---

[217] Herodotus (VII.226) gives a slightly different version of this anecdote.

[218] The Latin word for a Spartan female is *Lacaena*.

[219] Theodorus of Cyrene (or Theodorus the Atheist), c. 340 B.C.—c. 250 B.C., a Cyrenaic philosopher and disciple of Aristippus of Cyrene who was expelled from Athens and moved to Alexandria. He was apparently sent by Ptolemy I Soter of Egypt as an envoy to King Lysimachus. *See* Val. Max. VI.2.

[220] Lysimachus of Thrace (c. 360 B.C.—281 B.C.), Macedonian general who became king of Thrace. He was killed at the Battle of Corupedium (near Sardis in Asia Minor).

this sort did not matter to him. Diogenes[221] was even more harsh. His sentiments, indeed, were the same as those of Socrates; but as a Cynic he was more caustic, and ordered that his body should be dumped unburied somewhere. His friends asked him, "Dumped for the birds and wild animals that feed on carrion?" "Absolutely not," he replied. "Put my staff near me so I can run them off." "And how will you do this? You won't have any sensation of anything!" they protested. "So then what's the problem with the mutilation of my corpse," Diogenes answered, "if I'm unable to feel anything?"

When he was dying at Lampsacus, Anaxagoras[222] responded brilliantly when his friends asked him if he wanted to be taken to his homeland Clazomenae if he passed away. "That is quite unnecessary," he said, "for the road to the underworld is the same distance, no matter the starting point."[223] Regarding burial's main purpose, we must be guided by one rule: that it pertains to the physical body, whether the soul has died or still lives. Yet it is clear that, whether the soul has been extinguished or has departed, there is nothing left of sensation in the body.

44. But all of these issues are riddled with errors. Achilles ties Hector to his chariot[224] and drags him; I suppose he thought Hector could feel his body being destroyed. Thus Achilles avenges himself, or believes he is avenging himself, in this way. Yet a woman[225] expresses grief at this vicious desecration:

> I saw what I have endured watching
> With the greatest agony,
> Hector being dragged by a chariot
> Yoked four horses abreast.[226]

---

[221] Diogenes of Sinope (c. 404 B.C.—323 B.C.), one of the founders of the Cynic school. He was known for his frank criticisms of established values and customs.

[222] Anaxagoras of Clazomenae (c. 500 B.C.—428 B.C.), a pre-Socratic philosopher who was known to the Athenian leader Pericles. He was eventually exiled from Athens to Lampsacus in Mysia for philosophical and astronomical speculations that challenged the established faith.

[223] *Undique enim ad inferos tantumdem viae est.*

[224] *Illiad* XXII.395. Hector (son of Priam and Hecuba) was the best Trojan warrior, but was slain by Achilles, who then desecrated the corpse by dragging it with a chariot.

[225] I.e., Andromache, the wife of Hector.

[226] These lines are from Ennius's *Andromache*.

What Hector? Or how long will it be Hector? Accius[227] is better, and Achilles is eventually wise:

> Upon my word, to Priam I have certainly
> Returned Hector's remains,
> Now that I have deprived him of his life.[228]

You have not, therefore, dragged Hector, but only the corpse that had once been Hector. Behold another[229] that rises from the earth, and does not allow his mother to sleep:

> Mother, I call out to you, you that lightens
> Anxious care with sleep,
> Nor should you pity me: arise, and bury your
> child.[230]

When these verses, which can cast a pall of gloom over the entire audience in a theatre, are sung in a deliberate and doleful fashion, it is difficult not to believe that the unburied are miserable—

> Before wild animals and birds...

He is afraid he will not have good use of his body if his limbs are mangled. Yet he is not afraid if they are ritually burned:

---

[227] Lucius Accius (170 B.C.—c. 86 B.C.), an early Roman tragedian.

[228] These lines, according to F.E. Rockwood, may be from Accius's play *Epinausimache*.

[229] Referring to Deiphilus, son of the Thracian king Polymnestor, and Iliona, the daughter of Priam of Troy. Deiphilus was accidentally killed by his father.

[230] Lines from the tragedy *Iliona*, composed by the early Roman tragic poet Pacuvius (220 B.C.—c. 130 B.C.).

Do not, I ask you, permit my remains with their denuded bones
To be torn apart on the ground, coated over
With foul liquids of putrefaction.[231]

When he spews out such elegant seven-foot[232] verses to the accompaniment of the flute, I really don't understand what he's afraid of. We must therefore adhere to the rule that we should not worry about anything after death, even though many people take revenge on their dead enemies. In the writings of Ennius, Thyestes throws out curses in brilliant poetry.[233] He first calls for Atreus's death by shipwreck, which is certainly a terrible request, as this sort of death carries with it an appalling sense of what is happening. We then read these inane lines:

Fixed and disemboweled there at the summit of jagged rocks,[234]
Hanging by his side, sprinkling the stones
With putrid matter, ichorous pus, and atramentous blood.

The rocks themselves will not be more empty of sensation than a man who is hanging from them by his side—even though Thyestes thinks he is wishing torture on the man. It would be barbarous treatment, of course, if the person being tortured could feel what was happening. But when the victim feels nothing, there are no cruelties. How very inane, then, are these lines:

---

[231] Words spoken by the ghost of Deiphilus to his mother Iliona. These lines have an archaic quality in the Latin.
[232] Rockwood believes Cicero is mistaken here, noting that the verses are actually *octonarii*, or tetrameters.
[233] Atreus, son of Pelops, was king of Mycenae. Atreus sought a horrific vengeance against his brother Thyestes: he had Thyestes's two sons killed and served to their father at a banquet.
[234] Lines from Ennius's *Thyestes*. The two following quotes are also from this play.

Nor let him receive a tomb where he may have
A refuge for the body,
Where, when human life recedes,
The body may find reprieve from evils.

You see the extent of the mistake they are making here: he thinks the tomb is the body's refuge, and that a dead man finds rest there. Pelops[235] deserves a good deal of blame for not teaching and instructing his son on the attention that should be paid to different things.

45. Yet why should I focus on the opinions of individuals, when one can take note of the various errors of entire cultures? The Egyptians mummify their dead and store them at home;[236] the Persians inter them after they have been coated with wax, so that the corpses are preserved for as long as possible. The tradition of the Magi[237] is not to bury their dead until they have first been disfigured by wild animals.[238] In Hyrcania[239] the common folk take care of dogs for communal use, while the nobility keeps them for domestic use—and we know this is a superb canine breed. As his individual means will permit, each person arranges to have some of these animals in order to be disfigured by them. They believe this is the best sort of burial. Chrysippus[240] has catalogued many other types of burial customs— as his curiosity impels him to do for every historical topic—but these are so ghastly that we shrink from relating the details.

As far as we ourselves are concerned, the whole subject of burial should be treated with disdain; but it should not be neglected in cases of our friends. Those who live know that the bodies of the dead lack any kind of sense-perception. The living will honor these funerary practices to the extent that respectful deference must be shown to the

---

[235] Pelops was the son of Tantalus, founder of the house of Atreus. He was also king of ancient Elis in Greece.

[236] It is not clear what Cicero is referring to here. Mummies in Egypt were placed in tombs, not residential dwellings. *See* Herodotus I.140.

[237] Referring to the Medes, an ancient Iranian people.

[238] Corpses were exposed for consumption by wild animals and birds, sometimes in towers built specifically for this purpose.

[239] A province of the ancient Median Empire located on the southern shore of the Caspian Sea.

[240] A noted Stoic philosopher (c. 280 B.C.—c. 206 B.C.) from the city of Soli. He lived in Athens and was a student of Cleanthes.

dictates of tradition and popular opinion; but they will understand, at the same time, that such rituals have very little to do with the dead.

Yet death may be confronted with the serenest state of mind when a waning life can find consolation in the glory it has gained for itself. Anyone who has fully performed the obligation of perfect virtue has not lived too briefly. There have been many situations for me when death would have been appropriate—situations where I wish I had met it![241] For at that time there was nothing more to be gained; life's responsibilities had been completed, and all that was left was the battle with fortune.

Thus if reason is insufficient to convince us to pay no attention to death, then let the life we have lived thus far show that we have lived long enough, and even more than enough. Despite the fact that sense-perception has left them, the dead nevertheless possess their own special gifts of fame and glory, even if they are not conscious of them. For although glory has nothing that makes it intrinsically worth seeking, virtue still follows it like a shadow.

46. The crowd's true opinion about good men—if it ever forms one—is more something to be praised than a source of happiness to those who have died. However, I can't say—no matter how someone interprets it—that Lycurgus and Solon[242] lack glory as lawgivers and organizers of political systems, or that Themistocles and Epaminondas lack martial virtue. Neptune would sooner submerge the island of Salamis than the memory of the great victory at Salamis;[243] and Boeotian Leuctra would sooner be erased than the shining glory of the Battle of Leuctra.[244] Much more slowly will dim the glory of Curius, Fabricius, Calatinus, the two Scipios, the two Africani, Maximus, Marcellus, Paullus, Cato, Laelius, and innumerable others.[245] He who finds a way to imitate the positive attributes of these

---

[241] This sentence and the one that follows give the reader an idea of the anguish Cicero endured at the death of his daughter, the destruction of the republic, and the involuntary end of his career in politics and law.

[242] Solon (c. 638 B.C.—c. 558 B.C.), influential Athenian statesman and lawgiver. Lycurgus (fl. 820 B.C.) was the legendary lawgiver of Sparta.

[243] The famous Greek naval victory over the Persians in 480 B.C.

[244] Referring to the Theban victory over the Spartans in 371 B.C., where Epaminondas commanded the Thebans.

[245] Marcus Curius Denatus, three-time consul who defeated King Pyrrhus of

men, measured not by popular fame but by the legitimate praise of good men, will, if the situation arises, stride with a fearless spirit towards death, where we know that either the supreme good, or the complete absence of evil, may be found.

He might even wish to die when surrounded by his riches. For no amassing of benefits is so gratifying as is the vexation caused by their abatement.[246] This was apparently the meaning of the well-known statement made by the Lacedaemonian who, when the Olympic champion Diagoras of Rhodes[247] saw his two sons triumph on one day at Olympia, walked up to the old man to congratulate him and said, "Die, Diagoras, for you will not be rising to heaven."[248] The Greeks believe (perhaps too much) that success in these contests is a marvelous thing, or at least they used to believe so. The Lacedaemonian who spoke in this way to Diagoras thought that it was truly magnificent for one household to produce three Olympic winners. And he believed it was not advantageous for the father to continue living and subject himself to the cruel vagaries of fortune.

In a few words I have given you a response that, in my view, was satisfactory. You conceded that the dead were not in evil circumstances. But I have chosen to say more, because this point[249] is our greatest consolation during times of want or grief. We should bear sorrow with restraint when dealing with it ourselves, or when someone else suffers it for us, so that we do not appear to love ourselves too much. If we believe that the loved ones we have lost still possess some feeling of sensation among the evils that they are commonly thought to be under, then this would be an idea that causes unspeakable anguish. For my own sake, I wanted to pull out this opinion

---

Epirus at Beneventum in 275 B.C.; Caius Fabricius Luscinus, three-time consul; Publius Cornelius Scipio Africanus Maior, defeated Hannibal at Zama in 202 B.C.; Publius Cornelius Scipio Africanus Minor, destroyer of Carthage in 146 B.C.; Quintus Fabius Maximus Verrucosus, devised the effective strategy of avoiding engagement with Hannibal in Italy; Lucius Aemilius Paulus Macedonicus, defeated Perseus of Macedon in 168 B.C.

[246] *Secundis vero suis rebus volet etiam mori; non enim tam cumulus bonorum iucundus esse potest quam molesta decessio.*

[247] Olympic victor in boxing in 464 B.C. *See* Aulus Gellius III.15.3.

[248] I.e., "you might as well die now, because you will never again be so happy."

[249] The point stated in the previous sentence, that the dead are not in evil circumstances.

completely by the roots—and perhaps this is why I have spoken longer than necessary.[250]

47. A. You think you've spoken too much? I certainly don't see it that way. The first part of your discussion made me wish for death; the second part made me sometimes not resistant to the idea, and sometimes not distressed about it. However, the final impression that your discourse gave me is that I do not consider death an evil.

M. So do we still need to add a rhetorician's conclusion[251] to our discussion? Or should we set aside this practice?

A. You should not abandon the art you've always honored—and rightly so. For to speak honestly, it was rhetoric that first conferred honor on *you*. But what peroration did you have in mind? Whatever it is, I'd like to hear it.

M. It is standard practice in the schools to present the judgments of the immortal gods on the subject of death. These views are not created by the instructors themselves, but are based on the works of Herodotus and many other writers. The first tale they recommend is that of Cleobis and Biton, the sons of the Argive priestess.[252] The story is very well-known. In accordance with religious custom, the priestess was brought by chariot to a designated annual sacrifice. The shrine where this took place was some distance from the town. The animals that were supposed to carry her were delayed. So the two youths I just named removed their clothes, rubbed their bodies with oil, and stepped into the yoke themselves. This was how the priestess was brought to the temple. Now as her sons were pulling the chariot, she prayed to the goddess and asked her to reward the sons for their piety with the greatest gift that a god could provide. After the youths had dined sumptuously with their mother, they drifted off into sleep. In the morning, they were discovered to be dead.

Trophonius and Agamedes[253] were said to have recited a similar prayer. After they had constructed the Temple of Apollo at Delphi, they performed rituals to the deity and asked for a substantial reward

---

[250] An emotionally charged statement, likely related to Cicero's grief at the death of his daughter.

[251] *Epilogus*, meaning conclusion, peroration, or epilogue.

[252] *See* Herodotus I.31.

[253] The sons of Erginus, king of Orchomenus, an ancient city in Boeotia. Plutarch refers to this legend, and to the one of Cleobis and Biton, in his *Consolatio ad Apollonium* 14.

for all their labor and effort. It did not have to be anything in particular, they asked, just what was best for man. Apollo made it clear that he would give them this gift in three days. And at first light on the appointed day, the two men were found dead. It is said that the god had pronounced his judgment; and indeed, Apollo was the god to whom the other gods had ceded the powers of divine prophecy.

48. There is also a certain fable told about Silenus,[254] who had been taken prisoner by Midas.[255] It is said that Silenus gave Midas this gift to win his freedom: he taught Midas that the very best thing for a man was not to be born at all, and the next best thing after this was to die as soon as possible. This was an opinion voiced by Euripides in the tragedy *Cresphontes*:[256]

> For it is right that we grieve for the house in honoring groups
> Where a living being is born to daylight,
> When reflecting on human life's myriad evils,
> But who has cut short appalling labors with death,
> Let his friends follow him with applause and happiness.

We find a comparable sentiment in the philosopher Crantor's *Consolation*.[257] He says that one Elysius of Terina,[258] when he was in mourning over the death of his son, came to a place of necromancy where the spirits of the dead are questioned. When he asked why this

---

[254] A companion and tutor to the god Bacchus (Dionysius). He was sometimes portrayed as a kind of sage with the ears or tail of a horse.

[255] Legendary king of Phrygia, who had the power of turning things he touched into gold.

[256] A tragedy by Euripides, of which only fragments remain. The plot involved the story of the hero Cresphontes, son of Aristomachus and king of Messene, who was killed along with his two sons by the nobles of his realm.

[257] The philosopher Crantor of Soli (?—c. 276 B.C.), scholarch of the Platonic Academy. The pupil of Xenocrates, he was the first (or one of the first) to write commentaries on Plato's works.

[258] Terina was an ancient city in Magna Graecia, located in what is now the southern Italian province of Catanzaro in Calabria.

terrible tragedy had happened, he was given these three lines of poetry inscribed on writing tablets:

> Men go astray in life with heedless minds:
> Euthynoüs, through death, attains fate's divine will.
> Thus did his life end with more advantage for himself and you.

Through the use of these lines, and quotations from similar authors, they declare that this issue has been decided by the immortal gods. Alcidamas,[259] an ancient rhetorician of the first rank, wrote a glowing commendation on death that contained a recital of human evils. His pages are deficient in the profound reasoning that philosophers normally collate for the occasion, but his work is not without a certain fruitfulness of speech. Illustrious deaths sought for the sake of one's country are usually seen by rhetoricians as not only sublime, but joyous as well.

This view is traceable to Erechtheus,[260] whose daughters avidly sought death to safeguard the lives of their fellow-citizens. We recall the story of Codrus,[261] who hurled himself in the middle of the enemy while dressed as a slave to conceal his identity. He would have been recognized had he been outfitted in the garments of a king; and an oracle had been pronounced that if the king were killed, Athens would be victorious. We should not overlook the case of Menoeceus;[262] when the same type of prophecy was spoken, he shed his

---

[259] Greek rhetorician from Elaea in Aeolis who flourished in the 4th cent. B.C.
[260] An archaic king of Athens. According to legend, his three daughters sacrificed themselves to bring about an Athenian victory during the war against Eleusis.
[261] Last of the mythical kings of Athens (c. 1089 B.C.—c. 1068 B.C.). The legend about him states that during the Dorian invasion of Attica, the Delphic Oracle said that the invaders would capture Athens if they spared its king. Knowing this, Codrus defeated the prophecy by seeking death in battle disguised as a peasant.
[262] Son of the Theban king Creon. When Thebes was attacked, Menoeceus committed suicide because the soothsayer Tiresias had said that the Thebans would be victorious if he did so. The sacrifice was necessary, he said, to appease the god Ares.

blood profusely for his country. Iphigenia[263] ordered that she be brought to ritual sacrifice at Aulis "so that, as her own blood was spilled, the enemy's blood would also be spilled."

49. Harmodius and Aristogiton are often mentioned by writers or speakers. The names of Leonidas the Lacedaemonian and Epaminondas the Theban also appear frequently.[264] But they are not familiar with our own notable Roman figures, and to recite the names would be a considerable task. We see that there are many who have opted for death with glory. Since their deeds can guide us, we must summon great eloquence, and from a favorable spot deliver a compelling speech to the multitude on this point: *that men should either start to wish for death, or at least stop being afraid of it.* For if the final day of life brings not extinction, but a substitution of location, then what could be more desirable?

But if, however, that final day is attended by complete erasure and utter annihilation of self, what could be sweeter than drifting into slumber while grappling with life's tedious labors and, closing one's eyes in this way, allowing oneself to be benumbed by eternal repose? If this is how it is, then the words of Ennius are preferable to those of Solon. Our bard writes:

> Let no one garnish me with tears,
> Nor with sobbing besiege my funeral.

But the wise Solon has this to say:

---

[263] Daughter of Agamemnon and Clytemnestra. She was supposed to be sacrificed to the goddess Artemis (Diana) after her father offended the goddess by killing one of her deer. The goddess then said that the Greek expedition would not reach Troy until Agamemnon sacrificed Iphigenia at Aulis, a port town in Boeotia.

[264] Harmodius and Aristogiton were two Athenian lovers and political assassins. They killed Hipparchus, the tyrant Hippias's brother, in 514 B.C., but their target had been Hippias himself. They were executed for the murder, but later came to be seen as patriots. *See* Thucid. VI.56. Leonidas the Spartan (?—480 B.C.) and Epaminondas the Theban (?—362 B.C.) were warrior kings of Sparta and Thebes, respectively.

Let my death be not free of tears:
Let us leave the mourning to friends,
So that they celebrate the funeral with lamentations.

If it so happens for us that God provides notice that we should leave this life, let us comply happily and while giving thanks. Let us reflect that we have been released from prison, and unshackled from our chains, so that we may either return to the eternal abode which clearly belongs to us, or be liberated from all sensation and worldly difficulties. But if, however, we receive no such summons, let us still believe that that day is a favorable one for us—even though to others it may appear dreadful—and to understand nothing is evil that originates from either the immortal gods or from nature, the author of all creation.

For we have not been born or created through luck or random happenstance. There surely is some power that looks after human beings. And this power would not have created and nourished a living entity that, after having endured to the end all manner of prodigious hardships, would simply plunge into the eternal evil of death. We should think of it rather as a sanctuary, a shelter that has been prepared for us.[265] If only billowing sails might carry us there! But if opposing winds should push us back, we must still be returned to the same place a short time later. *Can something that must happen to everyone possibly be miserable for one person?*

You now have my summation. I have provided it so you wouldn't think anything was overlooked or abandoned.

A. I have heard it, and your conclusion has definitely fortified me in my thinking.

M. I'm very gratified to hear that. But now let us make some allowance for the sake of our health.[266] Tomorrow, and for the rest of the days we spend here at Tusculum, let us deal with these issues, especially with those that lighten the burdens of grief, mental anxiety, and sexual desire. For this is the choicest fruit in all of philosophy.

---

[265] Cicero's alliteration in this sentence sparkles: *Portum potius paratum nobis et perfugium putemus.*

[266] I.e, let us take a break.

93

BOOK II

ON BEARING PAIN

BOOK II

1. In a work of Ennius, Neoptolemus[267] says that he has to philosophize—but only a small amount, since doing so all the time would not be to his liking. Yet when it comes to myself, Brutus, I really *must* philosophize. How better could I occupy my time, especially when I have little else to do? But I don't want to confine myself to just a few things, as Neoptolemus proposes. It is difficult in philosophy to learn a few topics without being exposed many of them, or all of them. A few things cannot be selected unless they are taken from many; nor will someone who learns a few topics fail to pursue the remaining ones with the same avidity.

Despite this, in a hectic life, and in one devoted to the military profession (as Neoptolemus then was), a little can often be advantageous, and can bear definite fruit. Now it may not be the same quantity of fruit that one could harvest from all of philosophy's rich groves; but it may still be a crop of sufficient volume to liberate us from lust, sorrow, or fear.

The dialogue that I recently conducted at Tusculum seems to have produced an admirable contempt for death, and this carries considerable value in liberating the soul from the shackles of fear. For he who fears what cannot be avoided can in no way live with a tranquil soul. He who does not fear death—not only because death is inevitable, but also because there is nothing horrible about it—has acquired a robust advantage in leading a happy life. Although I'm quite aware that many will stridently oppose these things I've said, that outcome cannot be avoided unless I were to write nothing at all.

If my speeches, which overtly aimed at popular favor—for speech-making is a civic skill, and the purpose of eloquence is to win the audience's approval—have been rebuked by some people who praise only what they themselves can imitate, and who limit their conception of good speaking to what their own shallow abilities allow, and who, when they are deluged with a flood of words and thoughts, say that they prefer their own banality and aridity to fruitfulness and abundance (which was the origin of the Attic style of

---

[267] Neoptolemus, the son of Achilles and the princess Deidamia, was a main character in Sophocles's *Philoctetes*. He is also known as Pyrrhus, and it was he who killed Priam of Troy after the fall of the city.

oratory; those who claimed to follow it were ignorant of it; they have now fallen silent, and have been laughed out of the courts), then what kind of future can I expect, when I'm lacking the popular support I could formerly rely on?[268]

For philosophy is satisfied with a few judges. By her own preference she avoids the multitude, which is hostile and wary of her. If anyone wanted to denounce all of philosophy, he would have the endorsement of the mob. And if he were to criticize the philosophical school that I align myself with, he could count on a good deal of help from the other competing schools.

2. In my *Hortensius*,[269] I responded to those who would attack philosophy in general; and in the four books of my *Academics*,[270] I believe I have adequately explained what needed to be said regarding the Academy. Yet I'm so far from not wanting any criticism, that in fact I now eagerly welcome it. For Greek philosophy would never have been so highly esteemed were it not for the vigorous dynamism it derived from the tussles and disputes of its most learned practitioners.

I therefore urge anyone able to do so, to wrest the glory of this venerable study from the exhausted Greeks, and carry it here to this city, in the same way that our ancestors, using their determination and assiduity, brought to Rome everything else that was beneficial. And indeed our renown in oratory, after having started from a very modest place, has reached a high point, so that now, as nature decrees in nearly everything, its flame grows feeble, and seems soon will flicker and burn out entirely. From this time forward, let philosophy find a birth in Latin letters; let us nurture this inception, and humbly accept having our ideas challenged and repudiated.

Those who are slavishly devoted to rigid, predetermined views—and so committed to keeping them that, just to be consistent, support such positions despite not really agreeing with them—will not tolerate this kind of activity with composure. But those of us who follow

---

[268] This sentence is one of those Ciceronian symphonies that is best translated while preserving its arduous length. The combination of brilliant language, rhetorical erudition, and personal anguish is without equal.

[269] A lost dialogue of Cicero, apparently written in 45 B.C., and named after Quintus Hortensius Hortalus, a Roman orator and politician. The subject of the treatise was how one may make the best use of free time.

[270] A treatise of Cicero discussing various epistemological questions and the development of different philosophical schools.

the dictates of probability, and cannot go beyond the point at which the contours of truth emerge, are fully prepared to contradict without stubbornness, and to be contradicted without anger.[271]

When these studies are brought over to our own country, we will not even miss the Greek libraries, which contain an unending multitude of books due to the multitudinous number of authors. The same things are repeated by many writers, with the result that books accumulate riotously. This will happen to us too, if many writers flock to these studies. If we can, let us encourage those who have some learning in the liberal arts, who can articulate ideas with elegance, and who philosophize with purpose and reason.

3. There is a certain group of men who want to be called philosophers. They are said to have authored many books in Latin. I certainly do not condemn these writings, for I have never read them; but because the very authors of these works write with neither clarity, systematic technique, taste, nor sophistication, I decline to expend effort for that which yields no enjoyment. Even persons of modest education understand what the adherents of this school say, and what ideas they subscribe to. Seeing how they put so little effort into conveying information to others, I do not see why they should be read, unless the reading takes place within a closed group of devotees who already believe the same things. Everyone reads Plato and the other Socratic philosophers, as well as those who succeeded them, even if they reject their ideas or show scant interest in them; but hardly anyone reaches out for the books of Epicurus or Metrodorus.[272] So the only people who read these Latin books are those who already subscribe to the ideas contained in them.

It seems to me, however, that whatever is produced in written form ought to recommend itself to informed readers. And even if we may not always be able to uphold this standard, I do not think we should be any less ardent in striving to maintain it. Thus my habit was to follow the practice of the Peripatetics and the Academy of debating both sides of every issue—not just because I thought this

---

[271] The final clause has a nice use of active and passive infinitives with prepositional phrases: *et refellere sine pertinacia, et refelli sine iracundia parati sumus.*

[272] Most likely referring to Metrodorus of Lampsacus (c. 331 B.C.—c. 278 B.C.), one of the four major Epicurean philosophers. There was a Metrodorus of Stratonicea (fl. 110 B.C.), who began as an Epicurean but then defected to the Academic school of Carneades. He is referenced elsewhere in Cicero's works.

was the only way of discovering the truth for each question, but also because I thought it provided the best training in speaking. Aristotle first used this approach, and it was continued by those who succeeded him.

Philo,[273] if I remember accurately (for I often heard him lecture), chose to teach the principles of the rhetoricians at one time, and those of the philosophers at another. My friends convinced me to follow this precedent; and in this way we occupied our time together at Tusculum. So we spent our morning in oratorical training; and in the afternoon we went down to the Academy,[274] as we did the day before. I will relate the discussion that took place there not as a narrative, but by presenting the actual words used by the speakers in the discourse.

4. Our discussion began in this manner as we walked leisurely about. Its beginning very much resembled what follows.

A. I can't describe how much I was satisfied—or rather, *sustained*—by the dialogue that took place yesterday. I'm fully aware that I've never been excessively attached to life. Yet when I realize that at some point life's light will expire and all its benefits disappear, a certain fear would sometimes darken my spirit, and pain would oppress my thoughts. But believe me, I've been so freed from this kind of suffering that now I think there is nothing I should worry about less than this.

M. I find that hardly surprising. For philosophy produces this result: it is the curative of souls, the remover of unimportant anxieties, the liberator from desires, and the expeller of irrational fears. But it will not cast its spell over everyone to the same degree. Its power is most felt when it has been embraced by a character inclined to it by nature. Not only does "fortune favor the brave," as the old proverb goes, but philosophy does precisely this to a much greater extent; its precepts reinforce, as it were, the *effectiveness* of courage. Clearly you were born with a certain sublime and exalted nature that disdains petty human affairs. A discourse conducted against death will therefore find an apt abode in a fearless soul.

But do you think these same ideas would have any real impact on those who invented them, formulated them, and wrote them down,

---

[273] Philo of Larissa (c. 159 B.C.—c. 84 B.C.), Greek Academic philosopher who succeeded Clitomachus as head of the Platonic Academy. Philo took up residence in Rome in 88 B.C. and eventually Cicero attended his lectures.
[274] A place at Cicero's villa where philosophical debate or lectures took place.

except for just a few thinkers? For how few philosophers can be found who have actually structured their lives, and arranged their personal habits, to comply with what reason demands! How few there are who think that the doctrines of their particular school were not intended to be a way of showing off knowledge, but were meant to be rules of life! How few who have the discipline to practice self-control, and obey the very rules that they preach to others! Some of them display such irresponsibility and arrogance that it would have been much better for them had they never been taught anything. Some are consumed with greed, and still others covet fame. Many are enslaved by lascivious impulses, to the extent that we find a shocking gulf between what they *preach* and how they actually *live*—something that I myself consider utterly contemptible.[275]

It is the same as if someone who claimed to be a grammar teacher spoke with atrocious language, or someone who aspired to be a musician sang out of tune. The shame is greater because the person is blundering in the very knowledge in which he claims proficiency. In the same way, the philosopher who violates his own rule of life is more despicable because he fails in the duty that he professes to teach to others, and because he openly declares a certain art of life, yet falls short when the time comes to practice it.

5. A. If what you say is true, shouldn't we be concerned that you are embellishing philosophy with false glory? What better evidence could be offered to show the futility of philosophy than the fact that some accomplished philosophers live in a state of moral debasement?

M. That hardly qualifies as evidence—for not every field that is planted will yield crops. Accius's quote below is not true:

Although good seeds have been scattered in inferior fields,
Crops of lustrous sheen will of their own nature still emerge.[276]

---

[275] The biographer Cornelius Nepos voiced similar sentiments. See my translation of his *Lives of the Great Commanders*, Charleston: Fortress of the Mind Publications (2019), p. 262.

[276] From the lost play *Atreus* of the Roman poet Lucius Accius (170 B.C.—c. 86 B.C.).

Thus not all trained minds will produce fruit. A related comparison may be stated in this way: no matter how fertile its soil, a field cannot be fruitful without cultivation. *So will the soul remain barren without instruction.* It is clear, then, that one is worthless without the other. Philosophy is the cultivation of the soul; it eliminates vices at their roots, and prepares souls to receive the proper seeds. It delivers these seeds to the soul, or I should say, *sows* them in it. And when they finally ripen to maturity, they will bear fruit of unrivaled quality. So let us continue as we began. Tell me what subject you want to talk about, if you wish.

A. I consider pain to be the greatest of all evils.

M. Greater even than dishonor?

A. I wouldn't venture to say that—and I'm ashamed that my view has been refuted so quickly.

M. You should have been more ashamed to persist in this way of thinking. For what is less worthy than for you to consider anything worse than dishonor, disgrace, and moral corruption? In order for you to avoid these things, what pain is there that we should not—I won't say shrink from evading, but—voluntarily *seek, tolerate, and embrace*?

A. I see things the same way. Yet although pain is not the greatest evil, it certainly is *an* evil.

M. Don't you see how much of the fear of pain you've set aside, just from having heard my short cautionary statement?

A. I see this clearly, but need to hear more.

M. I'll make the effort—but this is a serious subject, and I need a participatory soul that is open to what I have to say.

A. You will indeed have that. Just as I did yesterday, so will I follow your reasoning now—no matter where it takes me.

6. Then my first priority will be to expose the intellectual weakness of many philosophers from the various schools. The first of these—measured by both influence and antiquity—is Aristippus the Socratic. He never wavered in his conviction that pain was the greatest evil. After him, Epicurus supinely endorsed this enervating, effeminate concept. Even later, Hieronymus of Rhodes[277] preached that the greatest good was to be free of pain. He was certain that much evil was to be found in pain. All the rest—except Zeno, Aristo, and

---

[277] Hieronymus of Rhodes (c. 229 B.C.—c. 230 B.C.), a Peripatetic philosopher about whom little is known.

Pyrrho[278]—agreed with what you said earlier: that pain is indeed an evil, but there are other evils that are worse.

Thus it is evident that nature herself, and a certain sense of noble virtue, immediately rejected the proposition that pain is the greatest evil, and forced you away from this idea when dishonor was weighed against pain. Yet philosophy, that instructress of life, has consistently asserted such a view for many centuries.[279] If a man had persuaded himself that pain were the greatest evil, what kind of duty, glory, or noble distinction would be so important that he would seek it while enduring bodily pain? And if he truly believed pain were the greatest evil, what ignominy or disgrace would he be willing to accept in order to sidestep it? If pain is where the greatest evil is found, who will not feel miserable, not just when he is actually overwhelmed by extreme pain, but also when he knows pain could be coming? Who is there who cannot be affected by pain?

Accepting this logic leads to one conclusion: that absolutely no one can be happy. Indeed Metrodorus thinks a man is completely happy if he has a sound physical constitution, and if he is certain he will always have it. But who among us can have such certitude?

7. Epicurus argues his points in a way that to me seems aimed at stimulating laughter. In one place he claims that if the wise man is being roasted alive or tortured—you expect him perhaps to say he will endure it, or he will suffer through it, or he will not give in. By Hercules, that would merit praise, and be worthy of the mighty Hercules I just called as a witness! But this is not enough for the rigid, obdurate Epicurus. If a wise man happens to be inside Phalaris's bull,[280] he'll say: "It's so pleasant to be here, that I'm not troubled by this at all!" Literally "pleasant"? Or is "not unpleasant" an insufficient description?

These very same thinkers who insist that pain is not an evil are not in the habit of saying that it is pleasant to be tortured. They say it is unwelcome, difficult, odious, and "against nature," but still not an evil. But Epicurus, who says that pain is the only evil and the most extreme of all evils, believes the wise man will say it is "pleasant." I

---

[278] Aristo of Chios (fl. 260 B.C.) was a follower of Zeno of Citium, the founder of the Stoic school; Pyrrho of Elis (c. 360 B.C.—c. 270 B.C.) was a philosophical skeptic and founder of Pyrrhonism.

[279] I.e., the idea that pain is the greatest evil.

[280] A legendary torture and execution device constructed by Perillos of Athens for Phalaris, the tyrant of Akragas in Sicily from about 570 B.C. to 554 B.C. It was a hollow bronze bull in which victims could be roasted alive.

don't ask that you characterize pain with the same words used by Epicurus, a man who was a voluptuary, as you know.[281] He would certainly say the same thing inside Phalaris's bull that he would say inside his own bed. I do not imagine wisdom has such power to overcome pain. If a man is powerful in his capacity to endure, then duty is satisfied. I do not expect him to be delighted. For pain is without doubt a gloomy malady: cruel, bitter, hostile to nature, and difficult to bear and endure.

Consider Philoctetes,[282] whose lamentations we must make some allowance for. He had seen Hercules on Oeta crying out openly in the severity of his pains. The arrows he had received from Hercules gave this man no consolation, since

> From a serpent's bite, the blood-vessels of
> his viscera,
> Imbued with poison, produce revolting tor-
> tures.[283]

And these words he exclaims while seeking help and desiring death:

> Oh! Who will commit me to the briny waves
> From the cliff's lofty peak?
> Now, now I am spent:
> The wound's power, and the ulcer's fire
> Finally end my life.

---

[281] Although Cicero is trying to make a philosophic point, it is wrong for him to describe Epicurus as a *voluptarius*. By all accounts, Epicurus led a simple and abstemious life.

[282] A renowned Greek archer and participant in the military expedition to Troy. He was the subject of several Greek plays. According to legend, he received the bow and arrows of Hercules as compensation for lighting Hercules's funeral pyre. Philoctetes was abandoned by the Greeks on the island of Lemnos on the way to Troy; there are various traditions explaining why this happened, but all maintain that he received a serious wound on his foot. One version of the story says that Philoctetes was scratched on the foot by one of Hercules's poison-tipped arrows. Those interested in the story of the death of Hercules should consult Seneca's play *Hercules on Oeta*.

[283] These lines and the ones that follow are from Accius's play *Philocteta*.

It seems difficult to say that someone forced to grieve like this is not afflicted with evil—indeed, with *a great evil*.

8. But let us consider Hercules himself, who was completely debilitated by suffering at a time when he was moving towards immortality by his own death. What unforgettable words does Sophocles give him in his *Trachiniae!*[284] Who, when Deianira put on him a tunic impregnated with the Centaur's blood and it clung to his body, says:[285]

> O great miseries to speak of, and bitter to suffer,
> Which are undergone by body and soul!
> Not the terror of the implacable Jove,
> Not gloomy Eurystheus[286] carried such evil to me
> As this one senseless daughter of Oeneus.[287]
> She entangled me, without my knowledge,
> In this frenzied garment which clings to me
> With a sting and lacerates my flesh,
> And violently constricting, empties the air from my lungs:
> Now it has drawn out all my filthy-hued blood,
> So the body is spent, consumed by a horrible disaster:
> I meet my end, ensnared in a fabric of destruction.
> Not the right hand of an enemy,
> Not immense giants born of the Earth,[288]

---

[284] Another name for the play is *Women of Trachis*.

[285] This long verse passage is Cicero's Latin rendering of the *Trachinae*, 1046 *et. seq.* The event described is the death of Hercules. Hercules killed the centaur Nessus for trying to touch his wife Deianira when he (Nessus) was carrying her across a river. The weapon used was an arrow dipped in the poisonous blood of the Hydra. As he was dying, Nessus devised a scheme to kill Hercules from the grave: he convinced Deianira that, if she soaked a shirt in his contaminated blood and gave it to Hercules to wear, the shirt would act as a magic charm to prevent him from ever deserting her. Deianira believed him and carried out these instructions, which proved fatal to Hercules.

[286] King of Tiryns (or Argos). It was he who directed Hercules to perform the famous "Twelve Labors."

[287] King of Calydon in Aetolia, and father of Deianira.

[288] The race of "giants" were the offspring of Gaia (Earth). They were generated from the drops of blood produced when Uranus was castrated by his son Cronos.

Not the assault of the bipartite Centaur
Inflicted these bodily strikes,
Not Greek power, nor any foreign brutality,
Not a furious people relegated to the ends of the
earth[289]
Where I roamed everywhere, pacifying all its wild-
ness,
But I, a man, am sent to my grave by a woman's
hand.
9. O my son,[290] truly take up that name for your
father,
Nor let a mother's love take precedence over my
death.
Once seized by righteous hands, bring her to me.
Now I will know if you think me or her better.
Go on, dare, my son, cry for your father's mortal
agonies,
And feel pity! Nations will shed tears over my mis-
eries.
Oh! To articulate with my mouth the sobbing of
girls,
Whom no one saw wailing over any evil!
My masculine virtue expires, feminized and with-
ered.
Come closer, my son, appear before me, see how
miserable
Is your father's body, eviscerated and wasted!
All of you together see, and you, Father of the
Gods,
Throw, I beg you, a flashing thunderbolt in me!
Now the fearsome whirlpools of my pains revolve,
Now the heat moves slowly forward.
O formerly triumphant hands,
O broad chest, O back, O muscles of my arms!
Did the Nemean lion,[291] grinding his teeth, in your
embrace

---

[289] "Ends of the earth" (*terris ultimis*), meaning the Pillars of Hercules.
[290] Hyllus, the son of Hercules and Deianira.
[291] The first of the twelve labors of Hercules was killing the Nemean lion.

Violently blow out his last breath?
Once the terrible viper was killed,
Did this hand subdue Lerna,[292]
This destroy the two-bodied gang,[293]
This cast out the devastating Erymanthian mon-
ster,[294]
This drag from the dark region of Tartarus
The three-headed dog[295] produced by the Hydra,
This kill the dragon with its manifold coils
That guarded with its gaze the gold-laden tree?[296]
Our victorious hand cleansed by sacrifice many
other things,
Nor did anyone take spoils from our glory.

Can we really look down on pain, when we see Hercules himself
suffering through his agonies so resentfully?

10. Let Aeschylus give us his thoughts, not just as a poet, but also
as a follower of Pythagoras.[297] For tradition says this is so. In Aeschylus's writing,[298] how does Prometheus endure the pain he
receives from the theft of Lemnos?[299]

---

[292] The Lernaean Hydra. Killing the Hydra was Hercules's second labor. The
monster was found in the lake of Lerna in the Argolid. Lerna was also reputed to
be an entrance to the underworld.

[293] Two-bodied gang (*bicorporem manum*): centaurs.

[294] The fourth labor of Hercules was to capture the Erymanthian boar.

[295] Cerberus. Hercules's twelfth labor was to capture this three-headed dog.
Cerberus's father was the monster Typhon; Cerberus's brother was the multi-
headed Hydra of Lerna.

[296] Gold-laden tree (*auriferam arborem*): the tree with the golden apples in the
garden of the Hesperides. Taking these apples was the object of Hercules's
eleventh labor. The apples were guarded by a hundred-headed dragon named
Ladon, as well as by nymphs (Hesperides) who were the daughters of Atlas.

[297] It is not clear why Cicero considers Aeschylus a Pythagorean. Tischer (note
11, p. 119) considers the assertion unfounded (*Wahrscheinlich eine willkürliche
Annahme; wenigstens spricht in den noch erhaltenen Schriften des Aeschylus
nichts für dieselbe*).

[298] Referring to the *Prometheus Unbound*, a play of Aeschylus that exists only in
fragments.

[299] The well-known myth of Prometheus holds that he, a Titan, stole fire from the
god Vulcan on the island of Lemnos and gave it to humans. His brutal sentence

Where it is reputed that fire was bequeathed to
mortals in secret;
The shrewd Prometheus purloined it through guile
And paid the penalty—with his ultimate fate left
to Jove.

Paying the price for his offense, Prometheus, fastened to the
rocks of the Caucasus, says this:

Progeny of Titans, comrades of our blood,
Born of Heaven, look at what is fastened to craggy
rocks:
A captive, as a ship on churning waves
That cautious sailors, dreading the night, secure in
place.
Jupiter, the son of Saturn, so bound me here.
And the divine will of Jupiter took over Mulci-
ber's[300] hands.
By hateful plan he inserted these wedges,
And fractured my joints: by his ingenuity, I dwell
in this
Castle of the Furies, a miserable, punctured being.
Not only this: on the anguish-filled third day, in
dismal flight
The servant of Jove comes to mangle me with
crooked talons,
And feeds on my body with brute relish.
Then, having gorged on liver fat and amply sati-
ated,
Unleashes an infernal noise and takes flight sky-
ward,
He makes obeisance to my blood with his plumed
tail.

---

was to be chained to the rocks of the Caucasus, so that his regenerative liver
could be eaten by a bird of prey for eternity.
[300] An alternate name for the god Vulcan.

When the consumed liver is renewed through re-
generation,
Then he again returns to the revolting feeding-
ground.
So I feed this sentry of my dismal suffering
Which defiles my existence with everlasting tor-
ment.
For, as you clearly see, immobilized by Jove's
manacles,
I cannot ward off this dire bird from my chest.
Abandoned in solitude I greet the curse prepared
for me,
Seeking an end to this evil by lusting for death.
But far from death, I am banished by the divine
will of Jove.
And in these time-worn ages congealed in grim-
ness,
A dire calamity is imposed on my body,
From which droplets extracted by the sun's rays
fall
Which continually spatter the rocks of Caucasus.

11. We can hardly say that someone in such a condition was *not* miserable. And if he was indeed miserable, then pain must without doubt be an evil.

A. You are actually advancing my own argument. But soon I'll evaluate this. Until then, let me ask you, where did you get these verses? I'm not familiar with them.

M. I'll tell you, absolutely. Indeed, it's right for you to ask this. Do you see that I have much leisure time at my disposal?

A. And so what, then?

M. I believe when you were at Athens, you often spent time in the philosophic schools, correct?

A. Indeed I did, and with pleasure.

M. You noticed then that although no one had an impressive command of language, poetic verses were often mixed into their discussions.

A. Yes, this was a common practice with Dionysius the Stoic.

M. That's right. But he did it as if he were reciting a lecture, with neither discriminating selection nor elegance. Philo recited lines with the correct cadence—and he used poetry that was both excellent and relevant. And since I've become enamored with this kind of declamation[301] practice of my old age, I scrupulously imitate Philo's habit, and make use of our own poets. And when these were insufficient, I also translated many Greek lyricists, so that discourse in Latin would not be lacking in elegance in this kind of debate.

But do you see the negative element that poets introduce? They portray the strongest men crying, and they weaken our spirits. Their language is so seductive that they are not only read, but memorized line for line. So when the sentiments of poets are mixed with feeble domestic discipline and an isolated, self-indulgent life, the vigor of masculine virtue is entirely strangled. Plato quite rightly banished them from his model state[302] when he devised the best morals and the ideal circumstances needed for his republic. But we ourselves, educated along the same lines as the Greeks, read and learn poetry from youth, and consider this gentlemanly learning and education.

12. But why do we resent the poets? We can find philosophers—the teachers of virtue—who say that pain is the greatest evil. A short time ago, young man, you stated that you agreed with this. But when questioned by me whether you believed pain was a greater evil than even dishonor, you discarded your position with a word. Ask Epicurus the same question. He would say that a mediocre level of pain is a greater evil than the severest dishonor; for there is no evil in shame alone, unless sufferings accompany it.

Then what pain accompanies[303] Epicurus, when he states his view that pain is the greatest evil? I imagine there is no worse disgrace for a philosopher than to believe this. You gave me enough when you told me that you thought dishonor was a greater evil than pain. And if you will hold on to this idea, you will appreciate that one must fight against pain. We must not ask whether pain is an evil; rather, we must fortify the soul in order to bear pain's burdens. The Stoics weave their petty syllogisms to explain why pain is not an evil, as if the issue can be clarified with verbal artifices instead of looking at the nature of the subject.

Why are you misleading me, Zeno? When you claim that what I believe is an evil is actually *not* an evil, my attention is seized at once,

---

[301] In classical schools of rhetoric, a declamation was a speech or composition created by students in response to a specific proposition. See, e.g., the declamations (*Controversiae*) of Seneca the Elder.

[302] Referring to book 10 of Plato's *Republic*.

[303] I.e., what pain does Epicurus feel.

and I want to know how that which I believe is most miserable, is not really evil. "Nothing is evil," says Zeno, "except that which is morally corrupt and depraved." Here you are speaking nonsense. You are not providing relief for what distresses me. *I know* that pain is not wickedness—stop teaching me that! Teach me that there is no difference in whether I feel pain, or do not feel pain. "It is irrelevant," Zeno says, "to living a happy life, which is grounded only in virtue. But pain nevertheless should be avoided." And why? "It is bitter, against nature, hard to endure, sad, and callous."

13. This is an abundance of words, all used to identify in different ways what we, using one word, call evil. When you say pain is bitter, against nature, and something that can barely be tolerated or suffered, you are *defining* pain for me, not *relieving* it. And you are not being dishonest. But you should not have conceded the issue while priding yourself with words. *Nothing good except what is representative of virtue, and nothing evil except what is morally corrupt*: this indeed is something to wish for, but it does not convince by argument. It is better and more true to say this: all things rejected by nature are evils, and all things approved by nature are goods.

Once this idea is acknowledged and the verbal squabbling has ceased, it will be obvious that what they[304] correctly adhere to—what we call morally good, right, and suitable, and what we sometimes embrace under the name of virtue—will appear so transcendent that, by comparison, everything considered goods of the body and of fortune will seem meager and petty. It will also be clear that no evil, even if all evils are collected in one place, can compare to the evil of moral debasement.

Thus if, as you conceded at the beginning, dishonor is worse than pain, then pain is obviously nothing. For you will consider it shameful and unworthy of a man to moan, whine, lament, collapse, and be paralyzed with anguish. But if moral goodness, if dignity, if honor are still present (and as long as you conduct yourself by being mindful of them), then pain will certainly yield to virtue, and will wither away through the application of a determined spirit. For either there is no virtue at all, or all pain must be viewed with contempt.

Will you accept the importance of prudence, without which no virtue can be understood? What, then? Will prudence allow you to labor and toil away while accomplishing nothing? Will temperance

---

[304] The Stoics, referring back to II.12 above.

permit you to behave immoderately? Can justice be exercised by a man who, due to the influence of pain, divulges secrets, sells out his friends, and abandons many of life's responsibilities?

What do you think? How will you respond to the demands of courage and its associated qualities—greatness of soul, honor, persistence, and scorn for petty human affairs? When, battered by life, you are stretched flat on the ground, and are bewailing your situation in a doleful voice, will you really hear someone say, "O, what a strong man"? If you indeed become reduced to this state, no one will even say you are a man. Therefore, one must either part with courage, or pain must be laid to rest permanently.[305]

14. Don't you know, then, that if you lose one of your Corinthian vases,[306] you can safely retain the rest of your household possessions? But if you lose one virtue (although it is impossible to lose a virtue), if you concede that there is a virtue you do not have, you would not have any of them. Can you, then, call yourself a brave man, a man with a noble soul, a man who has patience and dignity, a man who looks down on the caprices of circumstance? Or Philoctetes?[307] I prefer to draw away from you right now.[308] But he was certainly not a brave man who stretched himself down

> In a damp hovel, an inarticulate frame from which
> Reverberate doleful tones soaked in sorrow,
> Grievance, sad sighs, and wistful murmurs.[309]

I do not deny that pain is pain. Why would we even need courage, if this were not so? But I say it is suppressed by patience, if only there is some amount of patience: if none exists, why do we celebrate philosophy, or why do we become conceited in its name?

---

[305] *Amittenda igitur fortitudo est aut sepeliendus dolor.* Meaning true courage is impossible if we are worrying about pain.
[306] Corinthian vases were made from a mixture of precious metals. They fetched high prices in Rome, and Cicero uses them here as a euphemism for costly luxuries.
[307] Meaning, "Can Philoctetes call himself these things either?"
[308] I.e., I prefer not to focus on you.
[309] These verses are from the *Philoctetes* of Accius.

Pain hurts. Let it stab deeply. If you are unprotected, present your throat to it.[310] If you are housed in Vulcan's armor[311]—that is, in fortitude—then resist it. If you do not do this, the protector of your dignity will abandon and desert you. Indeed the laws of Crete—which, as the poets tell us,[312] were sanctioned either by Jupiter or by Minos[313] in conformity with Jupiter's opinion—and the laws of Lycurgus[314] educate the youth by using painful exertions, hunting and running, hunger and thirst, and being forced to endure extremes of heat and cold. Fearful whippings are administered to Spartan boys at the altar,[315]

> Such that blood issues in profusion from the body's viscera,

even at times—as I once heard when I was there—to the point of death. None of them ever cried out, or even emitted a sob. So what do you think? Are boys able to endure this, but not men? Does custom prevail, but will reason not prevail?

15. There is some difference between work and pain. They have a very close association with each other, but there still exists a distinction. Work is a certain performance of the mind or body of a serious obligation or responsibility; pain, however, is an unpleasant activity in the body that is offensive to sense-perception. Those subtle Greeks,[316] whose language is more copious in vocabulary than ours, use one word for these two different things; they call industrious men "enthusiasts of pain," or rather "lovers of pain." We more

---

[310] Referring to a defeated gladiator.

[311] As Achilles and Aeneas.

[312] E.g., *Odyssey* XIX.179.

[313] According to tradition, Minos of Crete received his legal codes from the god Zeus (Jupiter).

[314] Lycurgus, the legendary lawgiver of Sparta (fl. 820 B.C.?).

[315] Spartan boys were required to undergo brutal training designed to harden them. Flogging in front of the altar at the sanctuary of Artemis Orthia was an annual ritual.

[316] There is a sly element of contempt in Cicero's language. Instead of using *Graeci* (the neutral word for Greeks), he uses the dismissive term *Graeculi*. The tone is meant to be sarcastic, for Cicero proudly states elsewhere (*On Moral Ends* I.10) that Latin is *more* endowed with expressive terminology than Greek.

appropriately call them "laborious"; for it is one thing to work, and something else to feel pain.

O Greece, you are sometimes lacking in the words you think you abound in! I tell you that feeling pain is one thing, and performing labor is something different. When the varicose veins of Caius Marius[317] were severed, he felt pain; when he led his military formations in scorching climates, he was laboring. Yet there is some likeness between these two concepts: for the regular habit of work makes the tolerance of pain that much easier. Thus those who gave Greece the design of her republics wanted to strengthen the bodies of Greek youth through rigorous labor. Spartan male citizens also applied this rule to their women, who in other cities are "insulated behind the shadows of domestic walls" in an ambience of the most delicate refinement.[318] But the Spartans wanted no part of that tradition:

> In young women of Lacedaemon
> For whom priority is the palaestra,[319]
> Eurotas,[320] sun, dust, and the military craft
> More than barbarian fertility.

We see, therefore, that pain is often intermingled with these arduous exercises. Those who practice them are shoved forward, hit, tossed around, or knocked down—and hard work itself engenders a certain imperviousness to pain.

16. Indeed, military service comes to mind. And here I am talking about our own army, and not that of the Spartans, whose columns march to the sound of the flute, with no exhortation to maintain rhythm except the use of anapestic cadence.[321] You can understand right away the origin of our word for "army": the amount of toil required for a forced march, what it means to haul more than a half-

---

[317] Roman general and statesman (c. 157 B.C.—86 B.C.) who held the office of consul seven times.

[318] Married women in ancient Greece were subject to social restrictions that discouraged activities outside the household.

[319] A wrestling school or gymnasium.

[320] A mythical king of Laconia, a region of Greece whose capital is Sparta. He had two daughters, Sparta and Tiasa. The city of Sparta was named in his daughter's honor.

[321] An anapest is a metrical foot used in classical poetry. As in modern armies, music was used to maintain formations. *See* Valerius Maximus II.6.2.

month's supply of food, what it means to carry whatever the mission requires, and what it means to bear equipment needed for fortifications. Our soldiers do not consider shield, sword, and helmet any more of a burden than their shoulders, arms, or hands. They say that weapons are the "limbs" of a soldier, and these are carried with speedy deployment in mind. If necessity compels their use, they drop the loads they carry so that their weapons will be as ready for combat as their own limbs.

What do you think of the military exercises of the legions? The forward march, the attack, the war-cry—how much labor is required to do these things! These drills shape the battlefield mental state that fortifies soldiers to face physical harm. If you place before them untrained soldiers of equal morale, the untrained ones will look like women. Why is there such a big difference between green enlistees and veteran fighters, as we have learned from experience? The age of a new recruit often usually gives them an advantage, *but it is habit that teaches a man to bear burdens and think little of being wounded.*

We see wounded men often carried off the line of contact with the enemy, and the unseasoned, untrailed soldier spews the most shameful whining, despite being lightly wounded. Yet the hardened veteran, braver because of his experience, needs only a doctor to bind his wounds. Such a man would say:[322]

> E. O Patroclus, I come to you for help, and from your hands seek relief
> Before I meet a fiendish destruction imposed by hostile hand,
> (And by no method can one stop the oozing blood),
> To find out if, through your knowledge, death is more likely to be avoided,
> For the wounded fill up the portico of the sons of Aesculapius,[323]
> And it cannot be entered.
> P. Without doubt this is Eurypylus. A man truly in pain![324]

---

[322] In the lines that follow, "E" is Eurypylus, and "P" is Patroclus.

[323] See *Iliad* II.732. The "sons of Aesculapius" are the surgeons Podalirius and Machaon.

[324] A meeting between Patroclus and Eurypylus is mentioned in the *Iliad* (XI.804). But the source of the lines quoted is apparently (according to Tischer) Ennius's *Achilles*.

17. When the grief continues unabated, see how he does not respond tearfully. He even offers a rationale for why hardship must be endured with a resolute spirit:

> E. He who plans the death of another man
> Ought to know the same fate is made ready for
> him,
> So as to share in an equivalent end.

I imagine Patroclus would carry him off, and deposit him on a bed to dress his wound. He would do this if he were a decent man; but nothing like this happens. He asks him what has happened:

> P. Tell me, tell me, how now go
> The fortunes of the Argives in the battle?
> E. It is impossible to convey in words
> The magnitude of the actions there performed.
> P. You are fading.

Then stop talking and dress my wound! Even if Eurypylus could do this, Aesopus could not.

> E. Where Hector's fortune our sharp array of battle inclined…

and he explains various other things in his pain—so intemperate in a brave man is a soldier's ambition. So, then, can the seasoned soldier behave this way, but the educated wise man cannot? He will indeed be better able to do it, and not just a little more able. At this point I am talking about the habitual response that results from training; I am not yet dealing with reason and wisdom.

Elderly women often bear hunger that lasts for two or three days. But carry off an athlete's food for only one day, and he will shout prayers to Olympian Jove, the deity for whom he is training. He will

115

whine that he cannot bear the deprivation.[325] Great is the power of habit in him. Out in the mountains, hunters spend the night in the snow; Indians tolerate their flesh being subjected to intense heat; the pugilist pounded by his opponent's wrapped fists moans hardly at all. But what can we say about those who regard an Olympic victory as equivalent to a traditional consulship?

And gladiators, who are either desperate men or barbarians— what terrible beatings they absorb! Look at how well-prepared men prefer to receive physical punishment than to evade it cravenly! How often is it made clear that they want nothing more than the satisfaction of their master or the people! Even when debilitated by wounds, gladiators make an effort to ask their owners what they wish them to do: if the master is content with their performance, then the gladiator is satisfied with death. What average gladiator has ever disgracefully moaned, or has ever changed his facial expression?[326] Which one ever acted cravenly, not as he was standing, but as he toppled over in death? Which one, when he fell to the ground, pulled in his neck after being ordered to accept the death-blow? How great, then, is the value of training, practice, and habit. So will it be possible that

> The Samnite, a vile individual, worthy of his life and place,[327]

can do this? Will a man born to notoriety have any part of his soul so impotent that he cannot toughen it with intense practice and systematic method? The spectacle of gladiatorial combat is likely to be considered barbaric and inhumane to some who witness it; and in its present form, I believe this to be true. Yet when criminals used to fight with swords, there was no more effective instruction against pain and death for the eyes (although perhaps many more effective ones for the ears).[328]

---

[325] Athletes were used to regular and plentiful meals.
[326] I.e., lost his composure and discipline.
[327] Tischer claims this line is from the satirist Caius Lucilius (*Sat.* 4.2), who lived from c. 180 B.C. to c. 103 B.C. Samnites tended to be poor mountain folk, and were well-represented in the gladiatorial profession.
[328] Cicero's attitude towards gladiators was probably shared by many educated

116

18. I have spoken of training, practice, and mental preparedness. If you can, redirect your attention now to explore logical reasoning, unless you want to respond to what we've stated so far.

A. Should I delay you? I certainly wouldn't want that, since your discussion is guiding me to true belief.

M. Let the Stoics obsess about whether pain is an evil, as they try to prove with their contorted and quibbling arguments (which leave no meaningful mental impact) that pain is not an evil. As far as I'm concerned, whatever pain may be, it is not as powerful as it seems. I say that men are very much swayed by a false picture of it in their mind's eye, and that all pain is endurable. Where should I start, then? May I briefly review the same subjects I spoke of earlier, so I can more easily make better progress in my discussion?

It is a commonly held view—not only by educated men, but also by the unlettered—that the ability to endure pain with composure is a trait of men who are brave, magnanimous, patient, and able to overcome life's reversals. Everyone believed that the person who endured pain like this should be held in high esteem. When such fortitude is demanded of strong men, and praised when displayed, isn't it then disgraceful to shrink in fear when pain approaches, or to be incapable of enduring it when it finds you? Although all proper mental dispositions are called "virtue," this designation is not correctly applied to all virtues; but all of them were named from the one virtue that surpassed the others. The word *virtus* (virtue) is itself formed from the word *vir* (man).[329]

Fortitude is man's most distinct virtue, and it has two key purposes: the disregard of death, and the disregard of pain. We must, then, adopt these habits if we want to master virtue—*or rather if we want to be men*, since the word for "man" is derived from the word for "virtue." You may ask how, and it would be a valid question. Philosophy indeed offers this sort of medicine.

19. Epicurus arrives.[330] He is certainly not a bad man, or perhaps it is better said that he is a very good one: his counsel does not exceed

---

Romans: they did not consider it respectable, but nevertheless felt that it had its uses.

[329] The meaning is better conveyed by retaining the Latin words for virtue (*virtus*) and man (*vir*) in this sentence.

[330] In this section Cicero uses a practiced technique: conducting a hypothetical question and answer sequence with a philosophical opponent (in this case Epicurus's words) to illustrate a point.

the scope of his knowledge. "Pay no attention to pain," he said. Who says this? The same man who says that pain is the greatest evil. This is hardly congruous. Let us hear more. "If pain is at its greatest intensity," he announces, "it must be brief in duration."

Say that to me one more time![331]

When you use the phrases "at its greatest intensity" and "brief in duration," I don't really understand what you are getting at. "Greatest intensity means that which has nothing greater in severity to it; and by brief, I mean that which has nothing shorter in duration. I have disdain for an amount of pain for which I need only a short amount of time to be free of—almost before it has arrived."

But what if the amount of pain is equivalent to what was felt by Philoctetes? "To me it clearly appears to be very great, but it still is not the greatest. For him, nothing hurts except his foot. His eyes could hurt, his head could hurt, his sides, his lungs, and everywhere else. So he is quite a distance away from being in the greatest pain." "Therefore," he says, "extended pain has more pleasure than annoyance." I can't say that such a distinguished man understands nothing, but I think he is insulting us with this logic. I say that the greatest pain (and I'm saying "greatest" even if there is another pain that is ten atoms[332] greater) is not necessarily brief. And I can name a number of good men who have suffered the greatest agonies from gout for a number of years.

Yet this crafty man never marks the boundaries of pain's magnitude or duration so that I might know how he defines "in the greatest pain" or "in the shortest time." Let us therefore disregard him completely, since he is saying nothing. Let us force him to acknowledge that the alleviation of pain must not be sought from someone who has announced that pain is the greatest of all evils, even if this same person might show some bravery in enduring bowel troubles and difficulty in urination.[333]

---

[331] A line from Pacuvius's lost tragedy *Iliona*.
[332] A reference to Epicurus's advocacy of atomic theory.
[333] *Tormina* (bowel trouble, colic); *stranguria* (strangury, the painful discharge of

A curative medicine must be sought from somewhere else, especially if we are trying to find what is most appropriate. *It must be sought from those who believe that what is morally right is the ultimate good, and what is morally corrupt is the ultimate evil.* When you are with these individuals, you will absolutely not dare to whine or twitch about in pain. Virtue itself will counsel you through their voice.

20. Even if you may have seen boys in Sparta, young men at Olympia, or barbarians in the arena receiving the most severe wounds and bearing them in silence, will you squeal like a woman if you happen to feel the pinch of some pain, instead of tolerating it resolutely and calmly? I hear this: "He cannot bear it; nature cannot allow it." Boys with aspirations of glory can bear pain; others tolerate it out of shame; and many accept it out of fear. Yet we doubt nature can carry the same burden that so many others have carried, in so many circumstances? Nature not only bears such hardships, *she requires them.* For there is nothing in nature more surpassing, and nothing more sought after, than integrity, merit, honor, and dignity.

Although I write many terms, I want to convey a single idea by using them; in this way will my meaning be expressed with the most clarity. What I wish to say, in fact, is that by far the best thing for man is what is inherently and *per se* desirable, what comes from virtue or is grounded in virtue, and what is commendable in itself. Indeed I might more succinctly say that it is the *only good,* instead of the ultimate good. Just as we speak this way when discussing moral goodness, so do we use contrary terms when discussing moral corruption. For there is nothing so abominable, nothing so repugnant, and nothing so unworthy of a man.

Initially you stated that there was more evil in dishonor than in physical pain. If you have been persuaded by my arguments, the remaining point is that you must acquire a disciplined control over yourself. It is said that we have two characters: one that commands, and another that obeys. Although I'm not sure if this saying is accurate, it does have some validity to it.

21. In fact the soul is divided into two components, one of which participates in reason, and another part that is unfamiliar with it.

---

urine). This sentence, with its mockery of Epicurus, shows Cicero's invective powers at their most formidable. The reference to colic and strangury has significance, for Epicurus mentioned these ailments as he was dying. See *On Moral Ends* II.30.96.

When we are counseled to "master" ourselves, the intent behind this advice is that reason should work to control rashness. For there is in all souls some ingredient of softness, gloom, and cravenness—a sort of enfeeblement and lethargy. If man had no other qualities, no creature would be so loathsome; but Reason, the protectress and queen of all things, is ever-present and exerts herself forcefully, advancing continuously until she has become consummate Virtue.

A man must consider it his responsibility to ensure reason commands the part of the soul that is supposed to obey. You may then ask, "How does he do this?" Just as the master guides the servant, the general guides the soldier, and the parent guides the son. If this part of the soul (which I have previously characterized as soft) shows signs of moral debasement, if it displays effeminate wailing and tears, then let it be shackled and regulated by the supervision of friends and family. For we often see men subdued by shame who could never be conquered by reason.

These types of men, therefore, should be restricted and monitored like household servants; and those who are made of sturdier material—even if they are not the most robust—should be advised to preserve their honor, like good soldiers recalled for military service. In the *Niptra*, the wisest man in Greece does not much complain when he is wounded. Instead he conducts himself with a more even temper. He says:

> Gradually testing the way with measured effort,
> So that a sudden shock will not assail me with greater pain.[334]

Here Pacuvius is better than Sophocles. In Sophocles's play, Ulysses laments a great deal over his wounds. Those who were carrying the wounded man—and who were aware of the importance of his person—firmly told him this when he was grieving mildly:

---

[334] This quotation and the others in the section are taken from Pacuvius's *Niptra* (lit. "The Footwashing"), which was a Roman adaptation of a play by Sophocles (apparently the *Odysseus Acanthoplex*).

You too, Ulysses, although we know
You have been seriously hit,
Are displaying a spirit exceedingly soft.
You, who has long been habituated to life
In the profession of arms.

The prudent poet understands that the practice of bravely enduring pain is an instructor that should not be neglected. And then the
wounded Ulysses, in his great pain, replies with moderation:

Keep back! Continue! The ulcer overwhelms,
Oh, expose it, I am in agony! It is excruciating.

He begins to slip away. Then at once he collects himself:

Cover up, and leave now.
Release. For by touching and jostling
You heighten the relentless pain.

Do you see that it isn't the body's pain that has been alleviated
and suppressed, but rather the *mind's pain* that has been controlled
and diminished? Thus, in the final passages of the *Niptra*, he also
scolds others, and says this while dying:

You ought to gripe about adverse fortune,
Rather than bewail it;
This is a man's responsibility;
Weeping was conferred on woman's nature.

The softer part of his soul obeyed reason, just as the honorable
soldier complies with the directions of a stern general.

22. Consider someone who is possessed of consummate wisdom.
Of course we have never seen anyone fitting this description, but the

philosophers have explained what kind of man he might be, if in fact he could exist. Such a man, then—or rather such absolute and consummate Reason he will possess—will command the inferior part of himself just as a conscientious parent guides upright sons. With no fuss and no annoyance, he will implement his plan with a nod. He will rise to his feet, gather his strength, prepare, and equip himself to oppose pain just as if it were a corporeal adversary.

What are the weapons he will select? Preparation, quieting his fears, and speaking in this way to his deepest self: "Beware what reeks of moral corruption, what has no vitality, and what is not manly." Let him ponder the different kinds of integrity that are important to a man. Let him put forward Zeno of Elea,[335] who endured everything rather than provide the names of his compatriots in destroying tyranny. Let him think about Anaxarchus,[336] who was from Democritus's school; he fell into the hands of King Timocreon[337] of Cyprus, and neither begged for any kind of mercy nor shrank from any variety of torture.

The Indian Calanus,[338] who was both uneducated and a barbarian, was born at the base of the Caucasus Mountains—and he was voluntarily burned alive. Yet if one of our feet is in pain, or one of our teeth aches, we cannot bear it: it makes us feel that our entire body is hurting. This is so, I think, because there is a certain effeminacy and softness that is displayed as much in pain as in pleasure. We disintegrate and dribble away in impotence, to the extent that we cannot endure a bee-sting without wailing.

Yet Caius Marius,[339] a man of peasant stock but without doubt a real man, when he was being operated on (as I mentioned above) refused from the outset to be physically restrained. No one before

---

[335] Zeno of Elea (c. 495 B.C.—c. 430 B.C.), a Greek philosopher of Magna Graecia famous for his many subtle paradoxes. He was allegedly arrested and tortured for conspiring against the tyrant Nearchus of Elea.

[336] Anaxarchus (c. 380 B.C.—c. 320 B.C.), Greek philosopher who accompanied Alexander the Great in Asia.

[337] Cicero actually means King Nicocreon of Cyprus, who lived in the 4th century B.C. The biographer Diogenes Laertius (IX.59) says that the king ordered Anaxarchus to be executed by being pounded to death in a mortar with iron pestles.

[338] Calanus (or Kalanos) (c. 398 B.C.—323 B.C.), Hindu ascetic philosopher and Brahmin who accompanied Alexander the Great for a time.

[339] Caius Marius (c. 157 B.C.—86 B.C.), famous Roman general and statesman who was consul seven times.

Marius is said to have undergone surgery without restraints. Why did others after Marius do the same thing? Because his prestige exerted great influence. Do you see, then, that evil springs from belief, and not from nature? The same Marius showed that the pain's sharpness was acute, for he did not put forward his other leg. Thus he tolerated the pain as a man of courage, but as a human being he had no desire to endure it without good cause.[340] The central lesson here is *that you must exercise complete command over yourself.* I have explained the nature of this command; and by thinking about what course of action is most worthy of patience, fortitude, and greatness of soul, a person not only tames his soul, but in some way is also able to diminish pain itself.

23. During a battle, the craven and timid soldier tosses away his shield after laying eyes on the enemy, and runs away as fast as he can, and thus dies with an intact body—whereas nothing like this happens to the soldier who remains in formation. Similarly, we see that those who cannot bear the onset of pain will cast themselves down, lying prostrate, crushed and paralyzed, while those who stand their ground very often walk away in triumph. For there are some similarities that the soul shares with the body. Heavy loads are more easily carried by bodies exerting themselves as much as possible; and if the effort diminishes, the burden presses down even more harshly. In the same way, the soul casts off the weight of all burdens through its own straining. But if the soul suspends this effort, it is unable to make forward progress.[341]

If we wish to know the truth, the soul must summon intense effort in carrying out every responsibility: this alone is the protector of duty. But what must be kept in mind above all is that we should do nothing with a sense of despair, nothing with timidity, nothing with faint-heartedness, and nothing with servile effeminacy; and most crucially, that this Philoctetean noise be refuted and rejected. There are times—although they are rare—when it is permitted for a man to cry with pain; but howling is unacceptable, even for a woman. This evidently was the kind of lamentation that the Twelve Tables[342] would not allow to be performed at funerals.

---

[340] This sentence is a good illustration of the distinction between the Latin words *vir* (man of courage) and *homo* (generic word for man): *Ita et tulit dolorem ut vir et ut homo maiorem ferre sine causa necessaria noluit.*

[341] Due to the fact that the soul is "weighed down."

[342] Rome's ancient legal code that was inscribed on twelve bronze tablets from 451 B.C. to 450 B.C.

Nor indeed does the strong, wise man ever openly cry out in anguish, unless it happens to be for the purpose of summoning strength, as when runners in a stadium howl as loudly as they can. Athletes do the same thing when they exercise. Boxers punching their adversaries vent sighs as they launch their wrapped fists,[343] not because they are in pain or because their morale is sagging, but because the entire body's power is harnessed by this vocal emission—and the strike lands with more vehemence.

24. What! For those who want to yell more forcefully, is it enough for them to strain their sides, jaws, and tongues, from which we hear the voice emanating with such power? With the whole body and every fingernail, as the saying goes, they assist the intensification of the voice. By Hercules! I saw Marcus Antonius[344] touch the ground with his knee when he was speaking passionately on his own behalf with regard to the Varian Law.[345] Just as stone-throwing *ballistae*[346] and other dart-hurling machines launch their projectiles with greater speed when their strings are stretched most tightly, so it is with the voice and with running. A punch lands with greater force when it has been thrown with more focused exertion.

This focused effort has such power that, in a time of pain, we should make use of a groan to fortify the spirit. But if it is a groan of sorrow, weakness, wretchedness, or despair, then I could hardly call him a man who has surrendered to these emotions. Even if this sort of moaning helped to diminish pain, we must still consider if it is suitable for a brave and impassioned man. Since groaning does nothing to lessen pain, why would we want to be humiliated for no reason? What is more dishonorable for a man than the tearful wailing of a woman? And this general precept given to us to deal with pain has a broader application: *everything, not just pain, must be resisted with a similar exertion of the soul.* Anger flares, and sexual desire is kindled—one must look for sanctuary in the same fortress, and the same weapons must be made ready. But since we are speaking about pain, we need not elaborate on these analogies.

---

[343] The fists of pugilists were wrapped with straps (*caestus*) during bouts.

[344] Marcus Antonius (143 B.C.—87 B.C.), Roman orator and politician.

[345] The *Lex Varia*, a law introduced by Quintus Varius Severus in 90 B.C. to prosecute Romans who were helping the rebelling Italian states in the so-called "Social War" (91 B.C.—87 B.C.).

[346] A *ballista* was an engine of war designed to hurl large bolts or stones.

To bear pain with calmness and quiet resolution, it does much good to ponder with one's entire soul[347] (as they say) how morally right it is. As I have previously said—and it *must* frequently be said—we are designed by nature to be ardent strivers for righteousness. And once we have seen something of this radiant sheen, there is nothing we are not ready to tolerate and suffer in order to obtain it. It is from this overpowering instinct and compulsion of our souls towards true glory and honor that such dangers are faced in battle.

Brave men do not feel wounds when they are in the thick of battle; or if they do feel them, they prefer to die than be dislodged in any way from a position of dignity. The Decii[348] saw the enemy's glittering swords when they rushed towards their battle-line; the glory and nobility of death lightened for them all fear of being wounded. Do you think that Epaminondas cried out in pain when he felt his life-force flow away, along with his blood?[349] He left his country in a dominant position over the Lacedaemonians, even though he had found it subservient to them. These are the solaces, these the palliatives, of the greatest pains.[350]

25. You will say: what is there in peace, what in the home, and what on our couch? You encourage me to return to the philosophers who do not often appear at the front line of battle. One of these types (a fickle man named Dionysius of Heraclea[351]), once he had learned from Zeno to be courageous, unlearned this teaching when he encountered pain. When he began to experience problems with his kidneys, he cried out in pain, raving that the views he previously held on pain were incorrect. When his fellow disciple Cleanthes[352] asked him what had led him away from his original position, he responded: "If I am still unable to tolerate pain even after putting so much effort into philosophy, then that is proof enough that pain is an evil. I've

---

[347] Lit., "with the whole heart" or "with the whole soul" (*toto pectore*).

[348] Mentioned above in I.37.

[349] *See* Cornelius Nepos, *Epam.* 9. Wounded at the Battle of Mantinea in 362 B.C., he had a spearhead lodged in his side. After learning of his victory over Sparta, he pulled the spearhead out, bled profusely, and died.

[350] *Haec sunt solacia, haec fomenta summorum dolorum.* With this sentence Cicero ends a chapter of marvelous literary power.

[351] Dionysius "The Renegade" (c. 330 B.C.—c. 250 B.C.), so called because he abandoned Stoicism late in life when he had to endure bodily pain.

[352] Cleanthes of Assos (c. 330 B.C.—c. 230 B.C.), the man who succeeded Zeno of Citium as head of the Stoic school.

spent many years pursuing philosophy, and yet I can't bear it. Pain, therefore, is an evil." Cleanthes then struck the ground with his foot, and is said to have spoken the following words from the *Epigoni*[353]:

Do you hear this, Amphiaraus, hidden under the ground?

He was referring to Zeno; and he deeply regretted that Dionysius had regressed from Zeno's views. This was not the case with our friend Posidonius, however. I have often seen him myself, and I will tell you an anecdote that Pompey liked to circulate. When Pompey left Syria[354] and arrived at Rhodes, he got the idea to hear Posidonius lecture. But when he heard that the philosopher was incapacitated due to serious problems in moving his limbs, he still wanted to pay a visit to such a distinguished thinker.

Pompey saw him, wished him well in deferential terms, and said he was chagrined that he could not hear Posidonius. But the philosopher replied, "You certainly *can* hear me! Nor will I let bodily pain force a man as distinguished as yourself to visit me in vain." Pompey further related that the old man, while lying in his bed, held forth ardently and in great detail on this question: *that nothing is good except what is morally right.* And when Posidonius's body throbbed with a spasm of pain, he would often say, "Pain, you do nothing to me. Even though you are troublesome, I'll never concede that you are an evil."

26. Without exception, all labors that strive for what is illustrious and noble indeed become tolerable. Don't we see that, where competitive gymnastics are held in high regard, those who participate in these contests never try to avoid pain? Men who value prestige in the activities of hunting or riding will not avoid pain in seeking a reputation in these endeavors. What will I say about our own ambitions,

---

[353] A play of Aeschylus adapted or translated by Accius. The character Amphiaraus was a seer from Argos who fell into the earth. According to Tischer (p. 141), this quote proves that Zeno was dead when Cleanthes spoke to Dionysius (*Das Citat beweist, dafs Zeno schon tot war, als Kleanthes dies Gespräch mit Dionysius hatte*).

[354] He made it a Roman province in 63 B.C.

or our own desire for official positions? What fire is there through which those who once collected single punctures would not run?

Africanus always had Xenophon, the pupil of Socrates, in his hands. He used to commend him for saying that the same labors in war were not burdensome to the same degree for a general and a soldier. The reason was that the general's rank itself made his burden easier to bear. Nevertheless it happens that a careless view of integrity prevails among the general population because they cannot appreciate its true quality. Since they believe that whatever is praised by the masses is morally good, they are easily influenced by popularity and the judgment of the crowd. If you should ever fall under the scrutiny of the public, I would not want you to be at the mercy of their verdict; nor would I want you simply to mimic their view of what is best. You must exercise your own independent reasoning. If you are satisfied that you have aligned yourself with what is right, then you will master not only yourself—a principle I urged earlier—but everyone and everything as well.

Let this principle guide your behavior: an embracing grandeur of soul, a certain loftiness of the spirit that reaches to the skies, which is best expressed by despising and looking down on pain, is the one thing in this world that surpasses all others in beauty. It becomes even more magnificent if it does not depend on the public's endorsement, and is not motivated by a desire to win praise, but instead generates its own pleasure by itself alone. Indeed, it seems to me that all things accomplished without specious displays and shameless notoriety are rendered more praiseworthy. It is not that one should hide from scrutiny; things that are done properly, in fact, are usually carried out in plain sight. Nevertheless no theater for virtue is greater than one's conscience.

27. With regard to one's tolerance of pain—which, as I have repeatedly stated, must be enlarged through purposeful concentration of the soul—we must first understand that this tolerance should show itself equally in every area of endeavor. There are many men who have received and endured wounds bravely, either due to a love of victory, a desire for glory, or to retain their own rights or freedom; and yet these same men, once the unremitting exertion of combat has dissipated, are unable to tolerate the aches of disease. The things they endured easily were not endured because of their adherence to reason

or philosophical study: their incentives came instead from raw enthusiasm and the quest for glory. Some pugnacious barbarians can fight with implacable fury with the sword, yet are unable to bear illness in a manly fashion.

The Greeks, conversely, who are not especially renowned for fearlessness, but are as astute as man's potential for this trait allows, cannot look directly at an enemy. Yet these same men can tolerate physical ailments with fortitude, as a human being ought to do. The Cimbri and Celtiberi[355] are jubilant in battle, but weep when visited by sickness. Nothing can remain constant that does not proceed from a definite rule. When you see persons guided by zeal or opinion who are not broken by pain while pursuing and achieving their goals, you should conclude either that pain is not an evil or that, even if one wants to call anything "evil" that is disagreeable or abnormal, this still is so insignificant that it is entirely overshadowed by virtue and not noticeable at all.

I ask you to meditate on these things day and night. This principle will disseminate more widely, and will have an application broader than the single topic of pain. If our intention in everything we do is to avoid moral corruption and seek honor, then it is right for us not only to scorn the torments of pain, but also the thunderbolts of fortune—especially since such an impressive fortress has been made ready from the dialogue we had yesterday. Suppose a god said this to some mariner who was being pursued by pirates: "Leap off the ship. Either a dolphin will carry you off, like Arion of Methymna;[356] or those horses Neptune sent to Pelops,[357] which are said 'to have conveyed the chariot atop the crests of the waves,' will pluck you from the water and take you where you wish. Set all your fear aside."

In the same way, you will see where you must seek sanctuary if you are oppressed by insistent and odious pain that is too intense to

---

[355] The Cimbri were an ancient German tribe; the Celtiberi were Celts of the Iberian peninsula.

[356] A mythic Greek poetic performer said to have been captured by pirates, and then rescued by dolphins when he leaped into the sea. *See* Herod. I.23 and Aulus Gellius XVI.19.

[357] Pelops was a mythical Greek king who desired to wed Hippodamia, the daughter of Oenomaus. Oenomaus had killed his daughter's previous suitors because of a prophecy claiming he would be killed by his son-in-law. Pelops asked for Neptune's help, and received from him a chariot and winged horses.

bear. This is more or less what I thought should be said right now. But perhaps you will hold on to your original point of view.

A. Not at all. I hope that, in these past two days, I've been freed from the fear of two things that had caused me a great deal of apprehension.

M. Tomorrow, then, we go on to the water-clock[358] that's used for timing speakers. We've agreed to do this, and I know it's owed to you.

A. Yes, absolutely. We will have that in the morning, then this at the regular time.

M. We'll follow your admirable preferences, and do things that way.

---

[358] The clepsydra (water-clock) was a timing device used in oratory practice.

ILLUSTRATIONS

The following four photos are views of Arpino (Arpinum),
Cicero's birthplace. (Courtesy of Gianni Di Poce)

The "Torre di Cicerone" at Arpino

Aristotle

Greek image of Atlas and Prometheus (See II.10)

A scholar with his books

Carneades (See IV.3)

Chrysippus (See III.22)

Epicurus

Marcus Junius Brutus

Plato

An alleged bust of Pompey (See I.35, II.25)

Posidonius (See II.25)

The death of Archimedes (See I.25 and V.23)

A Greek fountain scene (See V.36)

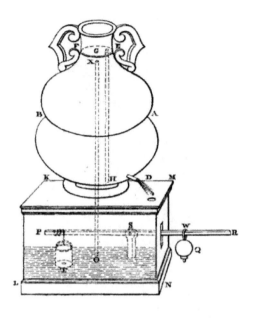

A water-clock, or clepsydra *(See II.27)*

Homer reciting his Iliad *(See I.26)*

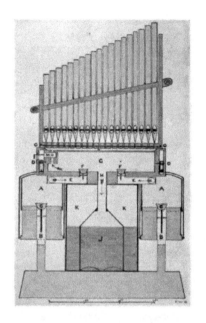

The Roman hydraulus, *or* water organ *(See III.18)*

BOOK III

ON THE UNBURDENING OF SORROW

BOOK III

1. Seeing that we are composed of body and soul, Brutus, what should I suppose is the reason why the art of healing and protecting the body is so sought after, and why this art's advantage in being discovered is attributed to the immortal gods? Why is it that the medicine of the mind was not much investigated before it was known, and not much cultivated after it was discovered? Why was it not accepted and endorsed by some, and viewed with overt mistrust and hostility by many others? Is it because we use our minds to judge the afflictions and pains of the body, but do not sense with our bodies the sicknesses of the soul? What happens is that the soul evaluates itself at a time when the very thing performing the diagnosis is unwell.

If nature had given us the abilities to understand and observe her thoroughly, and if we could make our way in life following her exemplary lead, there would certainly be no need for philosophical method or doctrine. She has, in fact, given us little internal flames; these we rapidly suffocate with our bad habits and opinions, with the result that nature's precious light is entirely smothered. There are innate seeds of virtue in our characters; if they were permitted to grow to maturity, nature herself would guide us to a fulfilling life.

However, once we have been born into this world and been welcomed by a father,[359] we are at once adrift in an ocean of depravity and destructiveness of opinion, so that we seem to suck in error with our nurse's milk. But when we return to our parents, and have been placed in the hands of teachers, then we become saturated with so many erroneous beliefs that truth surrenders to falsity, and nature herself defers to accepted opinion.

2. The poets should be counted here as well, since they offer a powerful kind of instruction and wisdom. Their words are listened to, read, committed to memory, and form powerful bonds with our minds. But when we add to this the public at large as a kind of all-important expert, and the multitude expresses general approval for that which is wrong, then clearly we have been corrupted by debased opinion.

---

[359] *Et suscepti sumus* is the phrase used, where the verb *suscipere* here literally means a father's taking a child into his arms and acknowledging it as his own (instead of abandoning it).

We thus rebel against nature, and convince ourselves that the people who best understand nature's workings are those who think there is nothing better for a man, nothing more worth seeking, and nothing more wonderful, than holding public offices, gaining military commands, or basking in the adulation of the crowd. The best men are drawn to this. As they strive for true honor—which nature diligently seeks above all other things—they become entangled in useless frivolities: they do not pursue an eminent likeness of virtue, but rather the chimerical illusion of glory. Real glory is not a shadow, but a distinct and lasting thing. It is the universal validation of the good, the uncorrupted voice of judges rendering decisions on transcendent virtue. It resounds as virtue's echo, so to speak. And because it follows in the wake of responsibilities properly carried out, it must never be belittled by good men.

Public fame, however, tries to imitate true glory. It is reckless and inconsiderate, and is a flatterer of vices and moral defects. It corrupts the form and beauty of honor by being a simulation of it. Some men, despite pursuing admirable goals, are blinded by its effect. Since they do not know where to begin or what qualities are important, some of them cause the complete destruction of their countries, while others bring about their own deaths. While seeking what is best, these individuals are led astray not by their objectives, but by errors in their chosen paths.

What do you think? Those who are driven by a love of money and a predilection for pleasure—impulses that so unbalance their minds that they totter on the edge of insanity, which is the expected outcome for all who are so deluded—can any remedy be found to treat them? Are the diseases of the soul less harmful than those of the body, or is it that the maladies of the body can be cured, while those of the soul cannot?

3. And yet the sicknesses of the mind are both more pernicious, and are of greater number, than those that afflict the body. Because they extend to one's soul and cause it distress, they are for this reason odious. As Ennius says, "And a sick soul is always amiss. It can neither grasp nor withstand anything, and it never stops longing for something."[360] Although I skip over others, what two afflictions are more dangerous than anxiety and desire? Since the mind has already discovered the art of treating the body, who can agree with the idea

---

[360] A line (according to Tischer) from Ennius's *Iphigenia*.

that the mind cannot cure *itself*? Is it not true that both nature and the body's inherent qualities are influential in the healing process? Don't we find that not all who allow themselves to be treated will promptly recover, while minds that want to be cured, and who follow the guidelines of wise men, are cured beyond all doubt?

There surely exists a medicine for the soul—it is philosophy. We must seek its help not from the outside, as we do with bodily ailments. We must exert ourselves intensely, deploying all our efforts and powers, so that we can act as our *own* healers. In my treatise *Hortensius*,[361] I believe I have satisfactorily discussed, in a general sense, why philosophy should be pursued and studied. From the time that work was composed, I have been continuously writing about or discussing the key questions in philosophy. But in these present books,[362] the debates that took place between myself and my friends at Tusculum have been accurately related.

Our dialogues on the two previous days centered on death and pain. The discussion that took place on our third day will form the content of the third book. We came down to the Academy[363] as the day was edging into afternoon, and I asked someone there to offer a topic for discussion. What appears below is the record of what was said.

4. A. It seems to me that a thinking person tends to be troubled by anxiety.[364]

M. And not by the other perturbations of the mind also, like terrors, passions, or rages? These are, more or less, the types of conditions that the Greeks call *pathē*.[365] I could call them "diseases," and this does reproduce the word's literal meaning. But that translation would not really conform with how we speak. Compassion, envy, elation, and bliss are all things that the Greeks call "diseases," in the sense that they are operations of the soul that are not controlled by reason. As I see it, however, we should properly say that these same movements of an aroused soul are "disruptions," and not "diseases" as that term is commonly used—unless you see things differently.

---

[361] A lost philosophical dialogue of Cicero that examined the question of how best to use leisure time.

[362] I.e., in the five books of the *Tusculan Disputations*.

[363] See II.3, above.

[364] The word *aegritudo* can mean either (1) physical sickness or disease; or (2) mental distress, anguish, or anxiety. In book III, Cicero generally intends the second meaning: a condition of mental distress.

[365] The Greek word πάθη.

A. I agree with what you've said.

M. Do you think the wise man is affected by these disturbances?

A. Very much so, I would say.

M. So this all-important wisdom you value shouldn't be considered so powerful, since it doesn't much differ from insanity.

A. In what way? Does every mental disruption look like madness to you?

M. It doesn't look that way just to *me*. It looked that way to our ancestors, too—and this is something that has often surprised me. From what I understand, our ancestors held this view many centuries before Socrates, the man from whom all philosophy related to life and morals flowed.

A. How did you come to this conclusion?

M. Because the word "madness" indicates an affliction and malady of the mind. That is, a disturbance and disease of the soul that they call insanity. Philosophers call all disruptions of the mind "diseases," and they believe that every fool suffers from them. Those who have diseases, however, are not healthy; and the minds of all foolish people are afflicted with disease. Therefore, all foolish people suffer from a condition of madness. They[366] believed that the health of the human mind was based on a certain tranquility and constancy; and they used the term "insane" to describe a mind that lacked these attributes. This is because good health was not possible in a disrupted mind, just as it was not possible in a disrupted body.

5. Nor were they any less perceptive in applying the terms "derangement" and "insanity" to a condition of the soul that lacked the mind's light. It should be concluded from this that those who coined the terms for these things had the same view the Stoics borrowed from Socrates and scrupulously kept: that all foolish persons were unhealthy. The soul that is in some way sick is no more healthy than a physical body suffering from a sickness—as I have said, philosophers designate all disturbed movement of the mind as "sickness."

We can see from all this that wisdom is the health of the mind. A lack of wisdom is a kind of debilitation, which is insanity, and also derangement. As happens to be the case in many other contexts, these conditions are much better articulated by Latin terms than Greek ones. That issue, however, will be discussed in another place. We now turn to our subject.

---

[366] "They" referring to "our ancestors" mentioned in M's previous statement.

The actual significance of the word—with regard to its quality and nature—announces the whole thing that we are seeking. We must realize that those whose minds have not been disrupted by the motion (so to speak) of a disease are healthy; those who have been adversely affected must be considered unhealthy. Nothing is better than how we commonly describe it in Latin, when we say that those who have completely abandoned themselves to either lust or rage have "lost power over themselves." Rage, however, is a subset of lust, since rage is defined as a "passion" for avenging oneself. Those who are described as having "lost control of themselves" are depicted in this fashion because they are not governed by the power of the mind, to which the entire soul's kingdom has been entrusted by nature to command.

I cannot easily say why the Greeks call this *mania*.[367] We describe the word's contours much better than they do: we draw a distinction between "madness" (which has a wider meaning, owing to its proximity to foolishness) and "furor." The Greeks try to so this, but the word they use is inadequate. What we call furor, they call *melancholia*,[368] as if the mind were affected only by black bile, and not often more profoundly moved by rage, fear, or pain. This is what we mean when we say that Athamas, Alcmaeon, Ajax, and Orestes were "in a furor."[369]

Someone in this state of mind was forbidden by the Twelve Tables[370] from managing his own affairs. Thus the Tables do not read "if one is insane," but instead, "if one be in a state of fury." They thought stupidity, even without mental constancy (that is, sound mental health) could still carry out life's basic responsibilities and common cares. But they saw the condition of *furor* as a blindness of the mind towards everything. Although this seems to be more serious than mental defectiveness, it is still of such a quality that a wise man can be gripped by a fury, but not by derangement. This is, however, a separate question. Let us return to our subject.

---

[367] The Greek word μανία.

[368] μελαγχολία.

[369] These are various figures from Greek mythology whom the gods afflicted with madness. Athamas killed Learchus, one of his sons, in a fit of madness; Alcmaeon went insane after committing matricide; Ajax was stricken with madness by the goddess Athena; and Orestes went mad after killing his mother Clytemnestra.

[370] Early legal codes that served as a foundation of Roman law.

6. If I recall, you said that the wise man had a tendency towards anxiety.

A. I definitely believe this.

M. Your belief is a view shared by many. For we are not born from stones. By nature there is in our souls something delicate and soft which, like a storm, can be upset by sorrow. The esteemed Crantor,[371] one of the noblest men produced by our Academy, was not speaking nonsense when he stated: "I do not at all agree with those who excessively praise that numbness to pain which neither can exist, nor ought to exist. I would prefer never to be sick. But if I am to be sick, I want the capacity for sensation that I previously had, even if my body is cut into, or if something is removed from it. For that kind of imperviousness to pain can't be reached without paying the price of dehumanizing the soul and stupefying the body."

But let us be wary that this kind of talk is not coming from those who excuse the weaknesses of human nature and indulge its infirmities. We ourselves should dare not only to cut off the branches of our miseries, but even to pull out every fiber of their roots. Perhaps some will still remain, for the roots of foolishness are deep; but the only fibers remaining will be those that must remain. Know this, then: unless the mind is cured—something that cannot be done without philosophy—there will never be an end to one's miseries. Therefore, since we have started on this path, let us turn ourselves over to philosophy for this healing process. We will be cured if we truly want to be cured.

And in fact I will say a bit more. Although anxiety will be my primary focus, I will not limit myself to this subject alone; as I have previously stated, I will discuss every disruption of the mind (or as the Greeks say, "sickness"). If it is acceptable to you, let us begin by emulating the habit of the Stoics, who like to offer a compact summary of their arguments. We will then wander according to our inclinations, as we usually do.

7. A man who is strong is a man who has faith in something. Due to a poor habit of speech, the word "confident" has acquired an improper usage; yet it is derived from the verb "to confide," which is approval. He who is motivated by a strong conviction is certainly not afraid, for there is a difference between being fearful and having confidence. Yet he who succumbs to anxiety also falls victim to fear.

---

[371] Crantor (?—c. 276 B.C.), philosopher and scholarch of the Platonic Academy.

When the appearance of certain things causes us anxiety, we are also afraid when they are hanging over our heads, or coming our way. So it happens that sorrow and fortitude are opposed to each other.

It is highly likely, then, that he who is inclined to grief is also inclined to fear—even to the cracking of the mind and the suffocation of one's spirit. Those who fall under the sway of these feelings also become enslaved to their powers; and as a result, they will be willing to admit defeat when confronted by adversity. He who concedes this must also necessarily accept the controlling influence of timidity and cowardice. The strong man does not permit himself to fall under the sway of these emotions—and therefore he is not vulnerable to sorrow, either. But no one is wise unless he is also courageous. Thus the wise man will not allow himself to be controlled by sorrow.

It is also necessary for the brave man to have a great soul; and he who possesses a great soul must be unconquerable. He who is unconquerable looks down on petty human affairs, and regards them as beneath him. Yet no one can look down on the things that cause him to be afflicted with sorrow. From this it follows that the brave man is never consumed by grief. All wise men are courageous; the wise man does not, therefore, fall under the influence of sorrow. Just as the eye, when irritated, is not in a suitable state for carrying out its designated role, and the other parts of the body (or the body as a whole) cannot perform their functions and missions when out of alignment, so also will the perturbed mind be unable to fulfill its responsibilities.

The duty of the mind is the correct employment of rational thought. The wise man's mind is always so aligned as to make the best use of reason. The mind of the wise man, therefore, can never be perturbed. But sorrow is a disturbance of the mind; the wise man, therefore, will never be afflicted with it.

8. This very likely leads us to a conception of the even-tempered man. The Greeks use the word *sophron*[372] to describe the even-tempered man, and they use *sophrosyne*[373] for the virtue I normally call either *temperance* or *moderation*, and sometimes call *restraint*. But it is possible to call this virtue *frugality*, which has a narrower meaning with the Greeks. They call frugal men *chresimoi*,[374] which essentially means *useful*. The word we use has a broader meaning,

---

[372] Σώφρων, meaning "prudent" or "sane."
[373] Σωφροσύνη, meaning "temperance" or "prudence."
[374] Χρήσιμοι.

since it embraces all abstinence and innoxiousness. The Greeks have no typical word for innoxiousness, but I think it is possible to use the word *ablabeia*,[375] which means *harmlessness*, since innoxiousness is a state of the mind which is disposed to hurt no one. Frugality also includes all the other virtues. If this trait were not so important, and if it were as narrowly restrictive as some people believe, it would never have been the widely praised cognomen[376] of Lucius Piso.[377]

Neither the man who has abandoned his post because of fear (which is cowardice), nor the man who fails to return money entrusted to his safekeeping because of greed (which is injustice), nor the man who commits a blunder because of temerity (which is foolishness), are typically described as "frugal." Frugality embraces three virtues: strength, justice, and prudence. This is a common characteristic of the virtues: they are all connected and woven together. Thus frugality itself is left as the fourth virtue. Its specific purpose seems to be to manage and restrain the restless movements of the soul, and to maintain steadfastness in every situation by constantly keeping passion within proper bounds.

The vice that stands in opposition to frugality is called *uselessness*.[378] The word *frugality*, I think, is derived from the Latin word *frux*, meaning fruit or crops; and certainly nothing better comes out of the earth. The word *uselessness* has a different origin. It will be a rougher pedigree, perhaps, but let us march forward; and if it amounts to nothing, we may consider it a joke. *Uselessness* is derived from that which is *useless* in such a person. As a result of this fact, such a person is said to be useful "for nothing." So he who is frugal— or, if you prefer, moderate and temperate—must be steadfast. He who is steadfast must be self-restrained. He who is self-restrained must be free of all angst, and thus also free of all disquiet. These are the attributes of the wise man. Mental anguish will, therefore, not be found in the wise man.

9. Thus Dionysius of Heraclea[379] reasoned correctly when discussing several lines of Homer where Achilles complains,

---

[375] Αβλάβεια, meaning "innocence," or "harmlessness."

[376] The surname of an individual, often derived from some achievement or trait. It can also mean a sobriquet or appellative.

[377] Referring to Lucius Calpurnius Piso Frugi (c. 180 B.C.—112 B.C.), consul in 133 B.C.

[378] *Nequitia.*

[379] See above, II.25.

And my heart swells from deep inside with sor-
rowful rage,
When I recall how I have been deprived of glory
and all renown.[380]

Dionysius reasoned this way: can a hand be in a healthy condition when it is swollen? Or can any swollen or inflamed limb be anything except damaged? When the mind is inflamed and irritated, it is like-wise in an unhealthy condition. The wise man's mind, however, is always free of this kind of injury; it is never inflamed and never dis-tended. It is the enraged mind, rather, that is like this. Therefore, the wise man will never allow himself to become enraged. For he who is consumed by rage is also desirous. The characteristic desire of the angry man is the longing to inflict the greatest pain on the person he believes has harmed him. He who has made this a goal must be quite elated when he successfully carries it out; and so it happens that he celebrates harm coming to another person. Because this is not some-thing that a wise man does, he does not allow himself to be consumed by anger.

But if the wise man feels anxiety, he could also be inclined to anger; and since he is free from anger, he is also from anxiety. For if the wise man could feel anxiety, he might also feel sympathy for oth-ers, or even envy (*invidentia*). Note that I have not used the word *invidia* for "envy," since that word is properly applied to someone who is being envied. The word *invidentia*, which is formed from the participle *invidendo*, is properly used here as a way of eliminating the ambiguity of *invidia*. The word *invidia* is derived from the idea of "looking"[381] too much at someone else's good fortune. We find this in the *Melanippus*:[382]

Who has cast an envious eye on my children's
youthful prime?[383]

---

[380] *Iliad* IX.646.
[381] Cicero likely is referring to the two Latin words *in* ("in") and *videre* ("to see").
[382] A tragedy by Lucius Accius.
[383] The line reads: *Quisnam florem liberum invidit meum?*

His Latin might have been better, perhaps, but Accius still expressed himself impeccably. Since the verb *videre* would take *florem* as a direct object, it is more correct to say *invidere florem* than *invidere flori*.[384] The weight of custom prevents us from speaking like this; but the poet asserts his own literary license, and has delivered his words with greater audacity.

10. The same person, then, is inclined to pity and envy; he who grieves over someone else's adversities will also be stung at another's good fortune. We recall that when Theophrastus felt sorrow at the death of his friend Callisthenes,[385] he was actually distressed over the stunning achievements of Alexander. For this reason he says that Callisthenes encountered a man of the greatest power and rarest good fortune, but one who could not understand how to make use of the good fortune that came his way. And just as pity is anxiety generated by someone else's adversities, so jealousy is anxiety provoked by someone else's good fortune. Therefore, he who is inclined to pity others is equally inclined to envy others. But the wise man will not be inclined to envy. He will not, therefore, be likely to feel pity. But if the wise man made a habit of feeling anxiety, he would also be in the habit of feeling pity. Anxiety, then, does not come near the wise man.

Now this is what the Stoics say, and they arrive at their conclusions through various mental twists and convolutions. These issues ought to be explained more broadly and with less narrow rigidity. Nevertheless we should primarily examine the views of those who, I might say, make use of a distinct strength and virility in their reasoning and opinions. Our friends the Peripatetics, who are unmatched in richness, erudition, and seriousness, are to me not very persuasive when they discuss the moderate conditions of either the distresses or the diseases of the soul. Every evil—even a moderate one—is still an evil. But the proper goal is that the wise man should contain no evil at all. Just as a body that is "moderately" sick cannot be said to be

---

[384] *Florem* is the accusative form (used for direct objects) of the noun *flos* (flower); *flori* is the dative form (used for indirect objects).

[385] Callisthenes of Olynthus (c. 360 B.C.—327 B.C.), a historian who accompanied Alexander the Great on his campaigns in the Near East. He was accused of conspiring against Alexander, and ultimately died in prison. Theophrastus (c. 371 B.C.—c. 287 B.C.) was a distinguished philosopher and naturalist (and Aristotle's successor as head of the Peripatetic school) who had befriended Callisthenes.

healthy, so is it true that a soul in this "moderate" condition cannot be said to be healthy.

Our own people were quite brilliant when they gave the name "anxiety" to mental distress, disquiet, and sorrow because of the similarities of these states to sick bodies. With substantially the same word do the Greeks identify all the mind's disruptions. They say *pathos*,[386] that is, "sickness," when describing any gloomy movement of the soul. Our way is better. For perturbation of the mind is similar to an ailing body. Sexual desire is not similar to a sickness, and neither is excessive joy, which is an elevated and lively delight of the mind. Fear also does not much resemble a sickness; it is more affiliated with anxiety.

It is only fitting that, just like a disease of the body, a disturbance of the mind has a name that is not unconnected to the concept of pain. Therefore, we must identify the source of this pain, since it is the agent that produces the mind's distress, and approach this task just as if we were trying to identify a disease of the body. Just as doctors believe that they learn the cure for a disease at the time they first discover its origin, so will we acquire the ability to treat anxiety once we identify its root cause.

11. The entire origin, therefore, is in *opinion*—this is true not just for anxiety, but for every other kind of mental perturbation. There are four types of these perturbations, with each having many parts. For every perturbation is a movement of the mind that is either lacking in reason, scornful of reason, or in defiance of reason. This movement is precipitated in two ways, either by an idea of good, or an idea of evil; therefore we have four perturbations that are divided equally. Two of these come from an idea of good, of which one is lively pleasure, that is, joy elevated by the belief in some present great good. The other is the immoderate desire for an imagined great good, a desire that does not obey reason. We can call this desire lust or wantonness.

These two categories, lively pleasure and lust, are stirred up by an opinion of good, just as the two others (fear and anxiety) are stirred up by the idea of evil. For fear is the belief in a great impending evil, and anxiety is the belief of a great present evil, and indeed a belief in a new evil of such a type that it seems justified to be distressed. It is of such a type that the person who is in pain believes he

---

[386] The Greek term πάθος.

really should be feeling pain. Our foolishness incites and sends us these perturbations like avenging spirits in human life; and we must fight them with all our strength and powers if we want to live this life we have been given in repose and quiescence.

But these remaining matters are better handled elsewhere. Let us dispose of anxiety, if we can. Indeed, let this be our objective. You have stated that you think the wise man is likely to be afflicted with anxiety, something that I do not at all agree with. It is a hideous, miserable, detestable thing that we should make every effort to avoid—with all sails and oars, if I may use these words.

12. What do you think of this man:

> Descendant of Tantalus, born of Pelops, who once seized
> Hippodamea from her father-in-law King Oenomaus
> By means of a coerced wedding?[387]

He was indeed the great-grandson of Jupiter. Will he then be so prostrate, so broken apart? He said:

> Don't come near me, my friends. Go away now,
> Lest my shadow contagion harm good men,
> With such strength does the power of evil adhere
> to my body.

Thyestes, will you condemn yourself and deny yourself of life, because of the magnitude of someone else's crime? Well? Don't you think that the son of Sol[388] was unworthy of his father's light?

> My eyes fade; my body withers with emaciation;
> The moisture of tears has engulfed my bloodless cheeks;

---

[387] From Ennius's *Thyestes*. See above, II.27 and I.44.
[388] "Son of Sol" refers to Aeëtes, king of Colchis.

On a neglected face, a beard unshaven and en-
crusted with dirt
Darkens a breast matted with filth.

Brainless Aeëtes! These foul things you brought down on yourself. They were not among the things that were delivered to your
doorstep by chance. They became an entrenched evil, once the swell-
ing of the mind had diminished. As I will demonstrate, however,
anxiety is found in the idea of a recent evil. But clearly you are
mourning the loss of your kingdom, not your daughter—for you des-
pised her, and perhaps justifiably. You could not calmly endure the
loss of your kingdom. Yet it is an impudent anguish that eats away
at a man when he is not permitted to rule over free men.

Indeed, the tyrant Dionysius of Syracuse, after having been
forced to leave his city, taught young students at Corinth—so unable
was he to continue living without this kind of authority. What could
be more impudent than the spectacle of Tarquin[389] waging war
against those who would not tolerate his overweening arrogance?
When the arms of neither the Veientines nor the Latins could put him
back on the throne, it is said that he moved to Cumae, and in that city
succumbed to decrepitude and sorrow.

13. Do you think, then, that it is possible for the wise man to be
crippled by sorrow? That is, with anguish? Now all perturbation is
suffering, but sorrow is torture. Lust contains intense ardor, spirited
joy contains levity, and fear contains debasement. But anxiety is associated with greater evils: putrefaction, torture, grievous suffering,
and repulsiveness. It shreds the soul, and leads it to complete destruction. Unless we cut it away and discard it, we have no hope of
liberating ourselves from distress.

Yet this, indeed, is evident: that anxiety starts when we think
some great evil is near and biting at our heels. Epicurus, however,
took the position that anxiety caused by the thought of evil was natural, meaning that someone who thinks about a great evil
immediately feels anxiety if he surmises that it has happened to him.
The Cyrenaics[390] reckon that anxiety is not caused by every evil, but

---

[389] Lucius Tarquinius Superbus, the seventh and final king of Rome, who died in
exile at Cumae in 495 B.C.
[390] I.e., the school of Aristippus.

by a *sudden* and *abrupt* evil.[391] This is no middling factor in elevating anxiety, for everything that is sudden appears more menacing. Thus these verses are deservedly admired:

> I raised them, and when I brought them up, knew they would die,
> And again when I sent them to Troy to defend Greece,
> I knew I was not sending them to dinner banquets,
> But to murderous combat.[392]

14. This premeditation of the future, then, alleviates the occurrence of evils whose arrival one has long anticipated. Thus we applaud the words that Euripides wrote for Theseus. And as we often do, we may render them in Latin as follows:

> As I remember what I heard from a learned man,
> I prepared myself for future miseries,
> Either a bitter death or a gloomy retreat into exile,
> Or always I contemplated some other burden of evil,
> So that if disaster should loom from a random occurrence,
> No unexpected concern might destroy me while vulnerable.

When Theseus says he heard something from a man with worldly wisdom, this is Euripides talking about something that he himself learned. He had been a student of Anaxagoras, a man who allegedly announced after having been told of his son's death: "I knew I had brought a mortal into the world." This declaration reminds us that this kind of tragedy is agonizing for someone who has not previously

---

[391] By a sudden and abrupt evil: *insperato et necopinato malo*, in the sense that the evil is unexpected.
[392] From Ennius's *Telamo*. In the *Iliad*, Telamon is the father of Ajax and Teucer.

meditated on it. It cannot be doubted, therefore, that *all things believed to be evil are more terrible when they come as unforeseen occurrences*. Although this is not the one thing that causes the greatest anxiety, nevertheless, because mental precaution and preparation can do much to curtail pain, a person should reflect deeply on all the possibilities that could happen to him.

Without doubt, this is that true wisdom which is both surpassing and divine; it consists in a profound awareness and understanding of human affairs, and in not being surprised by anything when it happens. It also means believing, before something actually happens, that anything can take place.[393]

> Therefore everyone, when their fortunes are at
> Their highest point,
> Should then reflect within themselves how
> They might tolerate the coming of adversity:
> A man returning from abroad should always
> Be mindful of dangers and damages, or his son's
> Transgressions, his wife's death, or his daughter's
> Sickness. Never forget these are vulnerabilities
> Common to all, so that one of them does not
> Hit a man like something completely unexpected.
> Whatever happens that exceeds our hopes,
> Should be counted as all profit.[394]

15. Since Terence has so suitably stated an idea taken from philosophy, will we, from whose wellsprings this sentiment was drawn, not articulate it more comprehensively, and feel it more deeply in our bones? This, indeed, is the face of the man of wisdom—the same face, we are told, that Xanthippe said her husband Socrates would display to the outside world. She claimed to see him with the same facial expression both when he left his house, and when he returned to it. He did not have the same dour countenance as old Marcus Crassus,[395] who laughed but once in his entire life, if we believe the

---

[393] In other words, "be ready for anything."

[394] Terence's *Phormio* II.241—246.

[395] Referring to Marcus Licinius Crassus Agelastus, grandfather of the more famous general and politician Marcus Licinius Crassus (c. 115 B.C.—53 B.C.) who died in the Battle of Carrhae. Due to his lack of humor, the elder Crassus was nicknamed Agelastus ("grim") by the satirist Caius Lucilius.

testimony of Lucilius. The demeanor of Socrates, by all accounts, was tranquil and serene. His expression was always the same, and with good reason, since no shift ever took place in his mind, the source from which his visage was created.

Therefore, as security against life's random chances and unhappy events, I indeed accept from the Cyrenaics those weapons which will permit me, with the aid of long premeditation, to shatter fortune's hostile incursions. At the same time, I believe this evil we have discussed is based on opinion, not on nature. For if it were based on objective truth, why would it become lighter by foreseeing it?[396] But something more precise can be said on this topic, if we first take a look at Epicurus's view. He thought that all men believing themselves surrounded by evils must be in a state of anxiety, whether the evils were awaited and expected to arrive, or were already present. Evils are not diminished by their longevity, he thought, nor are they lessened by our premeditation on them. And it was foolish to obsess over some evil not yet present, or an evil that would perhaps never materialize at all. Every evil is odious enough when it has arrived; but he who always thinks about the bad event that might happen, transforms it into a permanent evil. Yet if the event does not occur at all, he has embraced a voluntary misery for no reason. He is thus in a state of perpetual torment, either from experiencing the evil or from thinking about it.

Epicurus believes that the reducing of anxiety can be found in two courses of action: diverting the mind from thinking about troubles, and the "bringing back" of the mind to a contemplation of pleasures.[397] He thinks that the mind can obey reason and carry out its instructions. Reason therefore prohibits the mind's pondering of sorrows, diverts it from gloomy meditations, and dulls its penchant for ruminating on misfortune. Reason demands a retreat from this type of thinking. It compels the mind to seek a different course: that is, to consider a variety of pleasures, and to participate in them with all the mind's capabilities. Epicurus assures us that the wise man's life is filled with the memory of past pleasures and the fond hope of pleasures to come. We have articulated this view in our own way,

---

[396] *Si enim in re esset, cur fierent provisa leviora?* An elegant formulation.
[397] "Diversion" is used for *avocatio*, and *revocatio* is "bringing back" or "recalling."

157

and the Epicureans have declared it in their own style. But let us examine what they are saying; we will not concern ourselves with how they say it.

16. First of all, they are mistaken in placing blame on the premeditation of future evils. There is nothing so effective in numbing and assuaging sorrow as the persistent contemplation, conducted throughout one's entire life, that anything can happen. There is nothing so effective as meditation on the human condition, and nothing so effective as an awareness of the law of life and our mental preparation to submit to it. *The consequence of this is not that we become morose all the time, but that we are never inclined to feel morose at all.* Neither is he who contemplates the natural world, the multiformity of life, and the feebleness of humanity, depressed by thinking about these things. He is, in fact, ably carrying out wisdom's obligation.

He benefits in two ways: when he ponders human affairs, he enjoys the responsibility of philosophy, and when adversity comes, he is healed with a triple consolation. *First,* because he has for a long time thought about the chance of some disaster occurring, and this reflection is the most convincing way to dilute and alleviate all distresses; *second,* because he understands that human burdens must be borne with the dignity befitting a true man; and *third,* because he sees that what is culpable is the only real evil.[398] There is no culpability, however, when something happens that is beyond a man's ability to control.

With regard to this "calling back" that Epicurus mentions (when he dissuades us from obsessing about our misfortunes), we can say that it is non-existent. As we wrestle with those events we consider evils, it is not within our power to lie about them, or to forget them; they tear at us, oppress us, and incite extreme emotions. They kindle fires in us, and smother our breathing. You, Epicurus, tell me just to forget all this—a command that is against nature. And at the same time, you yank out of my hands the help nature has given us for alleviating chronic pain? There is indeed a medicine, slow-acting but nevertheless powerful, that is created with the long passage of time. You order me, Epicurus, to think about the good, and forget what is evil. You would be saying something worthy of a great philosopher,

---

[398] Meaning that the only things we should consider evil are our own personal failings, not events over which we had no control.

158

if you could perceive that those things are "good" which are most in accord with human worthiness.

17. Should Pythagoras, Socrates, or Plato say to me: "Why are you lying down helplessly, or why are you filled with sorrow, or why are you submitting to fortune? She might have slapped or pinched you, but she certainly can't have destroyed your strength. Great power resides in the virtues: if perhaps they are sleeping, awaken them. *Fortitude*, the most important of them, will then appear before you. It will force you to acquire a spirit of such strength that you will look down on, and see as insignificant, all things that can happen to a man.

"The virtue of *temperance* will then appear. She is also *moderation*, and was called by me 'frugality' a short while ago; she will not permit you to do anything that is depraved or foul. Yet what is more depraved or foul than an effeminate man? Not even justice will allow you to behave in this way. There seems to be little need for justice in this situation. Nevertheless she will say you are being unjust twice. You seek something that does not belong to you—for you were born a mortal, but want to be in the condition of an immortal.

"Besides this, you are complaining about having to return something that you received for temporary use. What response will you make to *prudence*, when she instructs you that she is a sufficient virtue in herself for living a good life, and thus a happy life? If prudence were dependent on others and restricted by outside factors, and did not originate from herself and return again to herself, so that she embraces everything within herself and looks for nothing anywhere else, I don't understand why she should deserve such effusive verbal flattery, or why she should be pursued with such acute vigor."

If you bring me back to these goods, Epicurus, I will listen to you, follow you, and accept you as my instructor. And as you ordered me to do, I will forget evils. I will certainly do this more easily, because I think they shouldn't be classified as evils. But you are leading my thoughts toward pleasures. What kinds of pleasures? Physical pleasures, I believe, or such bodily pleasures that are believed to come from past recollection or future hopes. Is there anything else? Did I accurately express your view? The followers of Epicurus like to deny that I truly grasp what Epicurus is saying.

He *does* say this. And when I heard Zeno[399] in Athens as an old man—he was an astute man, the shrewdest of them all—he would

---

[399] Zeno of Sidon (c. 150 B.C.—c. 75 B.C.), an Epicurean philosopher from Phoenicia.

assert these ideas in a loud voice: that person was happy who enjoyed present pleasures, and had confidence that he would enjoy them either for his whole life, or for most of his life, without the intrusion of pain; or, if pain should intrude into his life, it would be brief if it were severe, but if the pain were drawn out, it would be flavored more with agreeableness than with evil; and that thinking about this would make a person happy, especially if he were content with good things already enjoyed, and if he feared neither death nor the gods. You have Epicurus's conception of a happy life, expressed in Zeno's words. So it isn't possible to deny any of this.

18. What should we think, then? Will the notion and thought of this kind of life be able to comfort either Thyestes or Aeëtes, whom we mentioned earlier? Will it be able to console Telamon, who was expelled from his country and became a destitute exile? Those who encountered him would say in amazement:

> Here is Telamon, the man whom glory lifted to the skies,
> A man whom people laid eyes on in wonder,
> And Greek faces turned towards his visage?[400]

But if someone discovers—as the same writer says—that "as his affairs fell, so did his spirit,"[401] then he must seek a medicine from those sober ancient philosophers, not from these hedonists. What is this "abundance of good" that these voluptuaries are talking about? Imagine that the greatest good is to be without pain. Although this condition is not called pleasure (we do not need to discuss all these details now), is this really the place we've been brought for soothing our grief?

It may be, of course, that pain is the greatest evil. Does that mean that the man who is *not* in pain immediately enjoys the highest good, if he is untainted by evil? Why do we deliberately turn our backs when the time comes to explain these implications, Epicurus? Why don't we admit that we consider pleasure what you usually say pleasure is, once the blush on your face has gone away?[402] Are these your words, or are they not? In that work which contains all your doctrines

---

[400] Verses from Accius's *Eurysaces*, according to Tischer.

[401] *Simul animus cum re concidit.*

[402] A colorful idiomatic expression in Latin: *os perfricare*, "to wipe the blush from one's face," meaning to abandon shame. Cicero cannot resist mocking Epicurus and brings to bear all his powers of rhetoric and philosophical inquiry.

(I will now take on the responsibility of translator, so that no one will think I'm fabricating) you state the following:

> Nor indeed can I form any idea of what is called "good," if we subtract from it the pleasures acquired by taste, the pleasures that come from listening to music, the pleasures acquired from the observation of visible objects or their enchanting motions, or other pleasures recognized by the whole man using any of his senses. Neither is it possible to say that happiness of the mind alone is to be considered a good. I know that a mind is "happy" when it nourishes hope for all those pleasures I have mentioned above; or stated another way, the hope that nature can imbibe these pleasures while being free from pain.[403]

He expresses himself using words that are unambiguous enough to allow anyone to understand what he means by the word "pleasure." A short distance after the quote above, Epicurus adds this: "From men who were considered wise, I have often asked what good would be left over if they removed all those pleasures, unless they only wanted to leave us useless verbiage? I haven't been able to acquire anything from these men. If they want to talk about virtues and wisdom, they will state nothing but the path[404] in which those pleasures are produced that I mentioned earlier."

The same ideas are in what follows; and the entire book, which discusses the topic of the Ultimate Good, is filled with these kinds of words and opinions. To alleviate Telamon's anxiety, will you, Epicurus, bring him back to *this* kind of life? And if you notice someone in your household who is stricken with sorrow, will you hand him a sturgeon instead of one of Socrates's books? Will you encourage him

---

[403] A quote apparently from a lost treatise of Epicurus. But *see* Diog. Laert. X.130-133, which summarizes Epicurus's ideas on pleasure.

[404] I.e., the path to happiness. Stated another way, "the only path to happiness is through the pleasures I mentioned earlier." Cicero is also accusing the Epicureans of seeing virtue not as good for its own sake, but only as a tool for acquiring pleasure.

to listen to the sound of a water organ[405] instead of the words of Plato? Will you arrange different types of flowers for him to gaze at? Will you hold a bunch of flowers under his nose for him to smell, or burn fragrant aromas?[406] Will you tell him to wrap his head with roses and laurels? And certainly if you have other pleasures in mind...then without doubt, you will have taken away all his tears.[407]

19. Epicurus must acknowledge these claims, or expunge from his book these quotes I have accurately reproduced here. An even better option would be to tear up the entire book, for it is filled with solicitations to pleasures. It must also be asked how we can free a man from anxiety who speaks in this way:

> Certainly fortune now abandons me more than my lineage,
> For the kingdom that once belonged to me will teach you
> That from so high a station, such great resources,
> And such appurtenances of power,
> It still happens that fortune fell.

What now? Should we shove a cup of honeyed wine in front of him, to try to mitigate his anguish? Or something else along these lines? On another side, the same poet gives us these lines:

> Once so rich in resources, Hector, now needing your help.

We should help her, since she is looking for aid:

---

[405] *Hydraulus*, or water organ, was a pipe organ that converted the energy of moving water into pressurized air. Described by Vitruvius (X.8) and Pliny (*Hist. Nat.* IX.2.4).

[406] I.e., incense generated by the burning of aromatic resins.

[407] When Cicero is on the attack, he has no equal in the art of the invective. The scorn heaped on Epicurus in this paragraph is unmistakable.

Where do I look for, where can I find, a protector?
How am I to have confidence in help, escape or
withdrawal?
I am bereft of fortress and city,
To whom can I go? To whom can I petition?
My country's sacred shrines are fallen, and stretch
Shattered and dismembered upon the ground,
Temples have been consumed by fire,
High walls stand scorched,
Everything twisted in ruin,
And planks of fir warped by flame.

You know the lines that come after this, these most of all:

O father, O country, O house of Priam,
Temple secured by a vociferous hinge,
I saw you in uncouth plenitude
With roofs carved and adorned with angular de-
signs,
Sumptuously constructed in gold and ivory.

O exceptional poet! Even though he's disfavored by the perform-
ers who mumble Euphorion's verses! For he appreciates, on an
instinctive level, that everything unforeseen and unpredictable presents a more debilitating burden. What words does he add to this
exaggerated description of the royal riches, which many thought
would last indefinitely?

I witnessed everything consumed by fire,
Priam forcibly deprived of his life,
And Jove's altar desecrated with blood.

This is a brilliant verse. The words, the cadence of the lines, the
overall narrative—all these are tinged with anguish. Let us take away
her sorrow! But how can we do it? Let us place her on a plush, down-

163

stuffed bed; let us bring in a cithara-player; let us burn a dish of fragrant ointment; let us consider some mildly sweet drink and a morsel of food. These are the good things that will take away the most debilitating sorrows! For you said a short while ago that you didn't know any other good. If we could agree with Epicurus on what "good" means, then I ought to agree with him that we should be redirected from grief to a contemplation of life's goods.

20. Here someone will say: What should we conclude from this? Do you believe Epicurus wanted these things, or that his goals were lustful? I myself do not see it this way. I know many of the things he said were stern and exemplary. So as I've frequently stated before, what concerns us is his acumen, not his habits. Although he rejects the physical pleasures he has praised, I will still remember what he considers to be the highest good. He has not only referenced the word "pleasure," but explained for us the word's meaning. He clearly stated that he meant "taste, affectionate hugging, games, music, and physical shapes that agreeably excite the eyes." Am I making this up, or am I lying?

I want someone to disprove me. Why am I working at this, except to see that the truth is revealed in every discussion? This same philosopher[408] says pleasure does not increase when pain is taken away, and that the greatest pleasure is the absence of pain. Yet in these few words, we see three big blunders. One, because he argues against himself. He claimed he had no conception of any good unless his senses were titillated by pleasure; but now, however, he says that the greatest pleasure is the absence of pain.

Is it possible to hold two positions so at odds with each other? His second blunder is that he does not recognize the difference between *pleasure* and the *absence of pain*. For in nature there are three sensory conditions: the first is delight, the second is pain, and the third is neither delight nor pain. Epicurus thinks that the first and third conditions are equivalent. His third error is one that he holds in common with some other thinkers. Although virtue is something we seek intensely, and philosophy is cultivated for the purpose of gaining this virtue, Epicurus has disconnected the Ultimate Good from virtue.

Someone will now say, "But he usually says good things about virtue!" True, but so did Caius Gracchus when he distributed lavish

---

[408] Epicurus.

handouts to people and exhausted the treasury, while at the same time mouthing statements that he was protecting the treasury. Why should I listen to words, when I can see actions? Lucius Piso, whom we know by the name Frugi, had always campaigned against the Corn Law. When the law was passed, he himself showed up as consul to accept grain. Gracchus spotted Piso standing in the crowd. In a voice loud enough for others to hear, he asked Piso how it was logical for him to try to receive grain under a law he had formerly resisted. Piso responded, "I don't want you to split up my property among everyone, Gracchus! But if you're going to do this, I want my fair share." Didn't this wise and honest man adequately confirm that the Sempronian Law frivolously wasted the public's patrimony?

Read the orations of Gracchus. You will say he was the treasury's guardian. Epicurus denied that it was possible to live with satisfaction unless one's life was lived with virtue. He denied that fortune had any power over the wise man. He taught that simple nourishment was superior to a lavish intake of food. And he denied that there was any time when a wise man was unhappy. All of these ideas are certainly worthy of a philosopher, *but they are directly opposed to pleasure*. "But he is not referring to your conception of pleasure," someone will say. Well, he can be referring to *any* kind of pleasure. But he is, of course, talking about that pleasure containing no part of virtue. Consider this: if we don't understand pleasure, do we really understand pain? I do not think, therefore, that someone who judges the greatest evil using pain as a guide should be talking about virtue.

21. Those wonderful men, the Epicureans (for no class of men is less roguish), gripe that I speak zealously against their master Epicurus. So I am led to believe that we are competing for a public office or a formal position. It seems to me that the Ultimate Good is in the soul, but to Epicurus it lies in the body. For me it is in virtue, and for him in pleasure. The Epicureans are the ones who are fighting, the ones begging for the trust of their neighbors. There are many who will at once join together to help them. I am the one to say that I am not carping. What they are talking about is something I consider already resolved. What is the fuss about? Is this something related to the Punic War? When Marcus Cato and Lucius Lentulus[409] had different views on this issue, there was never any wrangling between them.

---

[409] Lucius Cornelius Lentulus Lupus, who was consul in 156 B.C. and died in 125 B.C.

The Epicureans are exceedingly bad-tempered, especially considering that the opinion they hold is not exactly a courageous sentiment; and they would not dare to promote it in the senate, in front of a large gathering, or before the army or the censors. But we will deal with these people at another time, and with such a spirit that no antagonism will develop. I will easily give way to words that are based on truth. I will only make this suggestion. If it is completely true that for the wise man everything is evaluated by comparing it to the body—or to say it more directly, the wise man only does things that are advantageous for himself, or evaluates everything based on how expedient it is—then, because these attitudes are not seen as worthy of praise, let them stop speaking so arrogantly, and instead rejoice privately to themselves.

22. We are now left with the opinion of the Cyrenaics, who teach that anguish results when some unexpected event occurs. As I indicated earlier, this assertion holds a great deal of merit. I also recall that Chrysippus's view was that unforeseen events strike us with more ferocity. But everything does not depend on this. We may concede that an unforeseen enemy attack generates more anxiety than an anticipated attack, and an abrupt tempest at sea provokes more fear in mariners than a predicted one. Many such examples can be cited.

Yet when you carefully consider the true nature of unexpected events, you will discover without exception that all such events appear greater than they really are. There are two reasons why this is so. First, because no reference measure is provided to evaluate the true significance of the event. Second, when it seems that precautions could have been taken if only someone had foreseen the event, the resulting evil gives our anguish a more bitter taste, since we believe we are at fault. The passage of time shows that this is indeed true. As time goes on the distress is mitigated, so that even if the same evils remain present, the resulting anguish is not only assuaged, but in many situations is entirely eliminated.

Many Carthaginians were enslaved to Rome; and after the capture of King Perses,[410] many Macedonians were in the same position. When I was a young man, I myself saw some Corinthians working as slaves in the Peloponnese. All of them might have expressed their sorrow using the same words found in the *Andromacha*:

---

[410] Perseus of Macedon (c. 212 B.C.—166 B.C.) defeated by Rome at the Battle of Pydna in 168 B.C., and taken into captivity by Lucius Aemilius Paullus.

I witnessed all these things…[411]

But perhaps by now they had finished uttering such lamentations. In countenance, speech, and every other aspect of their motions and dispositions, you might have said they were freemen of Argos or Sicyon.[412] The unexpected sight of the ruins at Corinth[413] moved me more than it moved the Corinthians themselves, for long consideration of them had allowed the passage of time to blunt the impressions made on their minds.

We have read Clitomachus's book which he sent to console his subjugated fellow citizens after the fall of Carthage. Recorded in it is a discourse of Carneades, which Clitomachus claims to have transcribed in his diary. The proposition of the discourse was that the wise man would likely feel sorrow at the ruin of his country. The arguments offered by Carneades against this premise are then recited. The medicine used by the philosopher to alleviate the shock of a current calamity is one which no one needs in a calamity that has persisted for a long time. If that same book had been sent to the Carthaginian prisoners a few years later, it would not have repaired fresh wounds, but scar tissue. Gradually, and by slow incremental steps, pain progressively subsides. This is so not because the underlying problem has usually changed, or can be changed, but because practice teaches what reason should have taught us: that the problems which once loomed so large are not as significant as they seemed.

23. Someone here will ask: so then why is reason needed, or why is any of that consolation needed which we normally give to people experiencing sorrow? Indeed, we generally have this saying ready at hand: *nothing should be seen as a surprise*. The man who knows it is inevitable for something like this to happen to someone: how will that man bear this setback more tolerably? This perspective takes away nothing from evil's sum total; it only presents the view that nothing has happened which should not have been imagined. Yet this kind of perspective has some consolatory value—in fact I believe it has very much value. Unforeseen things do not have enough power to produce all the distress that comes about. Their arrival causes more pain, perhaps, but they do not cause the things that happen to appear

---

[411] A quote from the *Andromacha* of Ennius.
[412] Sicyon was an ancient Greek city-state located close to the Corinthian Gulf.
[413] Referring to the damage caused by Rome's conquest of the city in 146 B.C.

167

more severe. They appear more severe because they are *recent*, not because they are *unexpected*.

Therefore, the method for arriving at the truth has two facets to it, not only for evil things, but also for things that appear good. We either examine the distinguishing features of the event and its degree of seriousness, as sometimes we see in the case of poverty, when we alleviate its burdens in debate by explaining how small and trifling are natural human wants; or, we turn away from the subtleties of formal discussion to the world of specific examples. Here we point to a Socrates, here a Diogenes, and here this quote from Caecilius[414]:

Under a grimy cloak is wisdom often found.

Seeing that the burden of poverty is uniformly the same everywhere, what explanation can there be for the fact that it was tolerable for Caius Fabricius[415] but unendurable for others? Here is something similar to the second way of alleviating distress: *that which teaches us that all the things that happen in this world are an inherent part of the human condition.* This assertion not only embraces an understanding of the human predicament, but it shows that the calamities other people have braved and endured are also tolerable for us.

24. Let us consider poverty. We know of many paupers who endured this condition with fortitude. What about the disdain for public office? We know of many who never sought such honors, and were happier for this choice. Praise is specifically given to those who chose a life of retired leisure instead of the hectic responsibilities of public office. Neither do they fail to mention the poetic lines of that most powerful monarch, in which he praises an elderly man and says the man is fortunate because he would reach the final hour of his life in a condition of obscurity and anonymity.

Similarly, they offer us examples of people who have endured the death of a child; for those carrying a tremendous burden of sorrow, their grief is assuaged by hearing cases of others who have faced

---

[414] Caecilius Statius (c. 220 B.C.—c. 166 B.C.), Roman poet and contemporary of Ennius. *See* Aulus Gellius XV.24, where Caecilius is ranked first among the comic poets: *Caecilio palmam Statio do mimico.*

[415] Caius Fabricius Luscinus, elected consul in 282 B.C. and censor in 275 B.C. He was considered an exemplar of incorruptibility.

equivalent trials. Thus, the courage of others makes calamities that have occurred seem much less dire than their originally estimated importance. So it happens that, with some deliberation over time, a person appreciates the extent to which his original assessment was mistaken. The well-known Telamon declares the same principle when he says,

I, when I gave birth to them,[416]

and Theseus:

I prepared myself for future miseries,[417]

and Anaxagoras: "I knew I had created a mortal."[418] Through a long period of scrutiny of human affairs, these men realized that in no way should such things be judged according the views of the masses. To me, it seems to be basically the same situation with those who think about things beforehand, as with those who heal over time; the difference is that a type of reason heals one of these, and nature heals the other. One realizes from all this—and this truth embraces everything we have been talking about—that *the evil we once believed was so overpowering is in no way so great as to prevent us from living a happy life.*

Our conclusion, therefore, is that the damaging effect of an unexpected negative event is greater. It is not as the Cyrenaics believe, that when two people have been hit with the same negative event, the only person who experiences sorrow is the one who was not expecting the event. Therefore it is said that some who are grieving have been touched with anguish even more profoundly when they hear of this universal human condition—this law that hovers over all of us from the moment of our birth—which is that no one can go through life avoiding evil completely.

---

[416] A line from Ennius's *Telamo*. See III.13.
[417] See III.14.
[418] See III.14.

25. This was why Carneades—as I know my friend Antiochus[419] has recorded—used to reprimand Chrysippus for praising these lines from Euripides:

> There is no mortal who does not experience sorrow
> And ailments too; it is the fate of many to bury their children,
> And create new life once more.
> Death remains the destination for all.
> To no purpose do these truths distress the human race,
> For Earth must return to earth,
> So life should be harvested by all, just as crops.
> Thus does Necessity command.[420]

He denied that this type of speech had any relevance at all with regard to soothing anxiety. He said that the real reason we feel sorrow is because we are exposed to a most cruel inevitability. The playwright's words were intended to console the disaffected by evoking the misfortunes of others.

Yet I see things much differently. Understanding the necessity of enduring the human condition prevents a man from taking a hostile stance against God, and reminds him that he is only a man. This realization very much lightens the burden of grief. The reciting of examples is not done to gratify the minds of the disaffected, but to enable a grieving person to understand that he must endure, calmly and patiently, the trials he sees many others have endured. Using all means, we must support those who, because of the magnitude of their grief, are ready to collapse and unable to hold themselves together.

Because of this, Chrysippus believes that sorrow is called *lupé*[421] from the view that it represents a weakening of the entire man. And, as I stated at the beginning, it can be completely torn out once we

---

[419] The Academic philosopher Antiochus of Ascalon (c. 125 B.C.—c. 68 B.C.), whose ideas figure prominently in Cicero's *On Moral Ends*. He attempted to reconcile the views of the Stoics and Peripatetics with traditional Platonism.

[420] Lines from Euripides's partially preserved play *Hypsipyle*. The subject of the play is the legend of Queen Hypsipyle of Lemnos, the lover of Jason.

[421] Λύπη, sorrow or grief.

have explained the cause of sorrow. *It is nothing other than an opinion and a judgment of an immediate and menacing evil.* Therefore bodily pain, whose sting burns very deeply, is endured when hope of the good still lives within us. A life lived honestly and magnificently rewards one with such a profound consolation that either no sorrow touches those who have lived this way, or pain only lightly stings the mind.

26. Yet when there is another belief added to this belief of great evil—that we should carry a burden of grief over what has happened, that it is right for us to do this, that it is our duty to do this—then does the disruption of crippling mental distress finally come about. The varied and detestable types of grieving arise from this way of thinking: failure to maintain personal hygiene, the effeminate habit of clawing hysterically at one's cheeks, and the agonized beating of the breasts, thighs, and head. Thus Agamemnon, in both Homer and Accius,

Ripping in sorrow, again and again, his uncut hair,

from which comes that gibe of Bion about the dimwitted king who, in his anguish, pulled out all his hair, imaging that baldness could assuage his grief! Those who do these things, do them because they are convinced they *should* do them. Thus Aeschines berates Demosthenes for offering sacrifices seven days after the death of his daughter. What nimble rhetoric, what eloquence of speech, what skillfully arranged thoughts, and what a torrent of words does he use in his attack!

You may conclude from this that the rhetorician is capable of anything he pleases. But no one could agree with this sort of tactic, except for the inherent belief that every good man should grieve over the death of relatives as deeply as possible. So it happens that other people prefer seclusion when their minds are in the throes of sorrow, as Homer says about Bellerophon:

The wretched one who roamed in grief about the
Aleïan fields,
Eating his own heart himself, shunning the traces
of men.

Niobe is depicted in stone, I believe, to convey the idea of eternal silence in anguish. But they think that Hecuba was changed into a dog due to a certain harshness and mental frenzy she possessed. There are other grieving individuals, however, who enjoy speaking with solitude itself, just as that nurse in Ennius:

> Desire now seizes me, miserable one,
> To announce Medea's miseries to heaven and earth.

27. They do all these things in grief, believing that they are right, true, and required. They do these things from some sort of *imagined* obligation; and we see the confirmation of this from the fact that, when those who want to feel sorrow behave more humanly or speak more lightheartedly, they once again revert to their morose behavior, and think that they have done something wrong by momentarily suspending their anguish. Mothers and teachers are even more likely to berate children if, during conditions of domestic grief, they show any geniality in their actions or speech: they will make the children cry not only with words, but even with lashes. Why do they do this?

When grief has run its course, and it is understood that further lamentation accomplishes nothing, doesn't it become clear that such mourning is completely voluntary? What does that character (in Greek *heauton timorumenos*[422]) in Terence say, the one who torments himself?

> I truly believe, Chremes,
> That I do my son less injury
> While I myself am miserable.[423]

So he makes a decision to be unhappy. Can a person decide anything that conflicts with his intentions?

---

[422] Ἑαυτὸν τιμωρούμενος, "The Self-Tormentor," a play by Terence composed around 163 B.C.
[423] *Self-Tormentor* 147-148.

I prefer to regard myself as worthy of any evil.

He considers himself deserving of misfortune unless he is miserable? You see, therefore, that evil originates in opinion, not from nature. What happens when some things prevent a person from expressing sorrow? We find in Homer, for example, that the daily number of deaths and burials produced a cessation of mourning. The poet tells us:

> For we know too many are dying every day,
> So that no one can be devoid of sorrow;
> Better it is to inter the dead in burial mounds,
> And with hardened sentiment, to limit grief
> To one day's tears.[424]

Thus it is within one's power to shake off sadness when one wants to, as the situation requires. And since this is something within our power to do, should we let ourselves miss any chance to unload burdens of care and sorrow?

It was clear that the friends of Cnaeus Pompeius—when they saw his strength ebbing away from his wounds,[425] just when that traumatic and miserable spectacle was unfolding—were much afraid for themselves, because they could see they were encircled by the enemy fleet. The only thing they did was to encourage the rowers to pull as hard as possible in order to reach safety.[426] Yet after arriving at Tyre, they began to mourn their loss and express grief openly. Thus fear could ward off their sorrow. Won't reason, then, be able to drive away sorrow from the wise man?

28. Yet what knowledge is more useful in helping us to abandon sorrow, than an awareness of the fact that we gain nothing from grief,

---

[424] Cicero's graceful Latin version of these lines from *Iliad* XIX.226 is:
Namque nimis multos atque omni luce cadentes
Cernimus ut nemo possit maerore vacare.
Quo magis est aequum tumulis mandare peremptos
Firmo animo et luctum lacrimis finire diurnis.
[425] Referring to Pompey's assassination in Egypt in 48 B.C.
[426] Plutarch says that a strong wind helped them as well (*Pompey* 80).

173

and that gratifying the impulse to be miserable is pointless? If a person can shake off grief, it is also possible not to gratify it in the first place. We must conclude, then, that mental anguish is a choice, something adopted voluntarily and derived from a sense of internal obligation. This is made clear by the patience of those who, once they have lived through many hardships and can more easily endure whatever happens, believe themselves to be somewhat protected from fortune's wiles. It is like that individual in Euripides who says,

> If this sad day were for me the first that came,
> And I had not piloted my ship through such wretched waters,
> It were a source of grief to throw off, as young horses
> Only recently made to feel a new harness;
> But now I am crushed, and bedazed with agonies.[427]

Because the fatigue of endured hardships makes sorrow lighter, we must realize that it is not the hardship itself that is the source of grief. Don't the greatest philosophers who still have not attained true wisdom know that they are in a condition of supreme evil?[428] They are not wise, and there is no greater evil than a lack of wisdom.

But they do not mourn this situation. And what is the reason? Because this opinion—that it is right and fair and an obligation to carry around anguish for not being wise—cannot be connected to this category of evils. Yet we do connect this opinion to the type of anguish found in bereavement,[429] and this sorrow is the severest of all. Thus Aristotle, in scolding the ancient philosophers who thought philosophy had reached the highest level of development as a result of their talents, says that they displayed incredible foolishness and arrogance. Yet he himself took the position that, due to the tremendous

---

[427] Tischer attributes these lines to Euripides's lost *Phrixus*.
[428] Restating the traditional Stoic position that a person was either wise, or not wise. In other words, there were no degrees of progress on the path to wisdom. Cicero uses several vivid analogies to illustrate this point in *On Moral Ends* III.14.48.
[429] I.e., the loss of a loved one.

progress that had been made in a few years, philosophy would be clearly perfected within a short time.

Theophrastus, in the final moments of his life, is said to have criticized nature for granting longevity to crows and stags, animals unable to make use of such a gift, while at the same time providing man, for whom long life mattered a great deal, with such a meager lifespan. If the duration of their lives were extended, all arts could have achieved the highest refinement, and human life might be instructed with every branch of knowledge. The old philosopher lamented that he was approaching the hour of death at the very moment he had begun to see the possibilities before him.

What do you think? Don't the best and most authoritative of the other philosophers concede there is much that they do not know, and that they are obliged to learn and relearn many things? And despite knowing that they are floundering in a morass of ignorance, which is the worst possible condition to be in, they are still not plagued with sorrow. This is because no belief in an "obligation to grieve" is mixed with their awareness of the situation.[430] And what about those who think that displaying grief is inappropriate for men? Taking this view were men like Quintus Maximus, who carried out for burial a son who was a consul; Lucius Paullus, who lost two sons within several days; and Marcus Cato, whose son died after he had been elected praetor.[431] I have collected other pertinent examples in my book *Consolation*.[432] What was it that soothed them, other than the fact that they believed it was improper for men to make displays of lamentation and mourning?

Thus, whereas some are inclined to give themselves over to grief because of their belief that it is the right thing to do, these men repudiated grief out of a conviction that giving in to it was shameful. We may conclude from this, therefore, *that sorrow arises from belief, not from nature.*

---

[430] I.e., because they are not crippled by the thought that they have an obligation to feel sorrow.

[431] The names here are the five-time consul Quintus Fabius Maximus Verrucosus (c. 280 B.C.—203 B.C.); Lucius Aemilius Paullus Macedonicus (c. 229 B.C.—160 B.C.), the conqueror of Macedon; and Marcus Porcius Cato Censorius (234 B.C.—149 B.C.), more commonly known as Cato the Elder.

[432] A lost philosophical work of Cicero, apparently composed in 45 B.C. to help him overcome the debilitating grief experienced upon the death of his daughter Tullia.

29. To dispute this conclusion, the following question may be asked: *who is so mentally unstable that he would choose to grieve voluntarily?* Nature brings us grief; and your friend Crantor, they say, believes we should yield to this sorrow. It weighs down on us, and insinuates itself into our lives: we cannot withstand its infiltration. Thus Sophocles's character Oïleus, who had earlier consoled Telamon for Ajax's death, was shattered by grief when he learned of the death of his own son. The following lines inform us of his mental transformation:

> No one is gifted with such wisdom,
> Who alleviates the sorrows of others with words,
> Does not himself, when changed fortune brutally strikes,
> Become shattered by his own sudden reversal:
> So that the words said to others are now bereft of consolation.

When they discuss these things, they are trying to show that nature in no way can be resisted. Yet they concede that men endure grief more terrible than what nature requires. What madness is it, then, that we also require the same thing from others?

Yet there are more causes for accepting a burden of sorrow. First, there is this preconceived opinion we have that something is "evil"— so that when we see this "evil" thing, and are persuaded it is before us, mental anguish necessarily follows in its wake. Second, people think that if they grieve with great expenditure of emotion, they are thereby appeasing the dead. An element of feminine superstition is also at work here: mourners are convinced they will more easily be able to placate the immortal gods if they concede that they have been shattered and incapacitated by a devastating strike.

Yet most do not understand how contradictory these opinions are. They heap praise on men who meet death with equanimity; but those who bear someone else's death with equanimity, they think should be rebuked. As if it were in any way possible for someone to cherish another person more than himself, as lovers often tell each other in their private talk! If you consider the matter, it truly is a wonderful thing, as well as something pure and heartfelt, to love those who should be dearest to us with a devotion equal to the love we feel for ourselves. But it is simply impossible for us to love someone else more than we love ourselves. Neither should we consider it a goal of friendship that my friend should love me more than himself, or that I should love him more than myself. If it were otherwise, life's balance would be disrupted, and all its responsibilities thrown into confusion.

30. But this is a topic to be taken up at a more suitable time. For now, it is enough not to impute our anguish to the loss of our friends, and not to be fond of them more than they themselves would want (if they were indeed aware of this). Certainly we should not love them more than ourselves. As for the assertion that words of consolation do nothing to soothe the distresses of most people, and the related point that consolers themselves admit they are miserable when fortune turns her cruel attentions to them: it is clear that both of these claims may be disproved. For the blame cannot be placed on nature—the fault lies with us. And one may rail against our own foolishness as much as one wishes.

Those who are not soothed by words of consolation are drawn to the idea of being miserable. Those who bear their own calamities differently from how they have advised others to bear similar calamities are, in general, no more blameworthy than greedy men who reprimand other greedy men, or glory-seekers who scold other glory-seekers. For it is an odd tendency of folly to notice the shortcomings of others, but to be oblivious to its own.[433] Since it is certainly true that grief dissipates with the passage of time, the best evidence is the fact that it is not just the passage of time that alleviates anguish, but also a person's long contemplation.[434] If we are dealing with the same situation and with the same individual, how can there be any change in the grief, if there is no change either in what caused the grief, or in the individual experiencing the grief? Long contemplation of this fact—that there is no inherent evil in the events that give rise to grief—cures our pain, not just the passage of time by itself.

---

[433] *Est enim proprium stultitiae aliorum vitia cernere, oblivisci suorum.*

[434] The gist of this opaque sentence is that we ourselves decide whether we wish to be free from grief, or be burdened by it. By "best evidence," Cicero means evidence verifying the theory he advanced earlier: that anguish is largely a human choice, and not something mandated by nature. In Cicero's view, continued reflection (*in cogitatione diuturna* or "long contemplation") is useful in lessening the pain of grief.

31. Here they will talk about medium levels of grief.[435] But if these things are natural, why is consolation needed to alleviate them? Nature herself will decide where the boundary is to be placed; but if such boundaries are based on sentiment, then the sentiment should be completely removed. I believe we have adequately proven that *grief is the idea of a present evil, and that this idea contains the notion that we have an obligation to grieve.*

Zeno correctly adds something to this definition—that this idea of a present evil should be a recent one. Zeno's disciples explain the word "recent" in the following way. They say "recent" is not just what happened a short time ago. As long as there is some power left in the supposed evil, as long as it retains its potency and preserves its vitality, it still should be called "recent." Consider the example of Artemisia, the wife of Mausolus, the King of Caria, who constructed that awe-inspiring, monumental tomb at Halicarnassus. As long as she lived, she lived in grief; and having been crushed by anguish, she would eventually die from its poisonous reverberations. This idea[436] was "recent" for her every single day—and the only point at which we can stop calling this idea "recent" is when the passage of time erodes it to insignificance.

These, therefore, are the responsibilities of those who provide consolation: to remove anguish entirely, or to alleviate or reduce it as much as possible, or to suppress it or not permit it to grow, or to redirect it to other manifestations. There are those who believe that the only task of the consoler is to try to convince the stricken person that the evil is not there at all. Cleanthes subscribes to this view. Some—like the Peripatetics—take the position that the evil in question is not very great. Some—such as Epicurus—say that we should divert our thoughts from evils to goods. Some—such as the Cyrenaics—think it is enough to demonstrate that nothing unforeseen has happened.

Chrysippus, however, teaches that the main objective in providing someone consolation is to eliminate this preexisting belief of the griever that he is fulfilling some proper and compulsory duty.[437] There are also some who collect all these consolation techniques—

---

[435] The Latin word is *mediocritates*.

[436] I.e., the idea of her own grief.

[437] This perceptive observation is an important one. Cicero has been arguing that, in many cases, people take on grief because they have some preexisting idea that they *ought to feel grief*. It becomes a form of mental flagellation.

for each man is moved by a different method—in a way that is similar to how I combined them all into one approach in my treatise *Consolation*. For my soul was in a state of extreme torment, and I was experimenting with every possible cure for my situation.

Yet selecting the right time is no less important in a sickness of the mind, as it is in a sickness of the body. As Aeschylus's Prometheus, when these words were said to him,

> And Prometheus, I think you believe this,
> That speech is able to cure intemperate passion,

responded:

> If indeed someone administers an appropriate medicine,
> And does not with clumsy hands worsen the wound.

32. Therefore, the *first* medicine in providing consolation will be to convince the person either that there is no evil, or that there is little evil. The *second* step will be to explain the universal condition of human life, and any specific issue that should be discussed with the person who is grieving. The *third* step will be to persuade that it is the greatest folly to drown oneself in grief for no purpose, when one understands that nothing can be gained from this. Cleanthes consoles the wise man who does not need consolation. If you persuade the griever that nothing is evil except what is morally debased, then you will remove not just his grief, but his folly. Another time is more appropriate for a discussion of this issue, however.

As I see it, Cleanthes has not understood that grief can originate from the very thing he concedes is the worst kind of evil. What should we say, Cleanthes? Socrates, we are told, persuaded Alcibiades that he was not a uniquely special man at all, and that even though Alcibiades came from a family of high social standing, there was no difference between him and any random attendant. Alcibiades was quite upset to hear this; and with his eyes full of tears, he begged

Socrates to show him the path to virtue and the way to banish moral corruption.[438]

Well, Cleanthes? Wasn't there evil in what was causing Alcibiades to feel sorrow? Well? What are Lyco's[439] words supposed to mean? Lyco downplays grief, and says it is caused not by evils of the mind, but by inconveniences of fortune and aggravations of the body. What do you say to this, then? Isn't it true that Alcibiades's anguish came from the evils and deficiencies of the mind? We have already said enough about Epicurus's opinion on consolation.[440]

33. "You are not alone in this situation": although this consolatory statement is often made to the aggrieved, and may sometimes be useful, we cannot say it is very dependable. As I have said, it is indeed advantageous, but not always, and not for everyone. There are some who reject it, and much depends on the context of how it is used. We should call attention to how everyone who carried grief wisely, actually succeeded in bearing this grief; we should not emphasize the obstacles that impeded each person's efforts. Chrysippus's way of consolation is based on truth and remains the most dependable method, but it is difficult to use in a time of anguish.

It is extremely difficult to convince a grieving person that he is only grieving because he *thinks* he should be grieving. One can see, then, that just as we do not always adopt the same "stance"[441] in court cases—for so we call our approach to different kinds of legal disputes—but instead adjust our legal theory to the situation, to the particular facts of the case, and to the character of the party involved, so also do we take the same approach when trying to assuage a person's sorrow. We must evaluate what remedy the person being cured will be able to accept.

Without our being aware of it, our discussion has strayed from the proposition you originally made. You were asking about the wise man who can see no evil where there is no shame, or else believes

---

[438] Cicero must have gleaned this anecdote from a lost source. It is found in St. Augustine (*Civ. Dei* XIV.8), but not in any pre-Christian text.

[439] Lyco of Troas (c. 299 B.C.—c. 225 B.C.), a Peripatetic philosopher who eventually succeeded Strato as head of that school. He is said to have died of gout at the age of seventy-four. *See* Diog. Laert. V.65.

[440] In this paragraph Cicero is trying to show the inadequacy of Cleanthes's and Lyco's views on the origin of grief.

[441] *Status*, which (according to the Ox. Lat. Dict.) can mean legal position, or any intellectual posture taken up by a person.

the evil is so small that it is overcome by wisdom, and is hardly perceptible. Such a wise man does not amplify his grief by opinion, and does not think it right that he should be excessively tormented or crushed by anguish. For him, nothing would be more humiliating. Although the specific question was not asked at the time (that is, whether something could be evil unless it was also considered morally base), it nevertheless seems to me that our reasoning has demonstrated this quite clearly: *whatever evil there may be in grief does not come from nature, but is caused by voluntary human judgment and erroneous belief.* Moreover, we focused on the most powerful type of grief, so that once we learned how to cope successfully with this type, we would consider it a simple matter to fashion remedies for other kinds of grief.

34. For there are established terms that are often used with regard to poverty, and certain words that are used when describing a life deficient in public honors or glory. There are separate and specific treatises relating to the topics of exile, destruction of one's country, servitude, physical debility, blindness, and on every event we may call a calamity. These topics the Greeks separate into different books, and into specific categories of disquisition. They seek out useful work; but despite this, their debates are delightful in every way.

Nevertheless, just as doctors treating an entire body will work to heal the most insignificant part, if that part happens to be afflicted, so philosophy operates in the same way. Once it removed grief in general, it took away the erroneous belief arising from some cause, whether it be the ache of poverty, the pain of humiliation, the black shade of obscurity in which exiles live, or any of the other circumstances I have mentioned. Yet for each of these situations, there is a distinct and suitable consolation, which you will indeed hear when you wish. Yet, in every one of these cases, one must look back to the same source: *that all anguish is absent from the wise man.* This is because it is empty, because submerging oneself in it does no good, and because it does not originate from nature's design but from our own mistaken judgments, our own beliefs, which act as some kind of enticement to sorrow when we have decided that we *ought* to be controlled by it. Once we have rid ourselves of that completely self-adopted belief, the melancholy pain we have discussed will then be removed.

Nevertheless, a residual hurt and a vague mental dejection will remain. Let people say that this is entirely normal, as long as the doleful, noxious, and destructive word "grief" is nowhere to be heard. For this word is incompatible with wisdom and cannot—if I may phrase it this way—coexist with it at all. And yet how pervasive are the roots of sorrow, how plentiful, and how harsh! Once the trunk of the tree has been knocked over, every root must be pulled out of the ground and, if necessary, with the aid of a rehabilitative dialogue for each root. Whatever value it may have, this is what I still have left: leisure.[442]

Its forms have many names, but there is a single operative rule in all varieties of sorrow. For jealousy is a variety of sorrow. Other varieties include envy, denigration of others, pity, vexation, mourning, lamentation, chronic bouts of malaise, bereavement, emotional turbulence, dejection, harassment, oppression, and despair. The Stoics define all of these terms, and the words I have used here correspond to each variety of sorrow. We may conclude that they are not all identical; and they differ in some way, which we will perhaps examine in another place. These, however, are those smaller offshoots of the roots I mentioned earlier; they must be assiduously hunted down and pulled out, so that none of them may ever emerge again.

This is a massive and difficult task. Who can deny it? And yet what worthy enterprise is not also incredibly arduous? Nevertheless philosophy declares that she will accomplish this task. So let us only accept her healing touch. But we have said enough for now. Other things will be ready for you, either in this place or in other places, as often as you may like.

---

[442] A frank acknowledgment from Cicero about his being forced out of public life.

BOOK IV

ON THE OTHER DISORDERS OF THE MIND

BOOK IV

1. Although I am used to admiring the inventiveness and virtues of our people in many areas, Brutus, my admiration has flourished most in those studies which were intensely pursued by them at a late date and were brought to this country from Greece. From the founding of the city, the decrees (and in part the legal codes) of the Roman kings established with divine assistance the auspices, the religious rituals, the popular assemblies, the appeals to the people, the senate, the assignment of cavalry and infantry units, and the complete structure of Roman military organization. After this, once the republic was freed from the grip of the kings, a prodigious and astounding progress was made towards all kinds of excellence.

But this is not the place for me to discuss the customs and institutions of our ancestors, or the discipline and constitution of the Roman state. These subjects have been adequately treated elsewhere, especially in the six books I have composed on the republic.[443] Now that I am firmly committed to philosophical studies, however, I can see a number of reasons why these studies, which came from a foreign source, seem not only to have been eagerly sought after, but also maintained and cultivated. Pythagoras,[444] a man of surpassing wisdom and virtue, was in their direct line of sight; he lived in Italy at the same time that Lucius Brutus, the distinguished founder of your family line, liberated his country.

Pythagorean ideas disseminated far and wide; and in my opinion, they percolated into our own state. This speculation is likely grounded in fact, and is indicated by the vestiges of Pythagorean influence that remain. Powerful and celebrated Greek cities, which collectively were called Magna Graecia,[445] flourished in Italy in olden days. The name of Pythagoras himself, and after him the fame of the Pythagorean school, carried a great deal of influence in those

---

[443] Referring to Cicero's *De Re Publica*, a dialogue in six books written between 54 and 51 B.C. This work does not survive in complete form.
[444] Pythagoras (c. 570 B.C.—c. 495 B.C.), founder of the Pythagorean school and one of the most famous philosophers of antiquity. He resided for a time in Magna Graecia (southern Italy). His school was known for its esoteric wisdom and ritualized practices.
[445] Magna Graecia ("Great Greece") was the name the Romans gave to coastal parts of southern Italy that had been settled by Greeks beginning in the 8th century B.C.

cities. How could anyone imagine that the ears of our Roman people would be deaf to those learned Pythagorean voices?

I personally believe that admiration for Pythagoreanism was the reason why posterity believed King Numa[446] to have been an adherent of that school. Romans were aware of the doctrines of Pythagoras and had a general understanding of the disciplines of his community. Their ancestors had passed down stories of Numa's wisdom and justice. But due to the antiquity of the era involved, they were unsure of the precise ordering of historical periods. This led them to think that Numa, who excelled in wisdom, had been an adherent of Pythagoreanism.

2. Our progress thus far has been based on speculation. Although many vestiges of Pythagoreanism can be compiled, I will not cite many of them, since this is not my current goal. According to tradition, they frequently employed poetry in a circumspect manner as a method of instruction, and liked to disengage their minds from arduous cogitation to unencumbered serenity by using song and lyre. The eminently reliable author Cato, in his work *Origins*, tells us that it was a custom of our ancestors at dinner parties for attendees to sing, in their turn, songs praising the virtues of great men while the music of the flute wafted over the room. It is obvious from this that songs and verses were set down in writing for the human voice. The laws of the Twelve Tables also make it clear that writing songs was already a custom by that time. For the Tables specifically provide that the creation of such verses should not harm someone else.

The fact that they played musical instruments before the sacred couches[447] of the gods and at the banquets of their magistrates also confirms that they had a certain level of cultural sophistication. This ceremony was a specific practice of the Pythagorean discipline I am referring to. There is a poem of Appius Caecus that is highly praised by Panaetius in a certain letter to Quintus Tubero—and it is my belief that this poem is essentially Pythagorean. There are many features of our Roman customs that find their origins with the Pythagoreans; these I will not describe, lest we appear to have adopted from others the things we are thought to have invented ourselves.[448]

---

[446] Numa Pompilius (c. 753 B.C.—673 B.C.), Rome's legendary second king.

[447] The word used is *pulvinar* (sacred couch). The ritual referred to was one where the Romans placed statues or busts of the gods on couches in public as part of a propitiatory ceremony called a *lectisternium*.

[448] Pythagoras was an Ionian Greek. As a patriotic Roman, Cicero is uncomfortable with the idea of giving a foreign sect too much credit for early influences on Roman customs.

But let us return to our original contention. How many great poets, and how many distinguished orators, have flourished among us in such a short period of time! One can easily see that once our people resolved to do something, they could succeed in whatever they set their minds to.

3. If it advances our purposes, we will discuss the other studies in a different place. We have taken this approach in the past. Among our people, the study of wisdom is of old date. Yet before the era of Laelius and Scipio, I cannot specifically recall anyone worthy of being called a true adherent of the art of wisdom. I know that as adolescents Diogenes the Stoic and Carneades the Academic were sent by the Athenians as envoys to the Roman senate. They had not participated in public affairs at that time. One of them was from Cyrene, and the other from Babylon. They would never have been summoned from their classrooms or selected for this responsibility unless philosophical studies had found favor with influential people in Rome at that time. They composed written works in various fields: some for civil law, some for their orations, and some for the records of their ancestors. And yet philosophy, the most rewarding of all the arts and the one that instructs us on how to live well, they practiced more by the way they lived their lives than through literary exercises.

Thus there are hardly any Latin literary works (or at least a very small number) dealing with that true and elegant philosophy which began with Socrates and now continues with the Peripatetics. (The Stoics are saying the same things in a different way, while the Academics arbitrate the controversies between Stoics and Peripatetics). We do not know whether this meager literary output was due to our people's preoccupation with time-consuming utilitarian projects, or whether it was due to the fact that intellectual activities were thought unsuitable for a populace lacking sophistication.

Yet during this period of silence the writings of Caius Amafinius[449] appeared on the scene. As his books gained circulation, public curiosity was aroused, and people were drawn most favorably to his ideas. We do not know whether this was because his teachings were easy to understand, or because new readers were enticed by the charms of intellectual pleasure; it may even have been because people simply made use of what they had, since nothing better was available.

---

[449] Caius Amafinius was an early Roman writer of the Epicurean school. He seems to have flourished in the late 2nd century or early 1st century B.C.

After Amafinius there appeared numerous writers who emulated the same method; their books proliferated and were disseminated to every part of Italy. The fact that their doctrine could so easily be understood and esteemed by the uneducated is strong verification that their arguments were not composed with care. Yet they believe this is a mainstay[450] of their doctrine.

4. But a person who believes something can advocate for it himself. We are all free to form our own conclusions. For my part, I will hold fast to my own guiding principle, and will not be tied down by the rules of one philosophical school which confine my thinking to a rigid paradigm: for every question, I will always seek what I believe is the most likely truth.[451] Just as I have employed this method on other occasions, so I dutifully made use of it here at Tusculum. We have engaged in disputations for three days; our fourth day of dialogue will be recorded in the present book. For when we walked down to the Academy, as we had done in the preceding days, we spoke as follows.

M. Whoever wants to propose a topic for debate—let him suggest one.

A. I don't believe that a wise man can be free of *all* mental perturbation.

M. It seemed from our dialogue yesterday that the wise man was free from grief. That is, unless you were just agreeing with me to save time!

A. No, I was not doing that at all. Your argument was to me very persuasive.

M. You don't think that the wise man can be stricken with grief?

A. No, I don't believe that.

M. If that can't trouble the mind of the wise man, then nothing can. What do you think? Can he be upset by fear? Fear comes from things that are absent—when these same things are present, they produce grief. Therefore, if grief is removed, then fear is also removed. Two perturbations are left, then: passionate joy and lust. If we discover that the wise man is not vulnerable to these two disturbances, then we can say that his mind will always be serene.

A. I agree with you completely.

---

[450] I.e., a strong point or bulwark.
[451] A clear statement of Cicero's eclectic skepticism.

M. What method to you prefer? Should we immediately raise our sails, or use our oars for a while, as if we were leaving port and heading for the open sea?

A. What are you trying to say? I don't see your meaning.

5. M. Because when Chrysippus and the Stoics discussed the disturbances of the mind, they spent a great deal of time in classifying and defining them. They actually devote little space in their discussion to *curing* the mind and in *preventing* its turmoil. The Peripatetics, however, offer a number of suggestions for placating the mind, and pass over the thorn-bushes of classification and definition. What I am trying to find out, really, is this: should I unfurl the sails of eloquence right away, or row forward a little bit more with the oars of dialectic?

A. Row forward a bit more with dialectic, definitely. What I want to know will be more fully explained if we use both techniques.

M. That way is better. But if something is unclear, you should ask after hearing it.

A. I will certainly do this. But you should talk about these obscure things more lucidly—as is your habit—than the Greeks talk about them.

M. I'll certainly make every effort. But a very diligent mind is needed, lest a person fails to grasp the entire argument if one important point is missed. What the Greeks call *pathê*, we prefer to call *perturbations* instead of *sicknesses*. In my explanation, I will follow the old analysis that originated with Pythagoras and was continued by Plato. They divided the soul into two parts; one they thought had the ability to reason, and the other they believed had no reasoning powers at all. In the reasoning part they placed *tranquility*, that is, a calm and quiet condition of harmony. The other part generated the passionate turbulence of rage and desire, emotions that are contrary and inimical to reason. These ideas will serve as our point of departure. In describing these perturbations of the mind, let us use the definitions and categories of the Stoics, who, as I see it, are very perspicacious in handling this question.

6. So this is Zeno's definition of perturbation. He calls it *pathos*, a turbulence of the mind that is averse to reason and against nature. Some thinkers more concisely define perturbation as an appetite that is more violent; when they say "more violent," they mean an appetite that is too far removed from nature's constancy.

They also say that the classes of perturbations originate from two supposed goods and two supposed evils. Thus there are four altogether. Lust and joy come from the good (i.e., joy of present goods, and lust of future goods, both come from the good). They believe that fear and grief originate from evils (i.e., fear originating from future evils, and grief from present ones). For the same things we fear when they are coming at us, also cause grief when they reach us.

However, joy and lust are conditioned on the belief of good. Lust, enticed and inflamed, is dragged off to what seems to be good, while joy celebrates and becomes ecstatic by obtaining what it wanted. Clearly, it is natural for every person to seek that which appears good, and to avoid what seems contrary to good. For this reason, as soon as something appearing to be good shows itself, nature instigates us to lay our hands on it. When this is done with prudence and level-headedness, the Stoics call it *boulesis*,[452] while we use the term *intention*.[453] This is something they believe only the wise man possesses. Their definition of this term is as follows: intention is a desire, controlled by reason, for some objective. Intention that is averse to reason and inflamed more vehemently is lust, or unchecked desire. And this is something we observe in every dolt.

Thus, when we find ourselves positioned to benefit from some good, this happens in two ways. For when the mind is moved in a placid and steady way in accordance with reason, then this is called delight.[454] However, when the mind exults vainly and lavishly, then this can be called intemperate or inordinate joy.[455] They define this as a mental ecstasy which is uncontrolled by reason. We by nature want what is good, and by nature decline what is evil. This declining, when it takes place under the influence of reason, is called caution,[456] and is something thought to be found in the wise man only. But caution that is governed by a craven and abject terror, and not by reason, is called fear. Therefore, fear is caution that lacks reason.

An evil that is present, however, has no effect on the wise man. Fools experience anxiety, and are affected by it when alleged evils visit them; their spirits, which refuse to follow reason, sag and

---

[452] βούλησις.
[453] The word Cicero uses is *voluntas*, meaning desire, will, volition, or intention.
[454] *Gaudium.*
[455] *Tum illa laetitia gestiens vel nimia dici potest.*
[456] *Cautio.*

189

wither. Therefore, the first definition of grief is this: *it is a withering of the mind in opposition to reason.* So there are four perturbations, and three steady, tranquil emotional conditions, because there is no steady emotional condition that is the opposite of grief.

7. But they take the position that all mental perturbations arise from judgments and opinions. So they define them with more care, so that one may understand not only how harmful they are, but also how much they are within our power. Anxiety is defined as a recent opinion of present evil, in which a person believes it is right to experience a weakening and constricting of the mind. Joy is a recent opinion of present good, in which a person believes it is right to feel jubilant. Fear is an opinion of an impending evil that seems to be intolerable. Lust is an opinion of a good that is coming, which would be a good if it arrived and were currently present.

I have identified the judgments and opinions of perturbations; but their significance is that perturbations do not consist of them alone. The resulting *effects* of these perturbations also reside in them. Grief produces a sort of sting of pain; fear produces a retreat and flight of the mind; joy produces an expansive cheerfulness; lust causes an uncontrolled craving. However, they claim that opinion (which we have included in all our stated definitions) is a kind of passive, indifferent consent.

For every perturbation, there are many dependent categories of the same type joined to it. For example, under *grief* we find *envy*.[457] We must use this rare word (*invidentia*) for teaching purposes: this is because *invidia* applies not only to the person who envies, but also to the person who is being envied. Also included under *grief* are jealous emulation, disparagement, pity, anguish, mourning, sadness, hardship, sorrow, lamentation, solicitude, annoyance, torment, desperation, and any other similar type of thing. Under *fear* we may list sloth, shame, terror, timidity, panic, alarm, dismay, and dread. Under *pleasure* we include malevolence (i.e., taking pleasure in someone else's misfortune), bliss, boasting, and similar things. Under *lust* we find rage, irascibility, hate, enmity, discord, craving, want, and other things of this kind.

8. They define these terms in this way. They claim *envy* is anguish produced by the awareness of someone else's good fortune, and which does not harm the person who is envying. If a person is

---

[457] *Invidentia.*

hurt by the sight of the good fortune of an individual he believes has wronged him, then that person would not correctly be said to be envying that individual. It would be like saying that Agamemnon was envying Hector. But if a person not harmed by another's benefits is nevertheless hurt by the other person's pleasure in having them, then he would certainly be said to be envious. *Jealous emulation* has two different meanings, so that the same term can indicate both praise and denigration. Jealous emulation is used in reference to the imitation of virtue; but will not employ it in this sense here, since it is admirable. Jealous emulation is also grief, if a person covets something that another person has, and the person who covets does not have it.

Disparagement, however, is what I intend to be the equivalent of the Greek term *zilotypia*,[458] or grief that originates from the situation where a person desires something that another person has, and the desirer himself also has the item. *Pity* is anguish that comes from the awareness of someone else's misery, where the misery is the result of a wrong. No one feels pity as a result of the punishment of a traitor or the murderer of a parent. *Anguish* is overwhelming dejection. *Mourning* is grief resulting from the unexpected death of something held dear. *Sadness* is grief with crying. *Hardship* is laborious grief. *Sorrow* is distress that torments. *Lamentation* is grief expressed with moaning. *Solicitude* is grief attended by intense rumination. *Annoyance* is distress that is persistent. *Torment* is grief attended by extreme physical discomfort. *Desperation* is grief that has no expectation of being relieved.

The categories classified under the heading *fear* are as defined as follows. *Sloth* is fear of imminent work. *Shame* is fear attended by dispersal of blood.[459] *Terror* is intimidating fear; and just as shame produces facial redness, terror causes facial pallor, tremors, and the involuntary chattering of teeth. *Timidity* is the fear of an evil that is near. *Panic* is fear that moves the mind out of place. In connection with this, we find this line in Ennius:

---

[458] ζηλοτυπία.

[459] Apparently referring to blushing. The definition of shame (*pudor*) does not appear in the Latin text. Tischer argues that a copyist in ancient times, and not Cicero, was responsible for this omission. For the definition of shame, he proposes *pudorem metum dedecoris* or *pudorem sanguinem diffundentem*. I adopt his suggestion and use the latter definition.

Panic banishes all wisdom from my dismayed
body.

Alarm is fear subsequent to terror and acts like its assistant. *Dismay* is fear that casts away thought. *Dread* is a permanent fear.

9. The various kinds of pleasure are defined as follows. *Malevolence* is taking pleasure in someone else's misfortune that brings no benefit to the person who takes such pleasure. *Bliss* is pleasure that calms the mind by seducing one's hearing. The pleasures of sight, touch, smell, and taste are of the same type as this enchantment of the sense of hearing. All of these are of one category which may be considered "liquid pleasures" in which the mind can be "immersed." *Boasting* is pleasure manifested in open exultation, and in an uncontrolled insolence.

The subcategories that fall under the heading of lust are defined as follows. *Rage* is the lust to punish someone believed to have caused a harm. *Irascibility* is anger that flares up and presents itself, and which is called in Greek *thumosis*.[460] *Hate* is long-standing anger. *Enmity* is anger looking for a chance for revenge. *Discord* is a more resentful anger formed in one's deepest heart and soul. *Craving* is lust that cannot be satisfied. *Want* is the lust of regarding someone who is absent. They make a distinction with regard to want; they say want is a lust formed from learning of things said of an individual or persons, which the Greek logicians call predicates (*katigorimata*[461]), as when someone feels a want to be in possession of riches, or a want to have obtained honors. Craving, by contrast, is the lust for the things themselves, that is, money and honors.

They claim, however, that intemperance is the source of all perturbations, which is an abandonment of all mental ability and proper reason. It is so against the rule of reason that the appetites of the mind can in no way either be controlled or contained. Therefore, just as temperance disciplines the desires and makes them submit to proper reason, so does its enemy—intemperance—inflame, incite, and upset the whole mental state. Anxieties, fears, and other perturbations therefore flow naturally from this.

10. When a person's blood is tainted, or if there is an excess of phlegm or bile, bodily sicknesses and diseases begin to appear. In the same way, the turmoil created by poisonous ideas contending with

---

[460] θύμωσις.

[461] κατηγορήματα.

each other deprives the mind of health and troubles it with sickness. Firstly, diseases originate from perturbations; such diseases they call *nosimata*.[462] Also originating from perturbations are the sentiments contrary to these diseases, and which are attended by a noxious disgust and revulsion for certain things.

Next there are the diseases that the Stoics call *arrostemata*.[463] These also have contrary disinclinations that may be considered opposites. Here the Stoics—especially Chrysippus—expend a great deal of energy in weighing the similarity between sicknesses of the soul and sicknesses of the body. Glossing over what they say as being of little import, I will discuss only the essence of the matter. As our beliefs churn with irregularity and tumultuous disorder, it should be understood that perturbation is always in motion. When, however, this fervor and agitation of the mind becomes habitual, and fixed in one's veins and in the marrow of the bones, then disease and illness begin to arise, as well as those disinclinations[464] which are the opposites of disease and illness.

11. The diseases I am discussing differ among themselves in an intellectual sense; but in fact they are closely connected, and arise from lust and joy. For when someone longs for money, and reason is not immediately summoned as a kind of Socratic preventive medicine to alleviate the lust, then this evil festers in the veins and adheres to the body's viscera. Sickness and an unhealthy moral condition will appear, things that cannot be eradicated once they have taken root. Avarice is the name given to this sickness. It is the same with other diseases, such as love of glory or lust for women, which the Greeks call *philogynia*.[465] In the same way do other sicknesses and diseases come about.

However, the sentiments that are the opposites of these things are believed to arise from fear, such as the hatred of women, as we observe in the woman-hater[466] of Atilius.[467] Another example would be the hatred of all humanity, which Timon[468] (who was called "The

---

[462] νοσήματα

[463] ἀρρωστήματα.

[464] *Offensiones*, meaning disinclinations, antipathies, aversions, or displeasures.

[465] φιλογυνια.

[466] μισογυνος.

[467] Marcus Atilius was a comic poet of the 2nd century B.C. about whom little is known. "Woman-hater" must refer to a character that Atilius either invented or imported from the Greek dramatists.

[468] Timon of Athens supposedly lived during the Peloponnesian War. The playwright Aristophanes portrayed him as an angry misanthrope.

Misanthrope") is said to have possessed. Hatred of strangers[469] is also similar. All of these sicknesses of the soul arise from a certain fear of the things that they shun and loathe.

Moreover, they define "sickness of the mind" as a vehement, enduring, and deep-seated belief which considers something that should not be pursued, as something that should be vigorously pursued. They define what arises from disinclination as a vehement, enduring, and deep-seated belief that considers something which *should not* be avoided, as something that *should* be avoided. This type of belief amounts to a judgment that presumes knowledge where no knowledge exists.

There are also certain subcategories of sickness: avarice, ambition, love of women, obstinacy, gluttony, drunkenness, gourmandism, and similar things. Avarice is a vehement, enduring, and deep-seated belief that considers money to be something which should be vigorously pursued. The definition of the other terms of this category is quite comparable. The definitions of disinclinations are of the following kind. Inhospitality is a vehement, enduring, and deep-seated belief that a visitor should be strenuously avoided. Hatred of women is defined in a comparable way, as for example the hatred felt by Hippolytus;[470] and the hatred of humanity is defined as that sentiment felt by Timon.

12. We now come to the metaphor of physical health, and will employ this analogy, although less than the Stoics do. Now some men are more susceptible to some diseases than are others. We therefore say some are more likely to get colds, and that others are more prone to colic. We say this not because they currently have these ailments, but because they often have them. Similarly, some people are inclined to feel fear, and others are inclined to some other perturbation. From this we see that some people have anxiety, and are said to be anxious; and some have what is called a *hot temper*,[471] which differs from anger.

It is one thing to have a hot temper, and another thing to be angry, just as anxiety differs from vexation. Those who sometimes feel vexation are not all anxious, nor are those who are anxious always

---

[469] *Inhospitalitas.*
[470] *Hippolytus* is a play by Euripides in which Hippolytus, the son of Theseus, expresses his resentments against women (e.g., lines 663-670).
[471] *Iracundia.*

feeling vexation. In the same way, there is a difference between intoxication and chronic insobriety, and a distinction between being a lover and being someone who is in love with another person.

This proclivity—of some people for one disease and others for another disease—is quite common. It applies to all perturbations. It shows itself in many vices, but it does not have a name. Some people are said to be envious, malevolent, jealous, afraid, and pitying because they have proclivities for these perturbations, not because they are always dominated by such sentiments. To use the metaphor of physical health: this proclivity of each person for his own perturbation is said to be a sickness, as long as we understand it to be a predilection for sickness. But when we are speaking about goods—where some people are better suited to one good, and others better suited to other goods—it may be named *facility*.[472] When dealing with evils, it may be called *proclivity*,[473] in order to imply tendency. In neutral situations, we should employ the preceding term.

13. Just as the body is threatened by disease, ailments, and deficiency, so too is the mind. Disease indicates a degeneration of the entire physical body. Sickness is disease accompanied by feebleness. Deficiency occurs when the body's parts are not in harmony with each other, which causes abnormality of the limbs, malformation, and defects. Thus the first two—disease and sickness—are produced by the "shaking up" and disruption of the body's entire health. Deficiency is recognizable by itself, although the body's health remains sound. In the mind, however, we can distinguish disease from sickness only as an intellectual exercise. Moral faultiness[474] is a habit or mental condition that is discordant during one's entire life and in conflict with itself.

And so it happens that, in one situation, sickness and disease are produced by a corruption of beliefs. And in the other situation, inconstancy and disharmony are produced. For not every mental vice brings with it an equal lack of stability, as we see in the case of those who are not far away from wisdom; we see a certain mental condition that is out of synchrony with itself while it is foolish, yet it is neither distorted nor wicked. But disease and sickness are parts of moral faultiness. It is a legitimate question whether perturbations are parts

---

[472] *Facilitas.*
[473] *Proclivitas.*
[474] *Vitiositas*, the state of having a defective character.

of the same category. Defects are enduring mental conditions, but perturbations are changeable, and thus they cannot be parts of enduring mental conditions. In evil, the metaphor of the body applies to the nature of the mind; and this metaphor is also applicable when we speak of goods. The attributes of the body are beauty, strength, health, firmness, swiftness. So they are also attributes of the mind.

A well-balanced body exists when all the things that determine health are congruent with each other. And so it may also be said of a well-balanced mind, when its judgments and beliefs are in concord with each other. This harmony of the mind is virtue. Some say that this is temperance itself; others say it amounts to obeying the rules of temperance, and following them closely, and not permitting it to be its own category. But whether it is one or the other, it[475] exists only in the wise man.

There is, however, a certain health of the mind that even fools can experience, when mental distress is cleared away by the remedies of physicians. Just as in the body, where a certain well-proportioned arrangement of the limbs together with a certain attractiveness of color is said to constitute beauty, so too in the mind the word "beauty" is affixed to a symmetry and constancy of beliefs and judgments, along with a certain firmness and stability that follows closely after virtue, or contains the inherent power of virtue. Thus the strength of the mind that corresponds to the hardiness, connective tissues, and efficacy of the body is also expressed in similar words. A fast reaction time[476] is called swiftness.[477] This word suggests praise when used in connection with one's mental capacity, due to the mind's adroit assessment of a large number of things in a brief amount of time.

14. There exists a contrast between body and mind, due to the fact that a healthy mind cannot be troubled by sickness in the way that bodies can. Disinclinations[478] of the body can happen without fault. But this is not true for disinclinations of the mind, as all sicknesses and perturbations come about from the rejection of reason. Thus we observe these things only in humans. Animals may behave in a similar way, but they are not troubled by perturbations of the

---

[475] I.e., virtue.
[476] *Velocitas.*
[477] *Celeritas.*
[478] *Offensiones,* meaning revulsions, dislikes, or antipathies.

mind. But there is this difference between intelligent men and stupid men: sharp-witted men resemble Corinthian bronze,[479] which takes a longer time to be corroded by rust. Percipient men are also not as quickly affected by mental distresses—and they recover from them faster. The same things cannot be said for stupid men.

Nor indeed does the mind of the intelligent man succumb to every disease and perturbation. It is not swayed by anything that is base or inhuman; indeed, some of its perturbations (e.g., compassion, grief, and fear) have the appearance of humanity at first. However, it is believed to be more difficult to cure sicknesses and diseases of the mind than it is to cure those serious defects that are contrary to the virtues. When diseases are still present, vices may be removed, since diseases are not cured as fast as vices can be removed.

In concise form, you now have the Stoic teachings on mental perturbations; they call these teachings "inferences of logic,"[480] because they are deliberated with minute thoroughness. As our discussion has now successfully steered away from these treacherous, jagged coastal rocks, let us follow the course of the remaining argument, as long as I speak with a directness sufficient to illuminate the penumbras of our topics.

A. That is straightforward enough. But if some things must be examined in greater detail, we will make inquiries at a more appropriate setting. For now we expect you to unfurl those broad sails you talked about a moment ago, and take us on our way.

15. M. There are many questions related to life and human customs which flow from the wellspring of virtue. I have said in other places, and will often have to say again, that virtue is a steadfast and consistent propensity of the mind; those who possess it are considered worthy of praise. It is praiseworthy by itself, and through its own

---

[479] Corinthian bronze (*aes Corinthium*) was a valuable alloy in Cicero's day. Its precise composition is unknown; it may have been an alloy of copper mixed with gold or silver, or simply a very high-quality bronze. Pliny (*Hist. Nat.* XXXIV.3.6) repeats, but disbelieves, a legend that the alloy was discovered by accident during the capture and burning of Corinth, when copper was supposedly seen to fuse with gold and silver. He claims Corinthian bronze came in three varieties: a white variety which resembled silver and was heavily mixed with it; a yellowish variety that contained gold; and a third variety that contained copper, silver, and gold in equal proportions. He says there was also a rare fourth variety, called by the Greeks "hepatizon," which was an alloy "blended by luck." (*fortuna temperatur*).
[480] *Logica.*

merit, separate from any kind of advantageousness. Proceeding from it are honest purposes, sentiments, actions, and all true reason, although virtue herself may be concisely defined as "correct reason."[481] The opposite of this virtue we speak of is *wickedness*. I prefer this word over "malice," which the Greeks identify as *kakia*.[482] For malice is the name given to a specific type of vice, whereas wickedness embraces all of them.

From this wickedness come mental perturbations. As I stated earlier, these are vehement and disruptive movements of the soul which reject reason and are inimical to tranquility of mind and the conduct of life. For they bring in anxieties and festering disquietude; they damage the mind and paralyze it with fear. They also inflame the soul with excessive appetites that we sometimes call desire, and other times call lust. It is a kind of mental impotence that is far removed from temperance and moderation. And if the mind has acquired what it ardently desired, it will be carried away with exhilaration, "so that nothing is reliable," about what it does. It is similar to what one writer said, who thought that "too much pleasure of the soul is the greatest mistake."[483] The remedy for these evils, therefore, is found only in virtue.

16. Yet what is not only more pathetic, but more shameful and repulsive, than a man stricken, debilitated, and crushed by anxiety? He who is terrified at the proximity of some evil, and whose mind dangles in a state of perpetual alarm, is closest to this condition of misery. The poets convey the power of this evil by portraying the image of a rock hanging over Tantalus in the underworld,

> On account of his debased actions, his weakness
> of mind,
> And his overbearing speech.

This is the standard punishment for human folly. For whenever the mind of man treats reason with abhorrence, the result is always

---

[481] *Recta ratio.*

[482] κακία.

[483] A quote apparently from the Roman playwright Quintus Trabea, who flourished in the 2nd century B.C. He is also mentioned by Cicero in *On Moral Ends* (II.4.13).

this kind of impending terror. And just as these debilitating perturbations (here I mean anxiety and fear), so also those more cheerful feelings (desire that is always searching hungrily for something, and vain ardor, that is, ebullient joy) do not differ much from mental disorders.

One can understand from this what kind of individual is the person whom we at one time call moderate, at another time modest or temperate, and at another time resolute or restrained. Sometimes I like to include all these designations with the term *frugality* as their heading. For if the virtues were not included under this term, it would never have achieved such general acceptance that we now have this popular proverb: *the frugal man does everything correctly*. When the Stoics say the same thing about their "wise man," it seems they are speaking about him with too much grandiosity and histrionics.

17. And so *this* man, whoever he may be, whose mind is calm with moderation and steadfastness, and who is truly at ease with himself, so that he neither wastes away in anxiety nor crumbles to pieces in fear, nor burns with a thirst for chasing some passion, nor pines away in the ebullience of futile ardor: *this*, indeed, is the wise man we are looking for. *He* is the happy man for whom no event in human affairs is so intolerable as to break his spirit, nor so immensely joyful that he is carried away with euphoria. For what can seem so important in human affairs to the man who contemplates all eternity before him, and who grasps the immensity of our universe? What objective in the list of human pursuits, or what circumstance that arises in the brief length of our short lives, could appear so important to the wise man, who always maintains his alertness of mind so that nothing unexpected, nothing unanticipated, or nothing entirely unfamiliar, might happen to him?

He casts his perceptive gaze everywhere, always searching for a suitable home and residence for himself, in order to live without anxiety and oppressive disquiet; and whatever unfavorable event fortune may send him, the wise man deals with this hardship responsibly and calmly. And he who does this will be free not only from sorrow, but from all other types of perturbations as well. A mind liberated from these burdensome distresses produces men who are perfectly and absolutely happy. But he who is in a state of mental turmoil, and estranged from complete and certain reason, loses not only his mental steadiness, but his physical health as well.

Thus the reasoning and arguments of the Peripatetics must be considered feeble and limp. For they say that minds will necessarily be afflicted with perturbations, but set a certain limit that perturbations will not progress beyond. Do you set a boundary for vice? Is there no vice in defying reason? Doesn't reason adequately warn us that there is no good which you should intensely desire? That there is no good which, once acquired, you should allow to carry you away with arrogance?

Doesn't reason teach us, again, that there is no evil capable of crushing you and casting you to the ground? Or that there is no evil you would barely have the mental strength to resist if it oppressed you? And that all these things may appear to be too hopeless, or too optimistic, through our own erroneous perception?[484] But if such a mistaken perception is for fools diminished over time—so that even if the original cause stays the same, they tolerate it just as well after it has persisted for some time as they bore it when it began—then a wise man should certainly not be affected by it at all.

For what indeed would this outer limit be? Let us investigate the final limit of sorrow, a subject that has been carefully studied. Fannius has written that Publius Rupilius experienced crippling anguish when his brother failed in his attempt to be elected consul: but he seems to have gone beyond a limit, for his life drained away as a result of this anguish. He should have carried his sorrow with more moderation. What do you think? And if he had actually endured this hardship with self-restraint, what would have happened if he had been *additionally* struck by the death of a child? A new anguish would have materialized.

Even if it were not an extreme one, it would still have produced a great intensification of the existing sorrow. What now? Now what if this were followed by serious bodily pain? Then by the loss of one's personal belongings? Then by the loss of one's eyesight? And finally exile from one's homeland? If each separate evil were to add to the aggregate sorrow, there would eventually come a breaking point where the amount was unendurable.

18. Thus, he who seeks an outer limit for vice is doing the same thing as believing that a person leaping from the rocks of Leucas can stop himself in midair if he wants to. Just as doing this is not possible, so it is equally impossible for a perturbed and disquieted mind to

---

[484] A sentiment similar to that expressed by Hamlet (Act II, scene ii) to Rosencranz: "Why, then, 'tis none to you, for there is nothing either good or bad, but thinking makes it so."

restrain itself, or to stop itself where it wants. And in all cases, things that are destructive in their progress are also nefarious from the time of their birth.[485] Anxiety, indeed, and other types of perturbations that have progressed for a long time are without doubt virulent. Once they take root, they immediately begin to act very much like a pestilence. For they advance under their own power from the moment reason has been abandoned.

By its very nature, weakness is lax and permissive; it is unsuspectingly carried out to deep waters by ocean winds, and lacks the ability to put an end to this calamitous drift. For this reason it makes no difference whether they[486] approve of moderate perturbations, or moderate injustices, or moderate laziness, or moderate intemperance: *because when someone draws a limit for vices, he thereby accepts such vices, to some extent.* This implicit acceptance of vice is an abhorrent practice in itself—but it becomes something even more terrible, because people find themselves walking down a slippery slope. Once they start down this slope for the first time, they easily glide along, and soon cannot find any way to stop.

19. Now what about the idea advanced by these same Peripatetics, that these perturbations we believe should be rooted out are (they say) not only natural, but gifted to us by nature for some productive purpose? This is the argument they make. They expend a great deal of verbiage in extolling the benefits of anger. They claim it is the "sharpening stone" of fortitude, and that the attacks of angry men on an enemy or traitorous citizen are conducted with greater intensity. Feeble are the pathetic rationales of those who think this way: "Giving battle is the right thing to do; it is appropriate to fight for laws, liberty, and country." These rationalizations have no power behind them unless fortitude burns brightly with anger.

They do not confine their argument to fighters alone. They think that no one gives severe orders[487] unless some of anger's harshness is present. Whether an orator is prosecuting a case or defending one, the Peripatetics will not approve of him unless he salts his delivery with barbs of anger. And even if the orator does not actually have this anger within him, they nevertheless believe he should *act* as if

---

[485] A graceful proverb: *omninoque quae crescentia perniciosa sunt, eadem sunt vitiosa nascentia.*

[486] I.e., the Peripatetic philosophers.

[487] I.e., during a crisis or emergency.

he has it with his words and movements, so that the orator's address provokes anger in the listener. They think that anyone who does not know how to display anger cannot be a true man; and what we call leniency, they call gentleness, a word that carries the taint of spinelessness.

They not only praise this kind of lust—for anger is, as I have already stated, a lust for revenge—but they also say that this type of feeling (lust or desire) was given to us by nature for reasons of the greatest practical utility. No one can do anything truly well unless he has a consuming passion for it. Because he was unable to sleep, Themistocles used to walk in public at night; and when people asked him why, he answered that Miltiades's[488] trophies[489] prevented him from sleeping. Is there anyone who hasn't heard of Demosthenes's insomnia? He said it pained him to find out any time he was bested by the industry of laborers getting out of bed before dawn.

Finally, the great names of philosophy itself would never have progressed so far in their researches if they had not had a burning passion for their subject. We are informed that Pythagoras, Democritus, and Plato explored the world's outermost regions; wherever there was something that could be learned, they believed they should travel there. Would they ever have done this if they were not motivated by the most fervent intensity of passion?

20. We have said that anxiety itself should be avoided as one would avoid a revolting and brutal beast. But they say it is something that has considerable utility—something that has been established by nature so that men, having committed a wrong, would feel the pain of punishment, reprimand, and dishonor. Those who can bear ignominy and infamy without pain, they believe, apparently have the capacity to commit crimes without fear of consequences. As they see it, it is better to be devoured by one's conscience. Thus the following exchange from Afranius comes directly from life. When the dissolute son says:

> Oh, how miserable I am!

---

[488] Miltiades (c. 550 B.C.—489 B.C.), Athenian military commander, famous for his leadership role in the Battle of Marathon.

[489] *Tropeum*, or trophy. A monument set up to commemorate victory over an enemy, usually decorated with images of spoils, such as armor, weapons, etc.

The strict father responds:

> However something may hurt him, let it hurt him
> no matter what.[490]

They also say that the remaining categories of sorrow are useful. Pity causes us to render aid to others, and to lighten the hardships of those who have been unfairly stricken by them. Even jealousy and disparagement have some utility, such as when someone sees either that he has not accomplished as much as someone else, or that someone has gained the same thing he has gained.

He who would remove fear, would thereby take away all diligence in carrying out life's duties; and this diligence is most exercised by those who fear laws, judges, poverty, disgrace, death, and pain. Although they make these arguments, they admit they should be cut back to some extent, but they also say that they neither can nor should be eradicated completely. They believe that the middle ground is best in the majority of cases. When they present their ideas, do you see them as meaningless? Or do their arguments have some merit to you?

A. There is some merit to their case, I believe. So I'll wait for your response to their points.

21. M. Maybe I'll find something to say. But before I do that, let me say this. Do you notice the degree of restraint shown by the Academics?[491] For they state clearly what is relevant to the subject. The Stoics reply to the Peripatetics. It is fine with me if these two schools fight with each other in gladiatorial combat; but from my perspective, what truly matters is to search for the explanation that seems most likely. What is there in this question that allows us to arrive at something resembling the truth? For the human mind cannot progress beyond this point.

Consider the definition of perturbation, which I think Zeno used correctly. He defined it this way: "perturbation is a disorder of the mind that is opposed to reason, and is against nature." He also gave a shorter definition, which was "perturbation is an excessively vehement desire." In this definition, *excessively vehement desire* is

---

[490] Meaning that "you've made your bed, now you have to sleep in it."
[491] I.e., the adherents of Plato's Academy.

understood to mean a desire that is far away from nature's harmony. What can they[492] say in response to these definitions? The words of these definitions belong to thinkers[493] who are discoursing thoughtfully and with perception. Their opponents use ostentation coming from rhetoric: *fires of souls and grindstones of virtue.* Or is it true that a brave man cannot be brave unless he starts to boil with rage? Indeed true for gladiators, although in these same men we often observe a mental steadiness:

> They speak together, congregate, ask about things,
> and ask for things,[494]

so that they appear to be more relaxed than irate. But in this category of men there could be someone like Pacidianus,[495] with a spirit that matches the following words of Lucilius:[496]

> I will indeed slay him and triumph, if this is what
> you want, he says.
> I believe this is what will happen:
> I myself will first absorb a strike to the face,[497]
> Before I finish my gladius's thrust into his foul
> innards and lungs.
> I hate the man, I fight enraged;
> And it takes no longer than for each of us
> To accommodate a gladius to his right hand:
> In my zeal and my hate, I reach this point
> And in my rage become like a wild beast.

---

[492] The Peripatetics.

[493] Stoics.

[494] The author of this line has not been identified.

[495] Pacidianus was a gladiator of the Gracchian era. He had a noted rivalry with a Samnite named Aeserninus. He is mentioned elsewhere by Cicero (*Ad Quint. Fr.* III.4.2; *Opt. Gen. Or.* VI.17).

[496] The Roman satirist Caius Lucilius (c. 180 B.C.—c. 102 B.C.) was a respected and original writer. The surviving fragments of his work show him to have been a major influence on Horace.

[497] The word for face (*os*) can also mean "mouth." Compare *Aeneid* X.323: *intorquens iaculum clamanti sistit in ore.*

22. Yet in Homer's epic we see Ajax without any of this gladiatorial rage: it is with a feeling of exuberance that he prepares to confront Hector in combat.[498] When he took up arms, his entry into the fray brought joy to his comrades and dread to his enemies, to the extent that Hector himself (as Homer tells us), his breast trembling with apprehension, regretted ever having agreed to fight Ajax. The two of them spoke to each other respectfully and in measured tones before beginning to fight. Even during the actual duel, they did not act with rage or manic vehemence. Neither do I believe that the legendary figure who earned the name Torquatus was enraged when he plucked the torque from the fallen Gaul's neck.[499] Marcellus[500] at Clastidium also did not derive his bravery from this emotion.[501] Africanus, whose career is of more recent memory, is certainly better known to us.[502] I can promise you that he was not burning with rage when during battle he protected Marcus Allienus Pelignus with his shield, and thrust his gladius into the chest of the enemy.

I may have some doubts in the case of Lucius Brutus.[503] Perhaps he attacked Arruns[504] with unbridled ferocity because of his overwhelming hatred of the tyrant; for I see that both of them died from stab wounds they gave each other in a close-quarters fight. So why do you introduce anger into the analysis? Does courage have no driving force of its own, unless it begins to act crazily? What do you think? Do you really think that Hercules, whose bravery carried him all the way to heaven (bravery that you try to characterize as rage),

---

[498] Referring to *Iliad* VII.210—235.

[499] A famous legend Cicero also cites elsewhere. Titus Manlius Imperiosus Torquatus, a politician (three times consul and three times dictator) and general of the Roman republic, killed a Gaul in combat in 316 B.C. and took his torque (neck ornament) as a trophy.

[500] Marcus Claudius Marcellus (c. 270 B.C.—208 B.C.), general and five-time consul of the Roman republic. He killed a Gaulish king in personal combat at Clastidium in 222 B.C.

[501] I.e., he did not get his courage from rage.

[502] Referring to Publius Cornelius Scipio Africanus Aemilianus (185 B.C.—129 B.C.), who captured Carthage in 146 B.C.

[503] Lucius Junius Brutus, a founder of the Roman republic and one of the first consuls in 509 B.C.

[504] Arruns Tarquinius (son of Tarquinius Superbus, the last Roman king). He and Lucius Junius Brutus killed each other in personal combat at the Battle of Silva Arsia in 509 B.C.

was angry when he grappled with the boar of Erymanthus or the Nemean lion?[505] Was Theseus enraged when he seized the horns of the bull of Marathon?[506] Make sure you do not have courage depend in any way on anger; for courage that lacks reason does not exist.

23. Petty human affairs should be treated with contempt; death should be regarded as of no consequence; and sufferings and labors should be thought of as bearable. When these ideas have been put in place by judgment and sentiment, then robust and steadfast courage follows: unless, perhaps, we believe that actions done vehemently, ardently, and courageously are accomplished through naked rage. To me even Scipio, the supreme pontiff—who demonstrated the truth of the Stoic principle that the wise man is never a private citizen—does not appear to have been angry with Tiberius Gracchus when he abandoned the feeble consul and, despite being a private citizen, ordered everyone who wanted to save the republic to follow him, just as if he were the consul.[507]

Whether I have acted courageously in my political career, I do not know. If I have acted with courage, I certainly have not done so under the influence of rage. Is there anything that more closely resembles insanity than anger? Ennius spoke aptly when he called anger "the starting-point of insanity." Facial hue, voice, eyes, respiration, and violence of speech and deed: what part do these things have in the estimation of mental stability? What is more contemptible in Homer than Achilles and Agamemnon, during their bitter dispute?[508] As for Ajax, indeed, rage led him to uncontrollable frenzy and death.[509]

Courage, therefore, does not need to be propped up with anger. It is adequately trained, prepared, and armed by itself alone. In some

---

[505] Hercules's fourth labor was to capture the boar of Erymanthus; his first labor was to kill the Nemean lion.

[506] Theseus's jealous step-mother Medea sent him to capture the vicious bull of Marathon.

[507] This refers to Publius Cornelius Scipio Nasica Serapio (c. 181 B.C.—132 B.C.), patrician-friendly politician of the republic and holder of the office of *pontifex maximus*. He led the mob that killed Tiberius Gracchus in 133 B.C., and later tried to purge the rest of Gracchus's supporters. Eventually sent away to Pergamum in Asia Minor, he may have been killed there by some of Gracchus's allies.

[508] Referring to their dispute over the girl Briseis in *Iliad* I.122.

[509] See *Odyssey* XI.540—565. Ajax was stricken with madness when he was not awarded the armor of the fallen Achilles.

way, of course, we may say that intoxication or lack of mental control are advantageous for bravery, because those who are drunk or not in control of their faculties often do many things with heightened vehemence. Ajax is always brave, but nevertheless bravest when he is aroused to fury. For

> He accomplished a great feat when the Danaans withdrew;
> He ensured safety for all;
> Ferocious to the point of madness, he resumed the fight.[510]

24. Should we say, then, that being in a mental frenzy is advantageous? Pore over the definitions of courage: you will learn that it does not need uncontrolled fury. Bravery is a condition of the mind in enduring hardships that is in alignment with the highest law; or, it is the preservation of a stable judgment in braving and defeating life's reversals that appear terrible. It may also be the discriminating awareness of those tribulations in life that are terrible and those that are not terrible, or the knowledge of those hardships that should be ignored completely while keeping a balanced judgment of them.

Or bravery may be, as Chrysippus says more briefly—for the above definitions were made by Sphaerus, a man with an unrivaled ability to craft definitions with a Stoic flavor. But in fact the definitions are very much alike, and they state notions that are common, more or less—so how, then, does Chrysippus define it?[511] He says that bravery is the knowledge of enduring hardships; or it is a state of mind in bearing and tolerating life's trials that fearlessly conforms to the highest law. However one may be tempted to denounce such thinkers, as Carneades liked to do, I suspect that they are the only real philosophers. For which of these definitions does not explain the notion—shrouded and concealed though it may be—that each of us has about courage?

---

[510] Tischer here references *Iliad* XV.727 *et. seq.*, and suggests these lines may be from a lost work of Pacuvius.

[511] The choppy, conversational flow of this sentence is deliberate. The paragraphs that follow are also intended to have an informal flavor.

Once it[512] has been made clear, who would seek anything else for a fighter, a commander, or an orator? And who would believe them unable to do anything brave without the help of rage? What do you think? Don't the Stoics—who declare that all men who are not wise are insane—synthesize all of these points in their reasoning? Remove mental perturbations, and especially anger. Now they will appear to be talking with no consistency.

Instead they try to convince us by saying that all foolish men are insane, just as all filth has a foul odor. But not always. Shake it up, and then you will know. A hot-tempered man is not always angry. Agitate him, and you see him in a furious state. Well? When this pugnacious anger[513] returns home, what is it like with your wife, your children, and your other family members? Or is it an advantage there, too?

Is there anything that the perturbed mind can do better than the stable mind? Or can anyone even be angry without mental perturbation? Therefore, since all vices come from our habits, and because no vice is uglier than rage, our people were right when they called angry men the only morose[514] men.

25. An orator least of all should be hot-tempered. Yet it may be opportune to simulate anger. Do I look angry to you when I argue court cases more sharply and vehemently? What do you think? And when the cases are finished and concluded, and I write down my orations, am I writing in anger?

> Does anyone crack down on this? Use the shackles![515]

Do you really think Aesopus[516] was irate when he played this theatrical role, or that Accius was enraged when he wrote these

---

[512] I.e., the definition of courage.

[513] The phrase used is *bellatrix iracundia*, identifying anger as a "warrior."

[514] The word used here is *morosus*, which the Ox. Lat. Dict. defines as "hard to please, difficult, pernickety, etc." It does not list "sad" or "morose" as a shade of meaning. Cassell's dictionary and Riddle's Latin—English lexicon define *morosus* as "peevish" or "captious," but they also include "morose" as a possible meaning.

[515] A line from the *Atreus* of Accius.

[516] This famous actor is mentioned in II.17, above.

words? These kinds of roles are beautifully played, and in fact better played, by an orator (if he is a true orator) than by any stage actor. But the roles are performed smoothly and with a calmness of mind.

And is it not reckless to praise lust? You offer me the examples of Themistocles and Demosthenes, and then you add in Pythagoras, Democritus, and Plato.[517] What are you trying to say? Do you consider dedication to one's studies "lust"? This effort to learn the greatest of things—as we see in these examples you are offering—still ought to be calm and tranquil. What philosopher will praise mental anguish, that one most detestable condition? Some believe Afranius was correct when he said:

> However something may hurt, let it hurt no matter what.

But Afranius was referring to a dissolute and ruined period of youth. We, however, are asking about the nature of a wise and level-headed man. Let a centurion—or a standard-bearer, or others[518] we need not mention, lest I reveal the rhetoricians' secrets—have this same rage. He who is unable to employ reason finds it advantageous to use a disturbance of the mind. As I have said before, we are inquiring into the nature of the wise man.

26. They say it is even useful to feel jealousy, to disparage another, or to feel compassion. Why should feeling compassion be favored over actually *helping* someone, if you can do it? Or can you not be generous without feeling pity? We should not shoulder sorrows ourselves on behalf of others, but we should alleviate the anguish of others if we can. But to belittle another, or subject him to perverse emulation that is similar to rivalry—what is "useful" about this? Being jealous is distress at another's good, when one does not have this good; disparagement, however, is distress at another's good, when one already has the good that the other man has.[519]

---

[517] Referring to IV.19, above.

[518] Orators and politicians, who know how to use rhetorical devices to mimic anger.

[519] Disparagement is being upset at the knowledge that someone else has what you have.

If you want to have something, who can approve of taking on anguish as a voluntarily choice?[520] For the greatest folly is a wish to have something that is not followed by action to get it. Who can rightly praise moderate levels of evils? Who cannot be lustful or desirous, if he has feelings of lust or desire? Who cannot be angry, if anger burns within him? Who cannot be anxious, if he is tormented by anxiety? Who cannot be afraid, if he is hounded by fear?[521] Should we think, then, that the wise man is lustful, angry, anxious, and fearful? Many things can be said, as extensively and broadly as one wishes, about the wise man's excellence. But in briefest form we may say that *wisdom is the knowledge of things divine and human, and the recognition of the cause of these things.* The outcome is that wisdom imitates what is divine, and considers all human affairs to be inferior to virtue.

Did you say it seemed to you that wisdom falls into perturbation as if it were a sea subjected to the force of winds? What is there that can shake up its composure and constancy? Could it be something unexpected or sudden? How could something like this happen to a man who has considered in advance the possible things that might occur? When they say that excessive things should be pruned away, and only what is natural should remain, my response is: what can be natural that may increase beyond measure? All of these views arise from the roots of errors, and they must be completely pulled up and removed—not pruned away or cut down.

27. But I suspect you are asking not so much about the "wise man" in the abstract, but about you yourself. You think that the wise man is free of all mental distress, so you want to be free of it too. Let us see to what extent the remedies of philosophy may be used to treat the sicknesses of the mind. There is some definite medicine. Nature has not been so hostile and ill-disposed towards humanity as to find so many healthful benefits for our bodies, and yet none for our minds. Nature has done our minds an even greater favor: curatives for the body are given from *outside* sources, while the restorative power of the human mind is

---

[520] I.e., who would recommend your taking on anguish, instead of trying to get what you want.

[521] This is a beautifully oratorical sequence: *Quis enim potest, in quo libido cupiditasve sit, non libidonosus et cupidus esse? In quo ira, non iracundus? In quo angor, non anxius? In quo timor, non timidus?*

contained within *itself.*[522] But the greater and more divine the mind's excellence, the more it is needs our diligent attention. If correctly used, reason understands what is best; if neglected, it becomes ensnared by a great many errors. All my words, therefore, must now be directed to your particular situation.

You claim to be asking about the wise man. But perhaps you are asking about yourself. There are various cures for dealing with these mental distresses I have set forth. Not every kind of anguish is cured in the same way; one medicine works for the grieving person, another for the pity-stricken, and another for the envious type. In all four perturbations, there is this distinction: (1) whether our discussion should apply to perturbation in a general sense (i.e., rejection of reason or an extreme appetite), or (2) whether it should apply to the individual perturbations, such as fear, lust and the rest of them. We should also consider whether it is better to try to take away what has caused the distress, or whether it is better to eliminate all types of distress.

Here is an example. Suppose someone feels anguish because he is poor. Do you try to convince him that poverty is not an evil, or that a man should not feel anguish about anything? Of course, this last option is the better one. For if by chance you can't persuade him about poverty, the man would have to give in to anguish. But if anguish is taken away by specific, pointed reasoning—similar to what I used yesterday—then the evil of poverty is also in some way lifted.

28. Yet every mental perturbation of this type can be removed with this treatment method: demonstrating that *neither what causes joy or lust is a good, nor what causes fear or anxiety is an evil.* Without doubt the definite and proper curing technique is teaching that these perturbations are themselves full of vice, and have nothing about them that is natural or necessary. As an example, we see that anguish is lessened when we clearly explain to grievers the weakness of a womanish mind,[523] and when we praise the constancy and dignity of those who endure the human condition with levelheaded balance. This attitude is common among those who think these things are evils, but nevertheless maintain that they should be carried with patient composure. Someone says that pleasure is a good, while another believes it is money. Regardless, the one can be dissuaded from intemperance, and the other can be dissuaded from greed.

---

[522] *Animorum salus inclusa in ipsis est.* I take *salus* here to mean more "restorative power" instead of "health."
[523] The phrase used is *imbecillitatem animi effeminati.*

More advantageous, however, is the other method and argument that simultaneously removes wrong beliefs and alleviates distress. Yet it rarely works, and it should not be used with the average person. There are also certain kinds of anguish which this medicine can in no way alleviate. For example, suppose someone felt anguish for not having any virtue in himself, no soul, no responsibility, or no honesty. Due to the evil resulting from this, he would indeed feel troubled. For him, however, a different cure would have to be applied; and it would have to be a cure that all other philosophers endorse, even if they might disagree on other matters. All of them should concur on this point: disturbances of the mind that defy right reason are vile.

So even if the things that cause fear or anguish are evil and the things that cause desire and joy are good, the disturbance itself is unhealthy.[524] We want the man whom we call magnanimous and strong to be steadfast, calm, and serious, a man who holds in contempt those reversals that may happen to us in life. But one who mourns, who fears, who desires, or who longs passionately cannot qualify as such a man. For these are the behaviors of those who believe human events should take precedence over their own souls.[525]

29. For this reason, as I have said before, there is one curative method used by all philosophers: that we should say nothing about what it is that disturbs the mind, but talk only about the actual perturbation itself. And so first, when we talk about lust, and our purpose is only to take it away, we should not ask whether the thing that causes the lust is good or bad, but should instead aim our attention on removing the sensation of lust itself. Whether the Ultimate Good is moral rectitude, or pleasure, or a blend of these two things, or whether it is the other three types of goods,[526] nevertheless, even if the appetite for virtue itself is excessively vehement, the same discourse should be used by all as a deterrent.

Yet when investigated accurately, human nature is found to be thoroughly capable of soothing the mind. So that a clear picture of

---

[524] The word used is *vitiosa*, which can mean "full of vice," "vicious," or "unhealthy."

[525] The last two sentences here have a compelling beauty, and an otherworldly Platonic power, that this translator finds magnificent. Consider: *Talis autem nec maerens nec timens nec cupiens nec gestiens esse quisquam potest*, with the drumbeat repetition of the negative conjunction *nec*.

[526] Referring to the goods of body, soul, and fortune, also mentioned below in V.9.

this may be grasped more easily, the common human condition and law of life must be explained in our discourse. Not without good reason, when Euripides related the tale of Orestes, Socrates is said to have recalled the first three verses:

> Neither any discourse so terrible that may be spoken,
> Nor outcome, nor evil mandated by heavenly rage,
> That human nature cannot find the strength to endure.

In persuading the victims of bad circumstances that they can and should endure them, it is useful to talk about other people who have borne similar hardships. The technique for calming anxiety was explained in our dialogue yesterday, and also in my book *Consolation*, which was written at a time when I was in the depths of personal grief and pain. For I was then no wise man. I used the remedy forbidden by Chrysippus, who disapproves of treating recent "inflammations of the mind," if I may put it that way. But I did it, and perpetrated an offense against nature in order that the magnitude of my grief might yield to the power of the remedy.

30. But fear, about which we should say a few words, shares a border with anxiety, about which we have already said enough. While anxiety is traceable to present evil, fear originates in future evil. Thus some thinkers used to say that fear was a specific subdivision of anxiety. Others called fear "nascent dread,"[527] because they considered it a sort of "vanguard" of subsequent trouble. Therefore, current bad circumstances are tolerated by using the same thought process we use in having contempt for bad circumstances to come. For in both scenarios, we must be on our guard to do nothing that is base, cowardly, weak, effeminate, pathetic, or contemptible.

Yet although one should call attention to the incongruity, feebleness, and negligibility of fear itself, it is a great advantage to have

---

[527] The word used is *praemolestia*. According to the Ox. Lat. Dict., this is the only attested usage of this term in classical Latin. It is likely a Ciceronian coinage. It is defined as "distress experienced by anticipation." Throughout the *Tusculan Disputations*, one often gets the sense that Cicero, with his nuanced appreciation of cognitive processes, would have concurred with many modern psychological theories of depression and its treatment.

scorn for things that are commonly feared. So whether it occurred deliberately or by chance, it very usefully happened that those things we fear most—death and pain—were debated on our first and subsequent days together. And if the findings of those discussions are accepted, we are to a great extent liberated from fear.

31. Until now we have examined the opinion of evil. Let us now examine the opinion of good; that is, the opinion of joy and desire. It seems to me that all reasoning related to perturbation of the mind contains one fundamental idea: that all perturbations are within our power, that they are maintained by our own beliefs, and that they are voluntary. This is an error that must be snatched away, and an idea that should not be accepted. And just as supposed *evils* are able to be withstood, so it is that in the case of supposed *goods*, those things considered crucial and joyous must be observed with a more relaxed frame of mind.

This characteristic, indeed, is something shared by both good and evil: if it is difficult to persuade the person that none of the things tormenting the mind should be counted as either good or evil, nevertheless different cures ought to be used for different sentiments. One cure is appropriate for the spiteful individual, a different one for the playboy, another for the excessively anxious, and yet another for the coward. For anyone following the most accepted line of reasoning about goods and evils, it would be a simple matter to deny that a fool can be influenced by joy, since he can never have anything good. But we are now speaking in a very general way. Let these things that are considered good—honors, riches, pleasures, and similar things—indeed be good. Nevertheless, jubilant and boastful rapture in acquiring such things is repulsive behavior. For example, if laughter were permissible in some situation, then outrageously boisterous laughter would look like an insult.

For the mind's extravagance in joy arises from the same shortcoming as does its contraction in pain. Excessive passion in seeking reveals the same superficiality as does exaggerated joy in expressing fondness. And just as those people overly debilitated by problems are correctly considered weak, so too are those who display inordinate exuberance in happiness considered weak.[528] As envy is a kind of mental defect, and taking pleasure in another's misfortune is a kind

---

[528] These three sentences are a complex and beautiful Ciceronian period: *Eodem enim vitio est effusio animi in laetitia quo in dolore contractio, eademque levitate cupiditas est in appetendo qua laetitia in fruendo, et, ut nimis adflicti molestia, sic nimis elati laetitia iure iudicantur leves.*

of thrill, both of these afflictions are normally remedied by explaining the extent of their savagery and ferocity. It is proper to be on one's guard, and improper to be afraid; it is right to rejoice, but not right to display ecstasy, because for instructional purposes we distinguish rejoicing from displaying ecstasy. We have previously made the point that a contraction of the mind is never proper. But mental elation can be proper. In the words of Naevius, Hector revels in one feeling:

> I am happy to be praised by you, father, a praise-
> worthy man;

while the character in Trabea revels in a different sentiment:

> The madam soothed with money will be alert to
> my command,
> What I want, what I seek: arriving, I push the door
> with my finger,
> And the portal opens. When Chrysis by chance
> gazes on me there,
> She will come to me hungrily, longing for my em-
> brace,
> And she will give herself to me.

Now he will say how beautiful he thinks this is:

> I will surpass Fortune itself with my own fortune.

32. Someone paying careful attention here will have a full awareness of how disgraceful this joy is. And just as those carried away with bliss when enjoying voluptuary pleasures are debased, so those who lust after them with inflamed minds are disgraceful. In fact the whole emotion commonly called love—and, by Hercules, I cannot call it by any other name—is of such superficiality that I really think nothing matches it. Caecilius says this about love:

He who says the gods are not the most powerful
Is either a dolt, or thinks like someone very im-
mature;
For Love determines the one whom it wants to be-
wilder,
Whom it wants to grant knowledge, whom it
wants to be insane,
Or whom it wants to send a disease,
And conversely, it decides whom it wants to be
loved,
To be sought after, and to be procured.

What an incredible rewriter of life is this poetry! It thinks love, the author of disgrace and superficiality, should have a seat in the council of the gods. I am talking about comedy, which would not exist at all if we did not accept this immoral self-indulgence. But what did the commander of the Argonauts say in tragedy?

You have protected me more out of love, than because of honor.

So what happened then? What a blazing fire of misery did this love of Medea ignite! And yet in the words of a different poet, she has the impertinence to tell her father that she acquired for a husband

A man whom Love had given, who is more capable and useful than a father.

33. But we should let the poets play their games—their stories allow us to see Jove himself involved in this disgrace. Let us rely on the instructors of virtue, the philosophers; they deny that love is part of depravity. On this topic they disagree sharply with Epicurus, who in my view is not being deceptive. For what is this love of friendship? Why does no one love a repulsive youth, or a handsome old man? To

me it seems this custom[529] arose in the Greek gymnasia, where these types of loves were open and condoned. Ennius puts it well:

The origin of shame is the revealing of male· nakedness in full view.

While these kinds of loves, as far as I see possible, may be modest, they nevertheless foment distress and angst, and all the more so because they are confined and repressed. And if I may overlook the love of women, for which nature has allowed greater license, who doubts what the poets say about the rape of Ganymede,[530] or does not grasp what Laius says and wants in Euripides?[531]

Finally, what do the most learned men, and the most powerful poets, reveal about themselves in their poems and songs? Alcaeus,[532] a brave man, well-known in his country—what did he write about the love of young men? Now if we look at Anacreon's[533] poetry, we see it is entirely concerned with love. And it is obvious from the writings of Ibycus of Rhegium[534] that he burned with an amorous love surpassing all others in intensity.

34. So we see that the loves of all these individuals are lascivious. Some of us philosophers—and indeed on the authority of Plato, whom Dicaearchus rightly criticizes—have appeared who would confer prestige on love.[535] The Stoics in fact say that the wise man should feel love; and they define it as an attempt to form a friendship

---

[529] I.e., love between men. See also Cicero's *De Re Publica* IV.4.

[530] In Greek mythology, the Trojan youth Ganymede was abducted by Zeus and taken to Olympus to serve as his "cup-bearer." The sexual overtones of the myth are what Cicero is referring to.

[531] Referring to the tragedy *Chrysippus*, a lost tragedy of Euripides. Laius, the king of Thebes, loved Chrysippus, the son of Pelops.

[532] Alcaeus of Mytilene (c. 625 B.C.—c. 580 B.C.), lyric poet from the island of Lesbos. He may have been a lover of Sappho, and is said to have originated the lyrical meter form called the "Alcaic stanza."

[533] Anacreon (c. 582 B.C.—c. 485 B.C.), Greek lyric poet from Teos in Ionia.

[534] Erotic poet who flourished in the second half of the 6th century B.C. Little is known of his life and activities.

[535] In the *Symposium* and *Phaedrus*, Plato proposed two types of love: one sensual, the other spiritual.

from an image of beauty. If there is anyone in this world who is without anxiety, without desire, without care, without a mournful sigh, he certainly might be a lover: for he is free of all lust. But our discussion here is about lust. However, if[536] there is some love (as indeed there is) which is not far or not too far from insanity, such as in the *Leucadia*:[537]

> If indeed there were some god,
> Whose care I might be.

But in this example all the gods should have cared about how he could enjoy love's delights!

> Ah, woe is me!

Nothing is more true than this. And he rightly says:

> Are you right in the head, you who recklessly cries in grief?

He seems insane even to his own relatives. But what tragedies he makes!

> You, sanctified Apollo, bring me hope, and you,
> omnipotent Neptune I invoke,
> And even you too, O winds!

---

[536] This conditional sentence with "if" is intentionally not followed by a main clause.

[537] The name of a lost play by the Roman writer Turpilius (or Sextus Turpilius), a contemporary and friend of Terence.

He thinks the whole world will harmonize its energies to support his love. He only excludes Venus, believing her to be unjust:

> For what reason should I call you, Venus?

He denies that Venus—because of lust—cares for anything. As if he himself said and did such disgraceful things for some reason other than lust!

35. But the necessary cure for someone affected by this is to show him how unimportant, worthless, and completely inconsequential is the thing he ardently desires, how easily it can either be obtained somewhere else or through a different method, or how it can be completely disregarded. Sometimes his attention should be directed to other studies, worries, cares, and activities. The sick who are not recuperating are often cured by a change of physical residence. Some also think that the memory of an old love can be dispelled by a new one, as one nail forces out another; but above all he must be instructed on how powerful love's unchecked fury can be. Of all the perturbations of the mind, there is certainly none more vehement.

And even if you do not want to denounce love—and here I am talking about the excesses of illicit sex, enticement, adultery, and finally incest, all of which have an ugliness that deserves to be denounced—the mind's distress in the throes of love is horrible in itself, even if you *leave out* these excesses. For to overlook the excesses that confirm love's fury, what shallowness do these things, which are looked upon as mediocre, inherently have!

> Injustices, distrusts, hatreds, suspensions of hostilities,
> War, and peace once again.
> If you attempt to do uncertain things by certain reason,
> You will achieve nothing more,
> Than if you, using reason, make an effort to be insane.[538]

---

[538] Terence's *Eunuchus* I.1.14.

Who wouldn't be deterred by the inherent perverseness of this mental unpredictability and fickleness? This feature also must be pointed out, as was said of every perturbation: that every emotion is due to personal belief, an accepted judgment, or a voluntary preference. For if love were something natural, everyone would be in love, and would be permanently in love, and would love the same thing. Nor would one person be deterred by shame, another by thinking, and another by gratification.

36. Whenever it upsets the mind, anger without a doubt resembles insanity. Its impact proves to be this kind of quarrel between brothers:

> A. In all the world's nations, whom have you exceeded in insolence?
> M. And whom have you surpassed in malice, as well?[539]

You know what comes after this. In alternate verses, the nastiest insults are thrown back and forth between brothers, so that it is obvious they are sons of the Atreus who devises a horrible punishment for his brother:

> A greater lump of evil should be mixed,
> Which should crush and subdue his harsh heart.[540]

In what way does this "lump" issue forth? Listen to Thyestes:[541]

> It was my own brother who urged me
> To hand over my own sons to despicable jaws.

---

[539] From Ennius's *Iphigenia*, according to Tischer.
[540] From Accius's *Atreus*.
[541] In Greek mythology, Thyestes was a king of Olympia. His brother, and king of Mycenae, was Atreus. Atreus, in an act of revenge, killed Thyestes's sons, then cooked the remains and served them to Thyestes, who unwittingly consumed them.

He lays out their flesh on a table. For how will anger not reach the same extreme as mad rage? Thus we rightly say that enraged persons have gone beyond all sense of restraint, that is, beyond the capacity for judgment, reason, and self-awareness. And these qualities should have controlling power over the entire mind.

We can remove the targets of aggression from the scene until the enraged person regains his composure—but what does "regaining composure" mean, except to reassemble once more the scattered parts of the mind in the right place? Or, if enraged persons have the ability to take revenge, they should be asked—and pleaded with—to postpone such action until their anger subsides. Yet the word "subsiding" suggests a mental fire ignited against reason's will. From this comes the praise given for what Archytas[542] said when he once was angry with his farm overseer: "How I would have dealt with you if I had *not* been angry!"

37. Then where are the people who say that anger is useful? Can derangement be useful? Or natural? Or can anything that violates rational thought be in accordance with nature? If rage were natural, how would one person be angrier than another? Or how would the desire for revenge have an end before it had accomplished its purpose? How would anyone atone for what he had done while enraged? We see this in the case of King Alexander, who could barely be prevented from hurting himself after he had killed his friend Clitus. Such power did his sense of remorse have. Once we understand this, who can doubt that this working of the mind is completely controlled by belief and personal choice? Who can doubt that the distresses of the mind, such as greed and the desire for glory, are traceable to the fact that what causes the mind's distress is something very highly valued?

So it should be understood that *all mental perturbation is traceable to a personal belief.* And if belief in oneself—that is, firm assurance of mind—is a type of knowledge and serious belief where approval is not recklessly granted, mistrust is also fear of an expected and impending evil. And if hope is the expectation of good, then fear must necessarily be the expectation of evil. Just as with fear, so with the rest of the perturbations: they are inextricably bound to evil. Therefore, as constancy is the defining feature of knowledge, so perturbation is the defining feature of error. Those who are by nature

---

[542] Archytas (c. 410 B.C.—c. 350 B.C.), a philosopher and mathematician of the Pythagorean school. He is credited with being a founder of mathematical mechanics, and his name persists in the so-called "Archytas curve."

said to be irascible, sympathetic, jealous, or something similar, possess an unsound mental disposition. Yet they are treatable, as Socrates was said to have been.

Zopyrus asserted he had the ability to discover a man's nature by looking at his physical form.[543] In a public gathering, he once charged Socrates with having various vices. The others present mocked Zopyrus, stating that they never observed these faults in him. But Socrates himself supported Zopyrus. He acknowledged that he harbored the alleged vices, but had banished them by using reason. Therefore, just as every person endowed with superior health can appear to have a greater susceptibility by nature for some physical affliction, so one mind has a greater propensity for one type of vice, and another mind for a different type of vice.

As for those who are said to be full of vice—not by nature's choice, but due to their own fault—their vices are traceable to false beliefs about goods and evils. Thus one man will lean more towards one type of mental turmoil and perturbation than another. As we observe in the human body, a chronic disease is more difficult to eradicate than a temporary perturbation; and it is easier to cure an unexpected inflammation of the eyes than it is to treat an inveterate ocular tumor.

38. Since we have now learned the cause of mental perturbations, and understand that they all arise from *judgments traceable to personal opinions and desires*, the objective of our discourse has been satisfied. Now that the ends of goods and evils are known—as far as such things can be known by man—we should realize that we can hope for nothing greater or more useful from philosophy than the issues we have discussed during the past four days. Death has been looked on with contempt, and pain has been soothed to a point where it is tolerable.[544]

To these achievements we have also added the alleviation of anguish—and no evil that affects man is more powerful than this. Although every perturbation of the mind is a serious matter and differs little from derangement, we are still in the habit of saying of other people afflicted by some perturbation—whether it is fear, joy, or desire—that they are just "excited" and "disturbed." But as for

---

[543] Zopyrus (5th cent. B.C.) was a physiognomist mentioned by Cicero in *On Fate* (V); see also Plato's *Alcibiades* 122b.
[544] Referring to the discussions in books I and II.

those who have given in to sorrow, we say they are miserable, afflicted with agony, wretched, or crushed by calamity.

Thus it does not appear to have happened by chance, but was proposed by you with a valid reason, that we should separately examine anxiety and other perturbations. For in this[545] we indeed find the source and wellspring of all miseries. But there is one treatment for anxiety and the other sicknesses of the mind: *understanding that they are all based on opinion and personal choice, and that we capitulate to them because it seems right to do so.* This destructive error, which functions as the root of all evil, philosophy promises to eradicate completely.

Let us, therefore, put our trust in its healing power, and allow ourselves to be restored. For once these evils have taken hold of our minds, not only can we not be happy, but we cannot even be in a stable condition. Either we should deny that reason can do anything (although on the contrary nothing can be done rightly without reason), or, since philosophy is based on the compilation of logical reasoning, we should, if we truly wish to be good and happy, seek from philosophy every kind of assistance and support for living well and happily.

---

[545] I.e., mental anguish.

BOOK V

ON WHETHER VIRTUE IS SUFFICIENT FOR LEADING A HAPPY LIFE

BOOK V

1. Brutus, this fifth day will see the end of our discussions at Tusculum, a day in which we treated the topic you recommend more than any other. I sense from the book you most accurately wrote and dedicated to me, and from our many discussions, that you believe virtue alone is sufficient for a happy life. Although proof of this is difficult to accept, considering the many and varied torments of fortune that occur, it is a statement of such merit that we should exert ourselves to prove it as efficiently as we can. Of all the subjects treated by philosophy, there is not a single one surrounded with more grandeur and consequence. Since this is what impelled the first adherents of the study of philosophy to bypass matters of secondary importance and dedicate themselves fully to investigating life's best state, surely they applied such care and effort on this question with the hope of a happy life as an incentive.

Because if the concept of virtue was invented and perfected by them, and if aid for living a happy life is contained in virtue, who would not think that the work of philosophizing was admirably established by them, and taken up by us? But if, however, virtue is subject to various and uncertain events and functions as a servant of fortune, and lacks the power needed to support itself alone, then I suspect that, when trying to seek a happy life, we would be better off extending our prayers to the skies instead of placing our faith in virtue. Indeed, when I consider the hardships of my own life with which fortune tested me so cruelly, I begin to have my doubts about your view. Sometimes I even begin to feel dismayed at the vulnerability and fragility of human beings. I fear that nature, since it has given us infirm bodies as well as diseases without remedy and intolerable pain, has also provided us with minds that equally experience the body's physical torments. And as a separate matter, our minds are interwoven with their own particular anxieties and distresses.

But when I am visited by such thoughts, I quickly correct myself, because I am basing my opinion of virtue's strength on the weakness of other people, and perhaps myself as well, instead of judging virtue on its own merits. For if there is such a thing as virtue—and your uncle, Brutus, has removed any doubt about that—then it keeps everything that can happen to a man under its control. It looks down on man's petty concerns, and holds them in contempt; and without any sense of guilt, it believes that nothing suits it except itself. We ourselves, however, enlarging every misfortune with our fear as it approaches and with our grief when it arrives, prefer to denounce the nature of things instead of examining our own errors.

2. But we must seek the remedy for this mistake, as we would for all our defects and errors, in philosophy. From the time of my earliest years, my desire and devotion compelled me to seek her comforting embrace. And with the severe difficulties of my present circumstances, having been thrown about by violent storms, I now seek refuge in that same port from which I once put to sea. O philosophy, my life's faithful guide! O pathfinder of virtue, and banisher of vices! What might have happened not only to me, but to the life of man in general, without your guidance? You have raised up cities; you have brought together dispersed peoples to share in common social life; you have joined them first in dwellings, then in marriage, then in written and spoken language; you were the inventress of laws; and you served as the teacher of morals and discipline. In you I seek shelter, from you I look for support, and to you I surrender myself—previously to a great extent, and now without any equivocation, and in the most intimate way.

One day lived rightly, and according to your principles, has more value than a perpetuity of mistakes. Whose assistance shall we call on except yours? You, who have gifted us tranquility of life and banished the fear of death? Yet philosophy has received so little praise in proportion to the benefit it has conferred on the life of man, that it remains neglected and even attacked by many. Who will dare to rebuke the creator of his life, tarnish himself with such unforgivable criminality, and demonstrate such malicious ingratitude as to impugn the one he should venerate, even if he is unable to grasp her teachings? Yet this grave error, as I see it, and this dense fog have settled over the minds of the uninformed because they cannot look back far enough in time, and do not understand that those who first articulated the principles of human life were philosophers.

3. Although we know that philosophy is of very old date, we still concede that its name is a recent innovation. For who can deny not only that wisdom is ancient in itself, but that its name is equally timeworn? It earned its beautiful name with the ancients by virtue of its insights into things both divine and human, and its understanding of

the origins and causes of events. Thus those Seven Sages[546] (whom the Greeks called *sophoi*[547]) were called wise and believed to be wise by our own people. Many generations earlier, Lycurgus (in whose time, before Rome was founded, it is said that Homer also lived) and in the heroic age Ulysses and Nestor were wise men, we are told, and were thought to be wise by their peers.

Nor would we have been told that Atlas supported the heavens on his shoulders, or that Prometheus was chained to a rock in the windy Caucasus, or that Cepheus[548] was fixed among the starry bodies in the sky with his wife, son-in-law, and daughter, unless their divinely-inspired revelation of celestial matters had transferred their names to fanciful parables. From these beginnings arose all those thinkers—men who were both considered wise and named so—who dedicated themselves to the contemplation of nature. And this name of theirs persisted until the era of Pythagoras, who supposedly came to Phlius (as we find it written in Heraclides[549] of Pontus, a student of Plato and an extremely learned man), and debated certain topics learnedly and extensively with Leon, the leader of the Phliasians.[550] Leon expressed admiration for Pythagoras's brilliance and eloquence, and asked him to state the art in which he placed the most trust. Pythagoras's response was that he was a philosopher, and not familiar with any art.

We are told that Leon was stunned by the strangeness of this word. He demanded to know who "philosophers" were, and how they differed from other people. Pythagoras's alleged response was that the life of man appeared to him to be like those commemorative games celebrated with the greatest assortment of sports and the general assembly of participants from all of Greece.[551] At this grand

---

[546] The name given by Greek tradition to seven men distinguished for their wisdom. Dispute existed as to who should be included, but these names always appeared: Thales of Miletus, Pittacus of Mytilene, Bias of Priene, Solon of Athens, and Chilon of Sparta. Periander of Corinth, Myson of Chenae, and Anacharsis the Scythian were also candidates for the list.

[547] σοφοί, meaning "wise men."

[548] In Greek mythology, the son of Agenor and husband of Cassiopeia, with whom he had a daughter, Andromeda.

[549] Heraclides of Pontus (c. 390 B.C.—c. 310 B.C.), Greek philosopher and astronomer.

[550] Leon was tyrant of the Greek city of Phlius.

[551] Referring to such Greek athletic festivals as the Olympic, Nemean, Pythian, or Isthmian games.

event, some men sought the glory and nobility of a laurel crown through physical exercises. Others were enticed there by the possibility of financial gain through buying and selling. And then there was another kind of person there, who composed the best type, who sought neither profit nor public acclaim, but were there only to observe. They carefully paid attention to their environment to see what was happening and how things were taking place.

In the same way, Pythagoras continued, just as if we were coming from some provincial city to a well-attended festival, so we ourselves have come from another life and nature to this life.[552] We see that some men are slaves to glory, and others to money. Yet there are those rare few who, looking upon everything else as insignificant, systematically probe into the real nature of things. These men refer to themselves as "devoted to wisdom," or in other words, *philosophers*. And just as at that crowded festival, said Pythagoras, where the most honorable men observe their surroundings without any fixation on material gain, so in life the contemplation and understanding of things is thoroughly superior to all other activities.

4. Pythagoras was not only the man who invented the name, but he was also the one who enlarged its scope. When he came to Italy after his dialogue at Phlius, he adorned that region known as Magna Graecia with the very best institutions and arts, in both a public and private sense. (It would probably be better to discuss his ideas and teachings at a different time, however). From ancient times until the advent of Socrates—who had attended the lectures of Archelaus, Anaxagoras's disciple—philosophy concerned itself with numbers and motions, and the question of how the universe had arisen and what its destiny might be. It assiduously probed into the size of the stars, the distances between them, their paths in the heavens, and all other celestial subjects.

Socrates, however, was the first man to summon philosophy down from the sky, place it in the cities, and introduce it into the home: he forced it to ask questions about human life, moral problems, and the dilemmas of good and evil. His versatile techniques of debate, the diversity of subjects he addressed, and the sheer scope of his intellectual brilliance—the legacy of which has been preserved in

---

[552] Apparently a reference to metempsychosis (the transmigration of the soul at death to another body), a doctrine taught by Pythagoras.

Plato's incomparable dialogues—have spawned many different philosophical schools with opposing doctrines. Out of these many schools, I have determined to follow the one I believe is most in accord with Socrates's teachings: not revealing my own personal views, removing the errors of others, and in every debate, trying to seek the answer that seems most likely.

Since this was the method employed most cleverly and eloquently by Carneades, I have regularly made an effort—and also recently here at Tusculum—to structure philosophical debates in accordance with this custom. Indeed, in the previous books I have written out our four-day dialogue and have sent you a copy. On the fifth day, however, when we took our seats in the usual places, the topic we were to debate was raised as follows.

5. A. To me it doesn't seem true that virtue can be enough for leading a happy life.

M. Oh really! As my friend Brutus sees things, it certainly is enough—and with all due respect, I have much more confidence in his judgment than yours.

A. Of course you do. But we're not concerned now with how much you love Brutus, but with the nature of what I've expressed an opinion on. And this is what I want you to discuss.

M. So be it. Do you deny that virtue can be enough for living a happy life?

A. I certainly do deny it.

M. What? Doesn't virtue give us enough help for living rightly, honestly, commendably, and, in the final analysis, a good life?

A. Yes, it does.

M. Then can you say that someone who lives an evil life is not miserable? Or do you deny that someone whom you admit lives a good life, must also live a happy life?

A. Why shouldn't I? Even someone in the middle of torments someone can live rightly, honestly, and commendably, and therefore can live well. As long as you understand what I mean by *good*. I intend it to mean *living consistently, seriously, wisely, and courageously*. These traits are also stretched out on the torture rack—and a happy life does not aspire to this.

M. So what do you think? I ask you this. Is the happy life abandoned, all alone, outside the prison's front gate and entrance when consistency, seriousness, fortitude, wisdom, and the rest of the virtues are hauled off to the torturer, and escape neither suffering nor pain?

A. If you are going to persuade, you ought to find some new points. The things you've said carry little persuasive power with me. This is not just because they are widely known. It is more because there is greater satisfaction in a taste than in a mouthful of this Stoic argument, just as there are some light wines that become unappealing when mixed with water. This collection of virtues, when placed on the torture rack, brings before our eyes images of the greatest eminence, so that it appears the happy life is rushing swiftly to them, and not allowing them to be abandoned. But when you take your mind away from this picture, and these images of the virtues, to reality and the truth of things, you are left with this stark question: is it possible for anyone to be *happy* while being tortured?

So let us ask this question now. Regarding the virtues, however, do not be worried that they might protest and complain that they have been abandoned by the happy life. For if there is no virtue in the absence of prudence, then prudence itself knows that not all good men are also happy. In fact prudence remembers very much about Marcus Atilius, Quintus Caepio, and Manius Aquilius.[553] And when the happy life—if it chooses to be persuaded by images rather than reality—tries to go to the torture rack, prudence itself stops it from doing so, and denies that it has anything in common with pain and torment.

6. M. I'm not opposed to having you continue in this way, although it's unreasonable for you to tell me how you want me to argue. But I'd ask whether anything productive was done in the past few days, or if we really settled on nothing at all.

A. Certainly we accomplished something, and in fact a considerable amount.

M. Well, if that's the case, this question has already been dealt with, and nearly brought to a point of resolution.

A. In what way?

---

[553] Marcus Atilius Regulus (c. 307 B.C.—c. 250 B.C.), Roman consul and general, considered a model of civic virtue for his devotion to duty. Defeated by the Carthaginians in Africa in 255 B.C., he was captured and released on parole, and honored his promise to return to Carthage to face execution; Quintus Servilius Caepio (consul in 106 B.C.), tried and exiled for his negligent leadership that led to the defeat of his army in 105 B.C.; Manius Aquilius (died in 88 B.C.), Roman general whose army was defeated by Mithridates in Asia. According to legend, Mithridates executed him by having molten gold poured down his throat.

M. Because turbulent movements and upheavals of the soul, incited and elevated by thoughtless instinct that spurns all reason, do not leave a bit of happy life in their wake. For who cannot be miserable when living in fear of death or pain, one of which is often near, and the other always hanging over one's head? Well, what do you think? And if the same person—something that often happens—fears poverty, dishonor, or disrepute, or if he fears physical incapacity or blindness, or finally if he fears slavery, which can affect not just individuals but even cohesive populations, then can anyone be happy while fearing these things?

What about the person who not only fears these things in the future, but bears and copes with them now in the present? Add to this also exile, grief, or the loss of a child: can he who is shattered by these trials, and ravaged by such grief, *not* be completely miserable?

Well, what do you think? When we see a man burning furiously with passion, lusting madly for everything with an insatiable desire—and when we see that the more efficiently he indulges in pleasures wherever they are, the more oppressive and fervent becomes his thirst for them—wouldn't you correctly call him completely miserable? Well? When someone is foolishly elated, reveling in inane joy, and exulting blindly, isn't he still that much more miserable, despite appearing happier to himself? Therefore, just as these people are miserable, so by contrast are those people happy who are *not* terrorized by any fears, *not* consumed by any anxieties, *not* incited by any lusts, and *not* corrupted by the worthless joys that come from languid pleasures.

Just as the sea is said to be tranquil when not a single breeze agitates its surface, so do we perceive a quiescent and placid state of the mind when there exists no perturbation capable of disturbing it. Therefore, if there is a man who considers the power of fortune, and who sees all human events that may conceivably happen as sufficiently tolerable that neither fear nor anxiety will affect him, and if this same man lusts after nothing, and is not dehumanized by worthless delights of the mind, then why would such a man *not* be happy? And if it is virtue that brings about this result, then why should not virtue itself, acting entirely its own, make us happy?

7. A. Certainly we can confirm one of your statements, which is that those who fear nothing, who feel no anxiety, who lust after nothing, and who are not dehumanized by empty joys, are happy. So I

concede this point. The other proposition, however, is no longer intact—for our earlier debates have shown that the wise man does not feel any perturbation of mind.

M. Then without doubt our investigation is over. It seems that the question has been fully examined.

A. This is very nearly true.

M. But this is the habit of the mathematicians, not of the philosophers. When the geometricians want to teach something—if what they taught previously pertains to their current subject—they assume what has already been demonstrated and proved, and only explain the things they have not already written about.[554] But philosophers, no matter what subject they have in hand, collect everything relevant to that subject, even if it has been debated somewhere else. If this were not so, why would a Stoic have so much to say on the question of "whether virtue is sufficient for living a happy life"? It would be enough for him to respond that he had already demonstrated that there was no good except what was morally right. Once this was proven, the logical consequence is that the happy life is sustained by virtue. And just as this is the logical consequence of the propositions, so it follows from this also that, if the happy life is sustained by virtue, then there is nothing good except that which is morally right.

Yet this is not how they choose to proceed. For their books separately discuss what is morally good, and the ultimate good. And when they show, from an examination of moral goodness, that virtue has sufficient power to enable us to live a happy life, they nevertheless handle this subject in a disjointed way. For every subject, especially one so important, must be treated with its own specific arguments and admonitions. Take care to remember that there is no declaration in philosophy enunciated with more clarity, or any promise in philosophy that is greater or more beneficial. For what is promised? Good gods! *That philosophy will ensure that he who obeys her laws will always be armed against fortune, that he will have all the strength needed to live a happy life, and that in the end he will always be happy.*

But I will see what she will accomplish. In the meantime I consider it a great thing that the promise is made. For although Xerxes was stuffed with all the rewards and gifts of fortune, he was not content with cavalry, an immense infantry force, a fleet of ships, nor a

---

[554] As we find in the writings of Euclid, where each proposition, axiom, or theorem builds on what has come before it.

233

bottomless treasure-chest of gold: in fact he offered a reward to any-one who might find him a new pleasure. Even if someone had done this for him, he still would not have been satisfied, for lust will never reach an outer limit. I wish we could offer someone a reward to create something that would enable us to believe this truth more deeply.

8. A. I indeed want this, but there's something I'd like to know. I agree with you that, with regard to the points you've offered, one proceeds logically from the other. By this I mean that, if what is mor-ally right is the only good, it follows that the happy life is created by virtue. So if a happy life is found in virtue, nothing is good except virtue. But your friend Brutus, following the view of Aristus[555] and Antiochus, does not see things this way. He thinks the happy life is found in virtue *even if* there happened to be some good besides virtue.

M. Then what can we say? Do you think I'm going to speak out against Brutus?

A. Well, you should take the position you believe in. It isn't for me to impose my views on others.

M. How these things are in harmony with each other, is some-thing for us to resolve at another time. For I often had this argument with Antiochus, and recently with Aristus when I stayed at his house in Athens during the time I was a commander. To me it seemed that no one could be happy when he was surrounded by evil. The wise man, on the other hand, could be surrounded by evil, if there hap-pened to be any evils of body or fortune. The reasons given for this assertion—reasons that Antiochus also recorded in many of his works—were firstly that virtue alone by itself can make life happy, but still not perfectly happy; and secondly, that most things are named from what which they are mostly composed, even if a small part is absent.

We see this is in things like strength, health, riches, honor, and glory. These things are not understood by numeric tally, but by in-herent quality. Similarly, the happy life—even if it may be imperfect to some degree—is nevertheless named from that which composes most of it. It is not necessary to explain this in detail here, although to me it seems this argument is not very logical. For I do not under-stand what the happy man requires so that he can be happier: if something is lacking, then he is not happy.[556]

---

[555] Aristus of Ascalon (c. 120 B.C.—c. 45 B.C.), brother and student of the more famous Antiochus of Ascalon. It is unknown whether he authored any works.
[556] The rigid Stoic view was that there were no degrees of happiness. Being "happy" meant being perfectly happy, with no deficiencies.

And as for their view that each thing is named and judged by what it is mostly composed of, there are situations where this view has merit. Yet they say there are three types of evils. If someone is hounded by every evil of two types—so that he is plagued by every hardship fortune can offer, and his body is debilitated and disabled by all varieties of pain—will we say that this man needs just a little something more to have a happy life, never mind an extremely happy life?

9. This is the view that Theophrastus was unable to justify. When he concluded that shocks, torments, torture, the destruction of one's country, exile, and the loss of a child had a tremendous capacity to make one's life evil and miserable, he did not dare to speak proudly or eminently, since he was thinking despondently and abjectly. To what extent he was correct, we do not ask; certainly he spoke consistently.

To me it is not acceptable to attack conclusions when you first concede the propositions. Yet this most elegant and erudite of all philosophers is not much attacked when he asserts that there are three types of goods. But then everyone reproaches him, first for the book he wrote about the happy life, in which he offers many arguments why the man who is stretched on the rack or tortured cannot be happy. In this book he is also alleged to have said that the happy life cannot ascend to the breaking wheel.[557] He does not say anything that precisely matches this, but his words carry the same general meaning.

If I've conceded that bodily pain is evil, and that shipwreck of fortune is an evil, should I be frustrated with him for saying that not all good men are happy, since those things he counts as evils can happen to all good men? Theophrastus is condemned in the books and schools of all philosophers because, in his treatise *Callisthenes*, he praised this sentence:

Fortune governs the life of man, not wisdom.[558]

---

[557] I.e., torture is incompatible with the happy life. The reference is to the punishment of being "broken on the wheel," in which the victim mounted a public scaffold where he would endure stages of bone-breaking tortures using a spoked "breaking wheel." This mode of execution was used from ancient until early modern times; its last recorded use was in Prussia in 1841.

[558] Tischer speculates that this may be a line from Ennius's *Penthesilea*.

No statement more despondent, we are told, has ever escaped the mouth of a philosopher. This is indeed correct, but I don't think anything could have been more logically stated. For if there is a measure of good in the body, and a measure outside the body in chance and fortune, isn't it appropriate for fortune—which is the master of things that both pertain to the body and are external to it—to have more influence, instead of human action?

Or do we prefer to fall in line with Epicurus's opinion? He often expresses high-minded views, and he does not fuss too much about consistency and lucidity in his pronouncements. He extols the desirability of a modest, simple way of life. This sentiment is certainly appropriate for a philosopher, but only if said by Socrates or Antisthenes,[559] not if it comes from the mouth of someone who teaches that pleasure is the ultimate good. He denies that anyone can live agreeably unless he also lives honestly, wisely, and justly. Nothing could be more grand, or more worthy of philosophy—if only he had not judged this same phrase (i.e., "honestly, wisely, and justly") by the measuring-rod of pleasure.

What is better than the expression "very little fortune intervenes in the life of the wise man"? But does someone say this who, once he has announced that pain is not only the greatest evil but also the sole evil, can endure over his entire body the most terrible pains at the same time he blusters most intensely against fortune? The same idea is stated in better words by Metrodorus. He says, "I have grabbed you, fortune, and have seized and blocked all your routes of entry, so that you cannot influence me." This would be a high-minded statement if it had come from Aristo of Chios[560] or Zeno the Stoic, who regarded only what was morally corrupt as evil. But *you*, Metrodorus—the man who restricts all good to the body's viscera and to the marrow of human bones, and who defines the supreme good as a robust condition of the body and a confident hope of its longevity—have *you* blocked fortune's routes of entry? In what way have you done this? A "good" like this could be taken from you at any time.

10. Yet the uninformed are led astray by these ideas. And due to the influence of such opinions, the number of uninformed individuals

---

[559] Antisthenes (c. 446 B.C.—c. 366 B.C.), Greek philosopher and student of Socrates.
[560] Aristo of Chios (fl. 260 B.C.), Stoic philosopher.

is very great. He who wishes to debate accurately should evaluate not what each philosopher says, but what each one should say. Consider the view that we have taken up in this debate: we want all good men to be happy at all times. When I say "good men," it is obvious what I mean by this phrase. We say men are "good" and "wise" when they are instructed and adorned with all the virtues. Let us consider who are said to be happy. I think the "happy" are those who are surrounded by good, and experience no trace of evil. No other significance should attach to the word "happy" when we say it, except a bountiful aggregation of goods and an absolute disengagement from evils.

Virtue cannot achieve this, if there is any good besides itself. For a furious tempest of evils will enter one's life, if we consider evils such things as poverty, nameless obscurity, debasement, solitude, loss of one's possessions, severe bodily pain, loss of one's health, lameness, blindness, the ruin of one's country, exile, and finally slavery. The wise man can find himself in any of these disasters—and even more calamities could be listed than just these. Chance allows them to happen, and random accidents can indeed intervene in the life of the wise man. But if these are evils, who can assure us that the wise man will always be happy, since he can be enmeshed in all of them at one time?

Therefore I do not easily concur with my friend Brutus, nor with the teachers we studied under, nor those ancient thinkers Aristotle, Speusippus,[561] Xenocrates,[562] and Polemo.[563] They consider all the things I listed above to be evils, while saying that the wise man is always happy. And if this distinguished and noble title[564] pleases them—most worthy in the cases of Pythagoras, Socrates, and Plato— let them induce the mind to look down on those things that captivate them with splendor: strength, health, beauty, wealth, honors, and power. And let them regard as nothing the things that are their opposites. Then they will be able to declare, with the loudest voice, that they fear neither the blows of fortune, nor the opinions of other people, nor pain or poverty; and that they see all things as located within

---

[561] Speusippus (c. 408 B.C.—c. 339 B.C.), Platonic philosopher and successor to Plato at the Academy in Athens.
[562] Xenocrates of Chalcedon (c. 396 B.C.—c. 314 B.C.), Platonic philosopher and scholarch of the Academy from about 339 to 314 B.C.
[563] Polemo of Athens (?—c. 270 B.C.), student of Xenocrates and scholarch of the Academy from about 314 to 270 B.C.
[564] Being called wise.

themselves; and that there is nothing outside their control that they consider good.[565]

Nor can I permit them under any circumstances to say things appropriate for a great and distinguished man, and identify as good and evil the same things as would society's vulgar multitude. Epicurus springs up, intensely moved by such glory. It seems to him that, if it pleases the gods, the wise man is always happy. He is captivated by the nobility of this idea—but he would never say this if he actually listened to himself. What makes less sense than a situation where a man who teaches that pain is either the greatest evil or the sole evil, believes at the same time that a wise man would cry out "How delightful this is!" when he is being tormented by pain? Philosophers should be evaluated not by single statements removed from context, but by their continuity and consistency.[566]

11. A. You're persuading me to see things your way. But take care that you yourself are not lacking in consistency.

M. In what way?

A. Because recently I read the fourth book of your treatise *On Moral Ends*. It seemed to me that, when arguing with Cato, you wanted to show something that I indeed approve of, which is that the only difference between Zeno and the Peripatetics is some new phraseology. If this is the case, what reason is there why the Peripatetics would not be allowed to say the same thing, if it follows from Zeno's arguments that virtue possesses great power for obtaining a happy life? In my view we should pay attention to the thing itself, not to words.

M. You are using sealed records against me, and dredging up things I have said or written elsewhere as evidence to impeach me. Take that line with others who argue using established rules. I live on a day-by-day basis. I may say whatever strikes my mind as likely—and for this reason only I am truly free.

Still, as we said a little while ago about consistency, I don't think the question we should be asking right now is whether the view endorsed by Zeno and his follower Aristo is true (i.e., the view that the only good is what is morally right). If this view is true, the question

---

[565] I.e., the only things we should count as "goods" are those things within our control.
[566] A useful adage: *Non igitur singulis vocibus philosophi spectandi sunt, sed ex perpetuitate atque constantia.*

we should be asking is how he constructed the entire question of living happily on virtue alone.

For this reason let us concede this point to Brutus—that the wise man is always happy. He himself will judge the extent to which his arguments agree with each other. Who is more worthy of the glory of this opinion than that man? Still, let us continue to express our belief that the wise man is also the happiest man.

12. And if Zeno of Citium, a foreigner and an unknown wordsmith, appears to have insinuated himself into ancient philosophy, let the full importance of this view be recalled from the authority of Plato. For the idea consistently emerges from Plato's works that nothing should be called good except virtue. In the dialogue *Gorgias*,[567] for example, when Socrates was asked if he thought Perdiccas's son Archelaus[568]—a boy seen as most fortunate—was happy, Socrates said, "I don't know, since I've never had a talk him." "What do you mean! Can't you learn this using some other method?" "Not at all." "So, then, you can't say whether the great king of Persia is happy?" "How could I do this, when I know nothing about how learned he is, or how good a man he is?" "What? Do you think that a happy life is based on that?" "I absolutely believe that the good are happy, and that the evil are miserable." "Is Archelaus therefore miserable?" "If he is unjust, then yes, absolutely."

Doesn't it seem to you that Socrates bases the happy life solely on virtue? What does this same man say in the *Epitaphios*?[569] He says: "For the man in whom all things needed for a happy life are found completely within himself, and who is not forced to hang in nail-biting uncertainty over the good or bad fortune of others, with his wellbeing contingent on someone else's life events—this man has found the way to live the best kind of life. He is that even-tempered man, that strong man, that wise man, who will accept the gain and loss of life's benefits—especially the gain or loss of one's children— and who will obey that ancient rule. He will never be too joyful or too morose, because all his hopes will always be built on himself alone." From this tenet of Plato, then, my entire discussion will be derived, as if extracted from a divine and majestic wellspring.

---

[567] 470d—470e.
[568] Archilaus I of Macedon, who ruled from 413 B.C. to 399 B.C.
[569] An *epitaphios logos* (ἐπιτάφιος λόγος) was a funeral oration. Here it refers to the long speech given in Plato's dialogue *Menexenus*.

13. What could be a better place to start than with our mutual parent, nature? The organisms she has produced—not just animals but also what comes from the soil and depends on its own roots— nature intends to be an ideal representative of its own category. So as for those low-hanging trees and vines that cannot lift themselves higher above the ground, some of them are evergreens, others display no foliage in winter but sprout leaves when warmed by the coming of spring. Nor is there any one of these plants that does not thrive due to some internal motion and the potential of the seeds contained within it, so that it creates flowers, fruits, or berries. And as long as no opposing force impedes these plants, they are perfect in all things, as far as their natural characteristics permit.

Yet the unadulterated power of nature may more readily be seen in the case of animals, since nature has bestowed on them sense. Nature has intended some beasts that can swim to make their habitations in the water; she has wished others that can fly to enjoy the boundless freedom of the air; she has willed others to crawl on the ground, and still others to move with measured steps. Of this multitude of sentient beings, nature has designed a portion to roam in solitude, a portion to congregate in groups, some to behave ferociously, others on the contrary to be gentle, and some to be masked and concealed within the earth. Each variety of these creatures clings to its own function— since it cannot cross over into the life habits of dissimilar animals— and each one conforms to nature's laws.

To every animal, nature has given something special—a unique trait to one here, a unique trait to another there—that serves to differentiate it from others. Each maintains this attribute as its own possession, and does not abandon it. Nature has given man something far more excellent—although the word "excellent" should be used in connection with things that can be meaningfully compared. For the human soul emanates from the divine mind; and, if it is right for me to speak this way, it can be compared with nothing else except God. If this soul has been so cultivated, and if its sight has been so nurtured, that it is not confused by the deceptions of life, then a fully developed mind will be the result. By this we mean absolute reason, which is equivalent to virtue. If everything is happy that lacks nothing and is complete and abundant in its particular kind, and if this is the characteristic sign of virtue, then without doubt all men in possession of virtue are happy.

Indeed I find myself here concurring with Brutus—that is, with Aristotle, Xenocrates, Speusippus, and Polemo. To me it seems also that men who possess virtue are uncommonly happy. For a man who is confident of his own goods, what could be lacking for living a happy life? Or who can be happy who does not have this kind of confidence? But he who divides up goods in three ways must absolutely be lacking in such confidence.

14. How will he be able to be confident in either the strength of the body or the steadiness of fortune? For no one can be happy except when good is stable, fixed, and permanent. So what are the views of these philosophers? It seems to me that a particular aphorism is applicable to them. When some merchant bragged about the number of ships he had sent to every far-flung coast, a Laconian[570] answered skeptically, "A fortune that depends on ropes is not exactly enviable."[571] Is there any doubt that something susceptible to loss should have no place in the category of things that supply a happy life?

For nothing that contributes to building a happy life should dry up, or be subject to physical destruction, or crumble to the earth. He who lives in fear of losing these things will find happiness beyond his grasp. We want, then, the happy man to be secure, unconquerable, enclosed, and protected, so that he remains unaffected not only by small amounts of fear, but by no fear at all. Just as a person is properly said to be "innocent" not when he commits a minor crime, but no crime at all, so we should call "unafraid" not the person who carries a small amount of fear, but rather the one who feels no fear at all. What else could fortitude be, other than a posture of mind that is prepared to face danger, and self-composed when enduring labor and pain, while never allowing fear even to cross one's mind? These capabilities would not exist unless all good were based exclusively on moral goodness.

But how can anyone have that desired and wished-for security who has, or can have, a multitude of evils coming to him? Security is the word I use to describe the absence of anxiety—a condition that forms the basis of a happy life. How will he be able to stand on his own two feet—with self-confidence, pride, and the bearing we expect of a wise man—and regard all things that can happen in life as trivial and insignificant, unless he believes in his heart that everything depends on himself alone? When Philip wrote to the Lacedaemonians, saying that he would impede all their efforts, did

---

[570] Laconia is the region of Greece in which the city of Sparta is located.

[571] *Non sane optabilis quidem ista, rudentibus apta fortuna.*

the Lacedaemonians in response ask him if he could impede them from killing themselves?[572] This ideal man we are looking for—will he not more easily be found with such an inner spirit, than an entire city-state?[573] What do you think?

And if we add temperance to this fortitude we are discussing, so as to moderate all our internal agitations, what could be lacking for living a happy life for someone whose fortitude protects him from anxiety and fear, when temperance will divert him from lust and prevent him from eagerly indulging his passions to excess? I would have demonstrated that virtue could do these things, had they not been adequately explained during our debates of the previous days.

15. So perturbations of the mind cause misery, and mastery of one's feelings brings about a happy life. Perturbation has a twofold path, because anxiety and fear are based on imagined evils, while eagerly desired joy and lust hinge on an erroneous understanding of goods. All of these things, however, clash with reason and level-headed counsel. When you see someone free from, unbothered by, and unconnected to emotional distresses so serious, antagonistic, and at variance with each other, will you doubt that he should be called happy? Yet this is the disposition the wise man always maintains: the wise man is, therefore, always happy.

In addition, everything good is joyous. What is joyous, should be admired and valued. What is admired and valued, is also glorious. If something is glorious, it is surely worthy of praise. What is worthy of praise, is certainly also moral rectitude. Therefore, what is good is moral rectitude. But the things that these other philosophers consider to be good, they do not even call morally right. The only good, then, is moral rectitude. We conclude from this that the happy life is contained only in moral rectitude. *Therefore, those things that someone can enjoy in abundance while remaining miserable, should neither be called goods, nor considered to be goods.*

Do you really doubt that someone who has health, strength, fine physical form, sharp and fully functioning senses—and in addition to this, if you wish, physical agility and speed—then give him riches,

---

[572] A slightly different version of this anecdote is found in Valerius Maximus (VI.4.ext.4). Philip II of Macedon attempted to burden Sparta with harsh restrictions. The Spartans told him that if he insisted on something worse than death, they would prefer to die.

[573] I.e., "Is it not easier to find one man with such an inner spirit, than it is to find an entire city-state of such men?"

honors, military commands, powers, and glory—if the person who has all these things is unjust, intemperate, timid, mediocre in intelligence or utterly stupid, then will you doubt that he should be called miserable? In what way are these things "goods," when a person who has them can still be completely miserable? Let us see whether a happy life should be composed of parts of similar kind, just as a pile of something is composed of grains of its own type.

And if this happens to be true, then it follows that happiness is solely made from good things that are morally right. If happiness is a mix of dissimilar things, then nothing morally right can be made from these things. If moral rectitude is taken away, how can happiness be imagined? For whatever is good, is sought after; whatever is sought after, is surely approved of. Whatever you approve of, must also be considered pleasing and acceptable. Dignity must therefore be granted to this. If this is true, then it must certainly be praiseworthy. We conclude from this, then, that moral rectitude is the only good.

16. If we do not firmly adhere to this view, there will be many things that we must call "good." I omit riches, and do not count them as goods, since any undeserving dolt can own them. The good cannot be possessed by just anyone. I omit aristocratic pedigree, and popular notoriety generated by a consensus of dimwits and dullards. Yet consider minor things, which still should be called goods, such as white teeth, beautiful eyes, attractive color, and the things Anticlea praises while washing Ulysses's feet:

Tenderness of speech, pliability of body.[574]

If we view these things as goods, what will we discover that is considered more important and grand in the seriousness of the philosopher, than in the opinion of the vulgar mob and multitude of imbeciles?[575] "But the Stoics call *excellent* or *preferred* those same things that others call goods." They certainly do, but they deny that

---

[574] Tischer says this verse is from Pacuvius's *Niptra*. See also *Odyssey* XIX.380 *et. seq.*

[575] I.e., if we view these things as goods, what greater accolades can the seriousness of a philosopher merit, than the opinion of the vulgar mob.

a happy life is completed with these things. These other philosophers, however, believe there is no happy life without them—and if it *is* happy, they deny that it can be extremely happy. We want it to be extremely happy, and this is proved for us by that conclusion of Socrates.

This was how Socrates, that architect of philosophy, made his point: just as each individual mind is inclined, so is the man himself; as the man himself is inclined, so is his way of speaking; actions are similar to speech; and one's life is similar to one's actions. The inclination of a good man's mind is praiseworthy, and thus the good man's life is praiseworthy. It is morally right, then, because it is praiseworthy. It follows from this that the lives of good men are happy.

Alas, so it is, may we have the trust of gods and men! Hasn't enough been understood from our previous debates here? Or was it only for the sake of idle diversion and consuming our spare time, that we've argued that the wise man is always free from all disturbances of the mind (which I call perturbations), and that wise man's mind is imbued with a most serene peace?

The man, therefore, who is temperate, resolute, fearless, without anxiety, without any yearning, and without lust—isn't this man happy? But the wise man always maintains this disposition: therefore he is always happy. How can a good man not evaluate everything that he does and feels by what is considered praiseworthy? He evaluates everything against the measuring-stick of "living happily." Therefore, the happy life is praiseworthy. And nothing is praiseworthy without virtue. Thus the happy life is achieved with virtue.

17. And therefore we also conclude this: there is nothing in a miserable life that is laudable or deserving of glory, nor is there anything laudable or deserving of glory in a life that is neither miserable nor happy. Yet in some lives we find something praiseworthy, deserving of glory, and truly meritorious, as in the case of Epaminondas:

> Stripped away by my guidance was the Laconian renown,[576]

---

[576] Words inscribed on the statue of Epaminondas at Thebes. *See* Pausanias IX.15. The reference is to Epaminondas's famous defeat of the Spartans at Leuctra in 371 B.C.

and in the case of Africanus:

> From the rising sun over the swamps of Maeotis,
> There is no man who can match my deeds.[577]

If there really is such a thing as a happy life, it is deserving of glory, praiseworthy, and meritorious—there is nothing else that should be praised or considered meritorious. Once this has been accepted, you know what follows from it. Unless this life (which is at the same time morally right) is also a happy life, then there must be something better than the happy life. Certainly they will concede that what is morally right is better. Thus there will be something better than the happy life—and can anything more perverse be said than this? Well, what do you think?

When they concede that there is enough power in the vices to make life miserable, shouldn't it be conceded that virtue has the *same* power to make a happy life? For contraries are the logical consequences of contraries.[578] At this point I ask what descriptive power there may be in the well-known "balance of Critolaus."[579] On one balance of his scale he places the goods of the mind, and on the other balance he places the goods of the body and other external goods. Comparing the two, he concludes that the balance holding the goods of the mind outweighs the other to such an extent that even if the world's lands and seas were added to the opposing balance, it would still make no difference.

18. So then what is stopping either this man, or that most prominent of philosophers, Xenocrates—who magnifies virtue so much, while neglecting and dismissing all else—from placing not just the happy life in virtue, but also the *extremely* happy life in virtue? Unless one does this, the result will be the ruination of the virtues. For the man who succumbs to anxiety must also succumb to fear, for fear

---

[577] The lines are from Ennius.
[578] *Contrariorum enim contraria sunt consequentia.* I.e., opposite consequences follow from things that are contrary to each other.
[579] Critolaus the Peripatetic was the third ambassador (along with Diogenes the Stoic and Carneades the Academic) sent by the Athenians to Rome (*see above* IV.3).

is the troubled expectation of future anxiety. He who is likely to succumb to fear is also vulnerable to dread, timidity, panic, and faintheartedness. It is as if he is waiting to be defeated now and then. And he does not believe that the famous saying of Atreus applies to him:

Let them take care in life to remain ignorant of defeat.[580]

But the kind of man we are referring to will be crushed, as I have said. Not only will he be crushed, but he will also become a slave. We want virtue always to remain free, always unvanquished: if things were any other way, virtue would be destroyed. If virtue provides enough assistance for living a good life, then it also provides enough assistance for living a happy one.

Certainly virtue is enough for us to live fearlessly. And if it is enough for us to live without fear, it is also enough for us to live with a great soul: indeed, in a way that we are terrified of nothing and always remain undefeated. It follows from this that there is nothing that causes regret, nothing that is lacking, and nothing that hinders us. Everything happens smoothly, perfectly, and prosperously, and therefore happily. But virtue can be enough for living bravely; therefore, it is enough for living happily. Just as foolishness never believes it has acquired enough, even after obtaining what it covets, so wisdom is always satisfied with what it has, and never has cause to regret anything.

19. Do you think there was a similarity between the one consulship of Caius Laelius, which happened only after he had been electorally defeated once before (when a wise and good man, which he certainly was, is neglected at the ballot-box, it is not the people being disregarded by the good consul, but instead the good consul being disregarded by the people)—nevertheless, if you had the ability to choose, would you prefer to be consul once, like Laelius, or four times, like Cinna?[581] I have no doubt about how you will respond—so I know I am talking to the right person. I would not direct

---

[580] A line apparently, according to Tischer, from Accius's *Atreus*.
[581] This sentence is equally unwieldy in the original.

this question to anyone else. Someone else might say that not only would he choose four consulships over one, but that he would rather have one day of Cinna's life than entire ages of a great many distinguished men.

Laelius, if he had touched anyone with so much as a finger, would have paid the price. But Cinna ordered his colleague, the consul Cnaeus Octavius, to be beheaded. Publius Crassus and Lucius Caesar,[582] men of the highest nobility whose virtues had been recognized both at home and in military affairs, were also killed. So was Marcus Antonius,[583] the most eloquent public speaker I ever heard, and Caius Caesar, who I believe to have been a true paragon of humanity, wit, charm, and refinement. Was the person who killed these men happy? Just the opposite, as I see it. He seems miserable not only because of *what* he did, but because he did it in a way that was *permissible*. Yet no one is permitted to commit moral offenses. Here we stumble due to an error of speech, for we say that one is permitted to do what is within his power to do.

Was Caius Marius happier when he shared the glory of defeating the Cimbri with his colleague Catulus?[584] Catulus was practically another Laelius, for he looked very much like him. Or was Marius happier when, as victor in the civil war, he responded furiously "Let him die!" not just once but multiple times to Catulus's friends who were trying to intervene on his behalf? And in this situation, he who submitted to these abominable words was happier than the person who so wickedly issued them. For it is better to yield to an injustice than to commit one. It was better to quicken one's pace a bit to reach death that was drawing near, as Catulus chose to do, than to behave like Marius and, by killing such a man, ruin the legacy of six consulships and dishonor the last years of his life.[585]

---

[582] L. Julius Caesar Strabo, consul in 90 B.C., and brother of the later-named Caius Julius Caesar Strabo. These deaths are discussed in more detail in *De Oratore* III.3, where Crassus is said to have died by his own hand. Cn. Octavius, P. Crassus, and L. Caesar were victims of Marius's purge of 87 B.C.

[583] Other ancient sources attribute his death to Marius.

[584] Referring to the defeat of the Cimbri at the Battle of Vercellae in 101 B.C. Caius Marius and Quintus Lutatius Catulus held joint command. Marius would eventually serve six full terms as consul.

[585] Catulus fell out with Marius and sided with Sulla's party in the conflict between Marius and Sulla (88 B.C.—87 B.C.). When Marius returned to power, Catulus died by his own hand rather than face retribution.

20. Dionysius, who was twenty-five years of age when he came to power, ruled as tyrant over the people of Syracuse for thirty-eight years. How beautiful a city, and how endowed with wealth was this polity, that he held in the grip of his absolute control! Although the testimony of reliable writers tells us that this man was quite temperate in his manner of life, as well as diligent and industrious in carrying out his designs, he nevertheless had an immoral and unjust nature. As everyone who understands the truth knows, the necessary consequence of this was that he was extremely miserable. For even when he believed he was capable of anything, he still could not obtain the very things he most desired.

He came from a good lineage and was born into an honorable station (although in this regard historians have provided conflicting information). While he enjoyed many good relationships with his peers and an easy familiarity with his relatives, and while he was amorously linked with some young men in the custom of the Greeks, he trusted none of them. He entrusted his personal security to slaves he picked from wealthy families and whose servile names he changed, as well as to assorted immigrants and uncultured barbarians. And so, as a result of his unjust longing for domination, he had practically walled himself within a veritable prison. Indeed, in order not to entrust his neck to a barber, he taught his daughters how to give him a shave. Bound to this degrading and pathetic chore, they trimmed their father's hair and shaved his whiskers as little female barbers.

Yet when these same girls grew to adulthood, he relieved them of the iron razor and directed them to scorch his beard and hair with hot walnut shells. He had two wives, Aristomache from his own city, and Doris of Locris. He would call on them at night, so that he could observe and investigate everything beforehand. He circumscribed his sleeping chamber with a wide trench, and placed over this trench a small wooden bridge to permit crossings; this walkway he would remove as often as he shut his chamber door.

Since he did not dare stand on a speaker's platform to address the public, his habit was to deliver speeches when positioned on a high citadel. When he wanted to play a ball game—as he often did with great enthusiasm—and set down his tunic, it is said that he handed his gladius to a youth who was very dear to him. When a friend jokingly said to Dionysius, "Well, certainly here is someone you can trust your life with," and the youth snickered at the remark, the tyrant had them both put to death. The friend was executed for having revealed the way to murder Dionysius, and the boy for having accepted the comment with a smirk. The tyrant felt great anguish for having done this. It was in fact the worst grief he had ever experienced, for he had slain that which he loved most affectionately. In such ways do the passions of volatile men clash unrelentingly with each other: when you yield to one, you must then fight against another. Yet this tyrant himself declared how happy he was.

21. When one of Dionysius's toadies, a man named Damocles, expounded on the tyrant's military forces, resources, the majesty of his rule, the extent of his assets, and the magnificence of his official residences, and denied that anyone had ever been happier than he was, Dionysius replied, "Since this life seems so appealing to you, Damocles, do you want to taste it yourself and experience my fortune?" When Damocles answered that he would indeed like to experience this, Dionysius told him to sit on a golden couch with beautiful woven coverings made with the most finely detailed artistry. He garnished this with some furniture pieces holding engraved gold and silver articles of table service. Then he ordered boys selected for their attractive physical appearances to take up positions at his table and wait on him. They were to watch for his nod and attend diligently to his needs.

Scented oils and wreaths were there, too, and incense was burned. The tables were piled high with the most desirable dishes, and Damocles saw himself as the most fortunate of men. In the middle of this arrangement Dionysius ordered a shining sword, suspended by a horsehair, to be lowered from the ceiling, so that it dangled over the neck of the happy man. He looked at neither the attractive servants, nor the finely-crafted tableware. He did not extend his hand to take what was on the dinner table. Then the wreaths fell from their positions. Finally Damocles begged the tyrant to let him leave, because now he did not want to be "happy." Isn't it true that Dionysius apparently declared that someone who always has some terror dangling over his head can never be happy?

But at that point it was impossible for Dionysius to redirect himself back to justice, and to give back freedom and the rule of law to his people. For as a reckless youth he had trapped himself by his actions; he had committed so many grievous mistakes that, if he ever began to act reasonably, he would never be safe.[586]

---

[586] I.e., he was riding a tiger and could never get off, lest the animal kill him.

22. Just how intensely Dionysius longed for friends—the possible betrayal of which he nevertheless profoundly dreaded—he revealed in an incident involving two Pythagoreans. Dionysius was holding one of them as the personal guarantor of a death sentence. The other Pythagorean appeared at the mandated hour of execution in order to release the guarantor from the obligation of his bond.[587] Dionysius told the two men, "How I wish I could be counted as a third friend to both of you!" How terribly sad was his decision to live a life without friends, to deny himself the nourishment of their companionship, and to renounce any chance of conversational intimacy! How particularly sad, indeed, for someone who had been educated since boyhood, and who was versed in the liberal arts!

In fact we are told that Dionysius was an ardent musician, as well as a tragic poet. How good he was is irrelevant. I am not sure why, but in this type of endeavor, more so than in others, each man regards his own work as beautiful. I have never known a poet in my life— and I was a friend of Aquinius[588]—who did not believe his own compositions to be the best. This is how it is with them: "Your creations delight you, and mine delight me." But to return to Dionysius: he cut himself off from all refinement and human life. He sought the company of fugitives, criminal types, and barbarians. He counted no one a friend who was worthy of freedom or who had the slightest desire to be free.

23. I will not compare Dionysius's life—and I can think of no life more hideous, miserable, and detestable—with the lives of men like Plato or Archytas, who were certainly men of towering wisdom and learning. I will, however, stir up from the sand and from his mathematician's rod a lowly little man from the same city who lived there many years later: Archimedes.[589] When I served as quaestor, I was able to locate his grave. It was blocked off on all sides and completely covered with underbrush and dense vegetation. It was unknown to the Syracusans, who denied any knowledge of its whereabouts. I was aware of certain verses I had heard were carved on his tomb, which stated that a sphere with a cylinder had been placed on the top of his sepulcher.

---

[587] This is the famous story of Damon and Phintias, also mentioned by Cicero in *On Duties* III.10 and by Val. Max. IV.7.ext.1.

[588] Apparently a notoriously bad poet; a scornful reference appears in Catullus (XIV.18).

[589] Archimedes of Syracuse (c. 287 B.C.—c. 212 B.C.), perhaps the greatest mathematician and scientist of antiquity.

After visually inspecting the entire area—for there are very many tombs at the Agrigentine Gate—I noticed a small pillar projecting slightly above the thickets, on which could be seen the images of a sphere and a cylinder. So I immediately said to the Syracusans—important men of the city were with me at that time—that what I was looking for had been found. Servants were called in with sickles to remove the vegetation and clear the area. When a path to the tomb had been made, we moved closer to the monument's base. The last part of the epigram had worn away, with only the first part remaining legible. Thus one of the noblest and most learned of Greek cities would have remained ignorant of the resting place of one of its most brilliant men, had the site not been identified by a man from Arpinum.[590]

But let us return to where our discussion wandered from its path. Who in the entire world, who has at least some degree of contact with the Muses (that is, with liberal studies and education), would not rather be this mathematician instead of this miserable tyrant? If we look into their habits of living and their actions, we see the mind of one of these men nourished by the complexities of mathematical reason, and delighted by the application of a formidable intellect. This is surely the most gratifying nutriment available to the human mind. The mind of the other man, however, was steeped in killing and injustice, and was tormented by fear both day and night.

Try it yourself, and compare Democritus, Pythagoras, and Anaxagoras with Dionysius of Syracuse. What kingdoms, or what riches, will you value more than the brilliant researches that gave them joy? That best element you are looking for must unquestionably be found in the best part of a man. What in man is better than a mind that is both wise and good? If we want to be happy, this goodness must be enjoyed. But the good of the mind is virtue; the happy life must therefore be maintained with virtue. From this source comes all things that are beautiful, honorable, and distinguished, as I said earlier, but apparently must say again with greater exuberance: and these things are full of joys. Since it is evident that a happy life is found in enduring and bounteous joys, it follows that this happy life is found in moral goodness.

24. So that what we wish to demonstrate may not be based solely on words, we must offer certain pertinent reasons, so to speak, which

---

[590] Cicero's native town was Arpinum; he is referring to himself.

will adapt our thinking to receive the requisite knowledge and understanding. Let us form a conception of a man brilliantly capable of the very best arts. Let us ruminate on this picture, and weigh him our imagination, for a short while. He must be, first of all, a man of marvelous intellect, for virtue does not readily accompany those with languid minds. Secondly, he should be passionately devoted to the pursuit of truth. From this comes that threefold offspring of the mind: *one* concerned with understanding the external world and explaining the laws of nature; *the second* in describing what we should seek and what we should avoid, and in creating a formula for right living; *the third* in judging the consequence of a proposition, and what may conflict with it, in which is found all nuances of debate and sureness of judgment.

With what delight, then, must the mind of the wise man be captivated when he lives with such activities and interests, and devotes his nights to them! When he observes the motions and cycles of the heavens, and sees the innumerable stars set in the sky, moving in harmony with the action of this celestial realm while maintaining their positions, seven others holding to their courses but with great distances between them in the height or lowness of their placements, and yet their roaming motions defining the established and certain tracks of their paths—without doubt, the awareness of this vast celestial edifice urged on the learned men of olden times, and persuaded them to strive for more knowledge and understanding.

From this emerged the systematic scrutiny into the origins and, so to speak, seeds from which all things arose, proliferated, and flourished; the probing into the inception of each type of thing, whether animate or inanimate, articulate or mute; what life and death are; what is the alteration and transformation of one thing into another; the earth's origin, and by what weights it maintains a proper balance; by what subterranean caverns are the seas sustained;[591] and, since all things are pulled downward, by what gravitational force do they move towards the earth's center, which in a spherical body is the lowest point.

25. To the mind immersed day and night in these thoughts, there arrives the Delphic god's precept that the mind should "know itself"

---

[591] Referring to the movement of water through the earth's subterranean cavities. *See* Seneca's *Nat. Quaes.* III.5 and III.2: *Aut stant omnes aquae, aut eunt, aut colliguntur, aut varias habent venas.* ("All waters are stationary, or moving, or collected, or exist in underground cavities").

and sense its connection with the divine mind, from which it is filled with a rapturous joy. Our contemplation of the power and nature of the gods ignites in us a wish to imitate their immortality. Nor does the mind believe it is confined to the brevity of this mortal life, when it clearly sees that, through unavoidable associations, the causes of things are connected with each other. Yet reason and intellect regulate these causes which flow from eternity to eternity. He who observes and contemplates these things, or rather he who directs his vision everywhere, to all the constituent parts and limits of creation—with what tranquility of mind does he in turn regard all human affairs, and those things that are closest to him!

From this arises man's understanding of virtue. The types and parts of the virtues flourish before him; he discovers what nature considers the Ultimate Good and the Ultimate Evil.[592] He learns what all duties should refer back to,[593] as well as the guiding principle that must be adopted to live one's life. When these issues and others like them have been thoroughly examined, what we must conclude—and what in fact was the object of our debate—is that *virtue itself is enough to sustain a happy life.*

The third requirement[594] follows after this. It spreads over and penetrates every part of wisdom. It is what defines something, differentiates between types, connects logical sequences, arrives at proper conclusions, and recognizes what is true from what is false: this is the method and science of disputation. What comes from this—besides a tremendous value in weighing propositions—is an especially noble pleasure, and one that is worthy of wisdom.

But these things are matters for leisure. Let this same wise man direct his attention to the protection of his republic. What could be more exemplary than this, since his prudence instructs him in what is useful for his citizens, his justice lets him misappropriate nothing belonging to the public for himself, and he practices so many remaining various virtues? Add to this the benefit of different friendships, in which cultured men discover the guidance that suits their perspectives and practically harmonizes with them in life, along with the incomparable appeal found in friendship's daily cultivation and nourishment.

---

[592] Topics discussed in great detail in Cicero's *On Moral Ends.*
[593] I.e., what is the purpose of duties.
[594] The third requirement of our wise man, as stated in the first paragraph of V.25 above.

What does a life like this need to make it happier? Fortune herself must give way to a life filled with joys of such plenitude and richness. If rejoicing in such goods of the mind—that is, in such virtues—is happiness, and if all wise men share in these joys, then it must be conceded that they are all happy.

26. A. Even when people are subjected to tortures and torments?

M. Did you think I was only talking about living with violets and roses? Epicurus wears the mask of a philosopher, and bestows this name on himself. Is it permissible for him to say—although indeed, as things are, I commend him for saying it—that there is no time when the wise man, even if he is burned, tortured, or dismembered, cannot announce, "I think this is no problem for me!" When he identifies evil with pain, and evaluates good by the standard of pleasure; when he laughs at our concepts of moral goodness and moral corruption; when he says we are occupied only with words and with spewing meaningless sounds, and that nothing should concern us except what the body feels as either smooth or rough—is all of this permissible?

Is it acceptable for this man, as I said, whose judgment is not much different from that of wild beasts, to forget himself and be contemptuous of fortune, when everything he considers good and evil is in fortune's power? Is it acceptable for him to say he is happy being in the throes of the most terrible tortures and torments—after he has already laid down the rule that not only is pain the worst evil, but the *only* evil?

Neither has Epicurus prepared for himself any remedies to assist in enduring pain, such as developing firmness of mind, the shame of moral corruption, the exercise and the habit of patience, the principles of courage, and a virile strictness. He says he consoles himself only in the remembrance of past pleasures, just as if someone suffering in hot weather, and barely able to endure the heat's intensity, would want to recall immersing himself in the bracing streams of my Arpinum. For I do not see how present evils can be soothed by the recollection of past pleasures. But since Epicurus—who would not be allowed to say this if he wanted to be correct—says that the wise man is always happy, what should be imagined about those who think nothing is desirable—and nothing should be counted as a good—that lacks moral goodness? My proposal is this: let the Peripatetics and the old Academics stop their babbling at some point, and dare to say openly and with a clear voice that a happy life will climb into Phalaris's bull.[595]

27. In fact there are three types of goods. In order for us to slip away from the Stoic snares—which I know I've used more than I normally do—let us affirm that these kinds of goods exist, as long as the goods of the body and external goods lie prostrate on the ground, and are only called good because they are to be favored. The other goods, the divine goods, announce themselves far and wide, and reach as high as the heavens. Why should I describe someone who has acquired these things as only *happy*, and not *extraordinarily happy*?

Yet will a wise man fear pain? For pain is what most opposes our way of thinking. Against our own death and the deaths of our family members, and against anxiety and the other perturbations of the mind, we seem to be adequately equipped and strengthened by our debates of the previous days. Pain appears to be virtue's most bitter adversary. It menaces us with flaming torches. It has the potential to erode our courage, greatness of soul, and patience. Will virtue surrender to pain, then? Will the happy life of the wise and resolute man capitulate to it? O righteous gods, what a contemptible shame!

The boys of Sparta say not a word when their flesh is painfully torn. I personally have seen groups of youths in Lacedaemon fighting with incredible ferocity, using fists, feet, fingernails, even teeth. They would have lost their lives before admitting themselves beaten. And what place is more primitive and untamed than India? Yet those among them who are considered wise men spend their years without clothing, and tolerate without pain the snows of the Hindu Kush[596] and the brutal force of winter. When they consign themselves to the flames, they are consumed by fire without even a murmur. And when the husband of an Indian woman dies, the women—for the men usually have more than one wife—enter into disputes to judge which wife the deceased man loved the most. The wife who prevails happily accompanies her husband to a place on the funeral pyre, escorted by her own relatives. The defeated wife withdraws in sadness.

---

[595] The legendary "bronze bull," an execution device supposed to have been possessed by Phalaris, the tyrant of Acragas in Sicily. It was a hollow bull into which the condemned was placed; a fire was then kindled under it, causing the victim to roast alive.

[596] The term used is *Caucasi nives* ("snows of the Caucasus"). Note that in II.10, Cicero uses the same term for the Caucasus Mountains.

Never has human ritual overcome nature, for nature is always undefeated. We have poisoned our souls by cowering behind protective shelters, by indulging in physical delights, leisure, apathy, and languid idleness; we have enfeebled and degraded our spirits with false beliefs and corrupting behaviors. Who is ignorant of the habits of the Egyptians? Their minds are imbued with contemptible irrationalities; they would sooner endure torture than harm an ibis, a venomous snake, cat, dog, or a crocodile. Even if they have accidentally caused such harm, there is no punishment they would refuse to accept as retribution.

I am talking about human beings. But what about the animals? Do they not endure bitter cold, gnawing hunger, lonely mountain wanderings, and wearying treks through dark forests? Do they not fight for their offspring with such intensity that they receive wounds, and avoid neither attacks nor physical strikes? Here I omit all those things that the ambitious endure for the sake of honor. I omit what those who lust after fame endure for the sake of glory. And I omit what those who burn with passion endure for the sake of lust. Life is full of such cases.

28. Eloquence has had its say. Let us now return to the topic from which our attention was diverted. I say that the happy life will give itself to torments. And in pursuit of justice, temperance, and especially fortitude, greatness of soul, and patience, the happy life will not stop when it looks at the face of the torturer. When all the other virtues go to face torture without fear, it will not pause, as I have said, outside the prison's entrance and front gate. For what could be more shameful, or more degrading, than to be left alone, separated from beautiful escorts? Yet this is impossible under any circumstance: the virtues cannot adhere together without a happy life, nor can a happy life be in harmony without the virtues.

They will not allow the happy life to turn its back on them; they will carry her off with them to whatever pain or torture they themselves might have to face. A mark of the wise man is to do nothing that can cause him regret, or nothing he does not wish to do. It is his practice to do all things graciously, reliably, seriously, and honorably, and not to anticipate anything as if it were certain to happen. It is characteristic of him to be shocked by nothing that happens (that he might see the circumstance as bizarre or new), to refer all things back to his own authority, and to stand by his own judgments. Certainly nothing comes to my mind that could be happier than this.

This conclusion is without doubt easy for the Stoics. For them the ultimate good is to live congenially with nature and in accordance with its rules. This, they say, is not only the wise man's duty, but is something truly within his power to do. In their view, it necessarily follows that when the ultimate good is within the wise man's ability, a happy life is also within his ability. The life of the wise man, therefore, is always made happy. You now have the arguments I believe are the strongest about the happy life—and at the present time they are also the most valid arguments, unless you have a better assertion to make.

29. A. I can't propose anything better. But I do have a request for you, if this is not a problem, since no restrictions limit you to any specific philosophical school—you sip from whatever school those things that for you have the greatest conformity to the truth. A short while ago, you seemed to call on the Peripatetics and the old Academics to have the backbone to say freely, and without hesitation, that wise men are always extremely happy. I want to hear how you believe it is appropriate for them to say this. By falling in line with the conclusions of Stoic logic, you have said much that contradicts their position.

M. Then I will use that freedom which only our school of philosophy is allowed to use. It judges nothing by its own declaration, but involves itself in everything, so that an issue may be evaluated by others on its own qualities, rather than appealing to the authority of an established thinker. It seems you want to know how it is—whatever may be the opinions of the disputing philosophical schools on the ends of good and evil[597]—that virtue is still sufficient protection for a happy life. We hear it was Carneades's frequent habit to discuss this idea. But this issue he was arguing against the Stoics, whom he vigorously attacked. His mind burned with passionate opposition to their teachings.

I myself will discuss this topic with an even temper. For if the Stoics have correctly determined the ends of goods, then the issue is resolved.[598] It must then be true that the wise man is always happy. If we can, let us examine the opinions of the remaining philosophical

---

[597] The text here has only *de finibus*, which for Cicero meant "on moral ends," or "the ends of good and evil," as defined and discussed in his *On Moral Ends* (*De Finibus*).

[598] The Stoic view of the end of goods is found in books III and IV of *On Moral Ends*.

schools, so that this grand concept of the happy life, so to speak, can harmonize with each school's views and doctrines.

30. As I see it, these are the opinions on moral ends that are upheld and defended. In the first place are four simple ones: that there is no good except moral rectitude, as the Stoics advocate; that there is no good except pleasure, as Epicurus claims; that there is no good except the lack of pain, as Hieronymus says; and that there is no good except the enjoyment of nature's primary goods (either all of them or the leading ones), as Carneades contended against the Stoics. These, then, are the simple ones. The others are mixed proposals.

Then there are three kinds of goods: the greatest are the goods of the mind; the second are the goods of the body; the third are external goods, as the Peripatetics and the old Academics do not much differ their usage of this term. Dinomachus and Callipho[599] have joined pleasure with moral goodness; but Diodorus the Peripatetic has connected freedom from pain to moral goodness.[600] These are the views that have some current traction, for the opinions of Aristo, Pyrrho, Erillus,[601] and a few others have faded into obscurity. Let us see what these thinkers can offer us. We will omit the Stoics, whose position I believe I have defended enough.

The position of the Peripatetics has also already been explained—except that Theophrastus, and those who subscribe to his beliefs, abhor pain and shrink from it in a very pathetic way. The rest of them may do what they generally do, which is to exaggerate virtue's dignity and majesty. When they have extolled it to the heavens, as eloquent men are in the habit of doing abundantly, any remaining issues are easily wiped away by comparison and treated with disdain. Those who say that praise should be sought after—even at the price of pain—may not deny that those who have acquired it are happy. Although they may be entangled in certain evils, this name of "happy" covers a wide area in what it connotes.

31. Commerce is said to be rewarding, and tilling the land is said to be fruitful—not if one of these activities always sidesteps every

---

[599] Two philosophers (Callipho is also known as Calliphon) mentioned in *On Moral Ends* (V.8.21) for the "joining of pleasure to moral goodness"; see also *On Duties* III.33.119.

[600] Diodorus of Tyre, who succeeded Critolaus as head of the Peripatetic school in Athens around 118 B.C.; he is also mentioned in *On Moral Ends* (V.8.21).

[601] Erillus (or Herillus) of Carthage (fl. 3rd cent. B.C.), Stoic philosopher and student of Zeno of Citium. Criticized by Cicero in *On Moral Ends* (IV.15.40) for "creating two separate Supreme Goods."

possible harm, or if the other always avoids any disaster from the weather, but because in each activity there is usually some profit to be realized. So can life rightly be called happy, not only if it is completely made up of goods, but if it is *usually* made up of an *ample* number of good things. It follows from the reasoning of these thinkers that a happy life will accompany virtue even to torture. On the authority of Aristotle, Xenocrates, Speusippus, and Polemo, the happy life would even descend, accompanied by virtue, into Phalaris's bull. Neither threats nor enticing favors will corrupt the happy life to a point where it deserts virtue.

The views of Callipho and Diodorus will be the same. For both of them embrace moral goodness to such an extent that they believe everything lacking it must be placed far behind it. The rest seem to be more hemmed in with these concepts, but still manage to swim to safety: here we mean Epicurus, Hieronymus, and whoever else chooses to defend the abandoned Carneades. There is not one of them who doesn't believe the mind to be the judge of true goods, and can teach him how to look down on those things that only appear to be good or evil. For what you think is the situation with Epicurus will also be the situation with Hieronymus and Carneades and—by Hercules!—all the rest of these thinkers.

For who is not prepared enough against death or pain? If it is acceptable to you, I will start with the man we call soft, the man we call a hedonist. What do you think? The man who calls the day of his death happy—does this man seem to you to fear death or pain? When he is stricken by the greatest pains, he holds those pains in check by the memory and recollection of his own discoveries. And he does not do this in such a way that it seems to be some extemporaneous invention. His understanding of death is to believe that sense-perception ends with the destruction of life; and that which lacks sensation is unrelated to anything we can judge.

He also has certain rules of guidance on the subject of pain. Its magnitude is alleviated by its brevity, and its duration by its mildness. When it is time to confront the two things that cause the most sorrow, are those pretentious thinkers[602] better equipped to deal with them than Epicurus? Or do Epicurus and the rest of the philosophers seem insufficiently prepared to confront all other things believed to

---

[602] Referring to the Stoics.

be evils? Who has no fear of poverty? Yet not one philosopher experiences such fear.

32. Indeed, with how little is this man satisfied![603] No one has spoken more about the simple way of life. When a person is far away from all those things that kindle a love of money, or from love, ambition, or things related to daily financial obligations, why would he much desire money? Or why would he even bother worrying about it? Was the Scythian Anacharsis able to ignore money? Are the philosophers of our own country not able to do it? One of his surviving letters is worded as follows: "Anacharsis sends his greetings to Hanno. I have the simple Scythian vestment for my garb, the tough skin of my feet for my shoes, the earth for my bed, and hunger for my morsel.[604] I live on milk, cheese, and meat. So you may come to me in tranquility. Give those gifts which you love so much to your own citizens or to the immortal gods."

Regardless of the school, almost all philosophers have been able to exhibit this same spirit, except those whose debased natures have deflected them from the use of proper reason. When Socrates once saw a large amount of gold and silver carried in a formal procession, he remarked, "How much is here that I do not desire!" When envoys from Alexander brought fifty talents to Xenocrates—which was an enormous sum in those days, especially in Athens—he brought the envoys to a dinner at the Academy. He set before them, without any pomp or ostentation, a quantity of food that was enough to be adequate.[605] When the envoys asked Xenocrates the next day to whom he wished the money to be paid, he said, "What? Didn't you realize from yesterday's little dinner that I don't need money?" When he saw they were dispirited, he agreed to take thirty minas, so as not to appear that he was spurning the king's largesse.

Diogenes, however, was more free with his tongue, as would befit a Cynic. When Alexander asked Diogenes to tell him what he needed, the Cynic replied, "Right now, just move away a little bit from the sun." Evidently, the king was blocking Diogenes's desire to sunbathe! In fact Diogenes was also in the habit of debating with the King of Persia about how much better off he was, in terms of his life

---

[603] I.e., Epicurus.
[604] The word used is *pulpamentum*, which is "a small piece of meat, etc., used to start a meal" (Ox. Lat. Dict.). "Appetizer" would also be acceptable here.
[605] And no more than adequate.

and fortune, than the monarch. He himself, Diogenes would say, wanted for nothing, yet nothing would ever be enough to satisfy the king. He felt no desire for the pleasures that would never be able to satisfy the king. And the king would never be able to obtain the pleasures known to Diogenes.

33. I think you know that Epicurus has identified separate types of desires. He has probably not done with complete precision, but his classification nevertheless is useful. He states that the three types of desires are as follows: natural and necessary, natural and non-necessary, and neither of these two.[606] Almost nothing is needed to satisfy the necessary pleasures, for the fruits of nature are easily procurable. The second category of desires, says Epicurus, is neither difficult to satisfy, nor difficult to be without. He thought the third category should be completely tossed aside, because these pleasures were absolutely worthless. Not only were they not necessary, but they were not even affiliated with nature.

Here the Epicureans engage in a great deal of debate. One by one, they demean the pleasures that are in the categories they dislike; yet they still seek an abundance of them. The obscene types of pleasures, which they spend a great deal of time discussing, are (they say) easy to do, common, and readily accessible. They think that if nature requires these things, they should not be judged by origin, position, or hierarchy; instead they should be evaluated by appearance, age, and form. Abstaining from these pleasures, they insist, is not problematic at all, should it be necessitated by one's health, responsibilities, or public reputation. Pleasure of this sort is altogether desirable, as long as there is no nuisance attached to it, but it never confers a real advantage.

Everything that Epicurus teaches about pleasure comes down to this. He thinks pleasure is always something to be desired and sought after for its own sake, simply because it is pleasure. And by the same reasoning, pain should always be evaded simply because it is pain. Thus a wise man should use pleasure and pain in mutual compensation, so that he avoids pleasure if indulging in it will produce greater pain, and tolerates pain when doing so produces greater pleasure.

All pleasing things, although evaluated by the body's senses, are still referred to the mind. So while the body rejoices during the time

---

[606] *Neutrum*, neither the first nor the second category.

it experiences present pleasure, the mind perceives this present pleasure equally with the body. The mind foresees pleasure that is coming, and does not allow past pleasure to dwindle. Therefore, since the expectation of pleasures anticipated in the future is seamlessly united with the memory of pleasures enjoyed in the past, the wise man will always have a stream of continuous and perpetual pleasures.

34. Similar ways of thinking are employed with regard to food. The magnificence and expense of banquets are looked on with contempt, because nature is satisfied with little finery. Who does not see, in fact, that all these things are flavored with necessity? When Darius as a fugitive drank turbid water contaminated by dead bodies, he announced that he had never imbibed anything so satisfying.[607] Before this it seems he had never been truly thirsty when drinking. Neither had Ptolemy[608] been truly hungry when he ate. When he was traveling through Egypt unaccompanied by his entourage, he was given plain bread in a local dwelling—and it seemed to him that nothing was more agreeable to him than this simple bread.

We are told that Socrates would walk strenuously until the evening hours. When he was asked why he chose to exert himself like this, he said that by walking he was buying hunger to accompany his evening meal, in order to make it taste better. What do you think? Aren't we aware of the Lacedaemonians' food at their communal meals? When the tyrant Dionysius[609] ate with them, he stated that their well-known black broth—which formed the principal part of the meal—was not agreeable to him. The man who had prepared the broth then said to him, "That isn't surprising, for there was no flavoring for your broth." "What flavoring are you talking about?" asked Dionysius. The cook replied, "Hard work on the hunt, perspiration, a run to the Eurotas, hunger, and thirst. The meals of the Lacedaemonians are flavored with these things."

This principle may be observed not only in human customs, but also in the habits of wild beasts. When something is tossed at them that is not foreign to their nature, they are satisfied with it and seek nothing more. There are some entire states, conditioned by custom, that find satisfaction in the practice of parsimony. Among them are

---

[607] Darius III of Persia was defeated by Alexander the Great near Erbil, Iraq in 331 B.C. and then fled.
[608] It is not clear which Ptolemaic king of Egypt is referred to.
[609] Dionysius I of Syracuse (c. 432 B.C.—367 B.C.)

the Lacedaemonians whom I just now referred to. The food of the Persians is discussed by Xenophon, who says that they add nothing but cress[610] to their bread.[611] Yet if nature wants something more gratifying than this, what an incredible quantity is produced by land and trees in accessible supply, and with such wonderful taste! To this we should add dryness, which is a consequence of moderation in eating. Then add soundness of health. Compare this with sweating, burping individuals, packed to capacity with food like overfed cattle. You will then understand that those who chase pleasure most ardently achieve it least of all, and that the agreeableness of food is found in the wanting of it, not in being satiated with it.

35. Timotheus[612] had a distinguished reputation in Athens and was the state's most important man. It is said that he once ate with Plato, and was very pleased with the banquet. When he saw him the next day, Timotheus said, "Your meals are truly pleasing, not only when they happen, but also on the day after." Why is this true? It is because we cannot think competently when stuffed with large quantities of food and drink. There is a wonderful letter of Plato[613] to the family members of Dion, in which essentially these words are written: "When I came to this place, the well-known 'happy life,' with its bounteous Italian and Syracusan meals, did not please me at all: being stuffed with food twice per day, never spending the night alone, and all those other things that go along with the kind of life that will never make a man wise, but will in fact make him much less restrained. With what nature, indeed, is a man so marvelously able to control himself?"[614]

How then can a life be pleasing when it has no prudence, or no moderation? From this we may perceive the error of the extremely opulent Syrian king Sardanapalus.[615] He ordered the following words to be inscribed on his tomb:

---

[610] *Nasturtium*, which is a kind of cress. The Ox. Lat. Dict. speculates it may be garden cress (*Lepidium sativum*), or possibly watercress.

[611] Xenophon's *Cyropaedia* I.2.8.

[612] Timotheus (?—354 B.C.), Athenian general and statesman. *See* Cornelius Nepos's *Lives of the Great Commanders.*

[613] The seventh of the pseudo-Platonic letters (326b).

[614] I.e., "it would take an amazing amount of self-restraint to remain temperate in such a situation."

[615] Son of the Assyrian king Anacyndaraxes. Sardanapalus's identity is uncertain; there is no Assyrian king of this name, but he may be Assur-danin-pal, son of Shalmaneser III.

These things I have: what I have eaten and what
has sated me,
And the joys of lust I have experienced.
But the many splendid other things I once owned
Have all been left behind.[616]

"What other statement," said Aristotle, "could you carve on the tomb of an ox, not on the tomb of a king?" He says that in death he has those things that, when he was alive, he did not possess any longer than when he was enjoying them. Then why are riches desired? Or what is it about poverty that does not permit us to be happy? Statues, I believe; you devote yourself to pictures. If there is someone who takes pleasure in them, can't men of slender resources derive more joy from them than those who are wealthy?

For in our city there is a great abundance of all these things exhibited for the public. Those who own such things privately do not see so many. They see them infrequently, when they visit their rural villas. And something still vaguely gnaws at them when they recall how they acquired these items. If I wished to defend the case for poverty, there would not be enough hours in the day. The point is obvious: every single day, nature reminds us just how few things she truly needs, and how easy it is to acquire them.

36. Will lack of fame, or commonplaceness, or unpopularity prohibit a wise man from being happy? Take care lest the adoration of the mob, and the glory you seek, prove to be more impediments than pleasures. Certainly it was vain of our friend Demosthenes to say he was happy to hear what was whispered by a foolish woman carrying water, as they often do in Greece. She muttered in a low voice to another person, "Here is the famous Demosthenes!"[617] What could be more unimportant than this? But what a great orator he was! Evidently he had learned how to speak in front of others, but not to talk much with himself.

We must understand, then, that popular glory should not be sought for its own sake, nor should we be afraid of living our lives in relative obscurity. Democritus said, "I came to Athens, and not a single soul knew me." How resolute and purposeful, this man who

---

[616] *See* Strabo XIV.5.9 for a reference to this funerary inscription.
[617] This anecdote is also mentioned in Pliny (*Letters* IX.23).

actually takes pride in being *without* glory! Should those who play the flute and the lyre be guided by their own judgment, rather than that of the crowd, when they control the cadence of their songs? Should the wise man, endowed with a much more elevated kind of knowledge, not search for what is most true, but for what the vulgar mob wants him to search for? Is there anything more idiotic than to believe that those whom you scorn individually as uncouth peons, will even amount to anything when lumped together as a group?

This wise man we speak of will look down on our meaningless ambitions, and will rebuff the honors that the public voluntarily offers him. But one does not know *how* to look down on these things, until one begins to feel regret.[618] The natural philosopher Heraclitus writes the following anecdote about Hermodorus, the most important man in Ephesus.[619] He says that all the Ephesians should be punished with death because, when they expelled Hermodorus from their city, they said this: "Let no man among us outshine anyone else; and if such a man emerges, let him be somewhere else, and among other people." Doesn't this same sentiment manifest itself with every group of people? Don't people malign all preeminence of virtue? What do you think? Consider Aristides—I prefer to use Greek examples than those from our own country—wasn't he expelled from his homeland because he was excessively just?

Those who do not get involved with the general public at all—what a great deal of trouble they are free of! What is sweeter than having the leisure to engage in literary pursuits? Here I am talking about the kinds of writings that teach us about the limitless extent of things and of nature, and in our own physical world, the writings that inform us about the sky, the lands, and the seas.

37. Once an individual looks on public approbation with contempt, and also views money with contempt, what else should he be afraid of? I imagine it would be exile—something counted among the greatest of evils. If it is evil because the goodwill of the people is harmed and violated, then we already explained a little while ago

---

[618] I.e., until one begins to feel regret for having accepted them in the first place. *Nos autem eos nescimus, ante quam poenitere coepit, contemnere.* This guilt-laden sentence seems to reflect Cicero's remorse at having so ardently chased honors and glory as a younger man.

[619] Hermodorus of Ephesus (fl. 4th cent. B.C.), a philosopher and original member of the Platonic Academy. He apparently authored a work on Plato; *see* Diog. Laert. II.160 and III.6.

how contemptible that is. But if it is miserable to be away from one's country, then the provinces are full of miserable people—of which only a few return to their original homes. Here someone may say, "But exiles have to forfeit their property." So what? Haven't we spoken enough already on bearing the burden of poverty?

If we examine the natural truth about exile itself—and not the dishonor of one's name—we may rightly ask: how different is it from living somewhere else as a permanent expatriate? The noblest philosophers have spent their years in this very situation: Xenocrates, Crantor, Arcesilas, Lacydes, Aristotle, Theophrastus, Zeno, Cleanthes, Chrysippus, Antipater, Carneades, Clitomachus, Philo, Antiochus, Panaetius, and Posidonius, as well as innumerable others who, once they left their homelands, never returned. Here you may say, "But I mean without *dishonor*." But can exile dishonor the wise man? This entire discussion is about the wise man, and this could not justly happen to him. For it is not proper to console someone who has been justly exiled.

Lastly, in dealing with all accidents of fate, the plan of those who evaluate the goals they pursue in life by "pleasure" is the easiest, so that they can live happily wherever this is furnished. Thus the words of Teucer can accommodate every situation:

Your country is wherever things are good.[620]

For example, when Socrates was asked which country was his own, he answered "the world." He considered himself a resident and citizen of the entire world. And what about Titus Albucius?[621] As an exile in Athens, didn't he devote himself to philosophical studies in a most contented spirit? Yet this good fortune would never have occurred if he had obeyed Epicurus's rules and remained politically inactive in the republic. In what way was Epicurus happier living in his own country, than was Metrodorus, who was living in Athens?

---

[620] A line from the poet Pacuvius's play *Teucer*. Teucer emigrated to Cyprus after coming back from Troy, and there founded the city of Salamis. *See* Horace, *Carm.* I.7.

[621] A self-important Roman orator who served as praetor in Sardinia around 105 B.C. He was exiled to Athens after accusations of corruption (*repetundae*, extortion of money from those subject to an official) were made against him.

As for who was happier, did Plato prevail over Xenocrates, or did Polemo outclass Arcesilas? How much can a society that expels its good and wise members really be worth? Take the example of Damaratus, father of our King Tarquin. Because he could not bear the tyranny of Cypselus,[622] he fled Corinth for Tarquinii, established himself there, and fathered children. Was it irrational for him to choose freedom in exile instead of servitude in his native land?

38. Now once minds have been brought towards pleasure, the disturbances of the mind—its anxieties and stresses—are eased by the inability to remember things. Thus it was reasonable for Epicurus to dare to say that the wise man always has more goods, because he always has pleasures. From this he thinks we should infer what we are looking for: that the wise man is always happy. Here someone might ask, "Even if he has lost the use of his eyes or ears?" The answer is yes—for the wise man looks down on these very things.

In the first place, let us consider this horrible blindness: what pleasures does it not experience? Some allege that other pleasures are found in the senses. But the things perceived by our sight do not depend on the pleasure experienced by the eyes, as is the case when we taste, smell, touch, and hear. In these situations, the body part experiencing the sensation also experiences the pleasure; but with the eyes, it does not work this way. For it is the mind that takes in what we see.

The mind may find pleasure in many different ways, even if one loses the ability to see. Here I am talking about a learned and erudite man, someone whose very existence is the activity of the mind. The wise man's thinking hardly ever needs the assistance of the eyes in his investigations. For if night does not deprive him of a happy life, why would a day similar to night deprive him of it? The following comment by the Cyrenaic philosopher Antipater[623] is a bit lewd, but its meaning is not irrelevant. When some foolish women were expressing anguish over his blindness, he said, "What is your problem? Does it seem to you that there is no pleasure at night?"

The venerable statesman Appius[624] was blind for many years. We know from the magistracies he filled, and from his actions, that he in

---

[622] Cypselus, a 7th cent. Corinthian tyrant who ruled for about thirty years; he was succeeded in 627 B.C. by his son Periander.
[623] Antipater of Cyrene (fl. 4th cent. B.C.), a follower of the school of Aristippus. *See* Diog. Laert. II.86.
[624] Appius Claudius Caecus ("The Blind") (c. 340 B.C.—c. 280 B.C.), Roman statesman and reformer, served as consul twice (307 B.C. and 296 B.C.) and once as dictator (c. 285 B.C.).

no way lacked the capacity to carry out his public and private responsibilities. We hear that Caius Drusus's[625] house was constantly filled with clients. When people who had problems to handle could not see for themselves, they employed a blind man as a guide. When I was a boy, the blind ex-praetor Cnaeus Aufidius[626] stated his opinions in the senate and was prepared to help his friends in their deliberations. He also wrote a work of history in Greek, and had an intimate familiarity with literary culture.

39. The blind Stoic Diodotus[627] lived for many years at my residence. It seems hardly believable, but he committed himself more intensely to philosophy than he had before, played the lyre just like the Pythagoreans, and had books read to him day and night, for his study of them did not require the use of his eyes. He also accomplished what seems hardly possible without vision: he continued teaching geometry, verbally instructing his students on the correct places to start and finish the lines they drew.

We are told that Asclepiades[628] (a not unimportant Eretrian philosopher), when someone asked him what blindness had done for him, responded that he added another boy to his group of attendants.[629] Just as the worst poverty would be tolerable if one could permit oneself to do what some Greeks do every day, so blindness could easily be endured if assistance with one's physical limitations were not lacking. Of course when Democritus lost his vision, he was unable to discern white from black. Nevertheless he could discern good from bad, just from unjust, morally good from morally corrupt, advantageous from disadvantageous, and great from small. He was allowed to live happily without seeing differences of color; he was not allowed to do this without a proper conception of things. And this man thought that the vision of the eyes *impeded* the perception of the mind. While other men often could not tell what was in front of their feet, he roamed through unbounded infinity, with no limits imposed on his explorations.

---

[625] Caius Livius Drusus (jurist and orator, brother of the reformist tribune Marcus Livius Drusus). *See* Val. Max. VIII.7.4.

[626] Praetor around 107 B.C. Mentioned by Cicero in *On Moral Ends* V.19.

[627] Stoic philosopher (?—59 B.C.) who lived in Cicero's house and instructed him on Stoicism and logic.

[628] Asclepiades of Phlius (c. 350 B.C.—c. 270 B.C.), Greek philosopher. *See* Diog. Laert. II.126. The Eretrian school was an obscure school founded by Phaedo of Elis, a student of Socrates; it was later relocated to Eretria by Phaedo's student Menedemus.

[629] I.e., attendants to help alleviate the inconvenience of his blindness.

Tradition holds also that Homer had been blind. But we see his painting, not his poetry: for what region, what shore, what locale in Greece, what dimension or form of fighting, what battle-line drawn up, what rowing of oarsmen, what movements of men and animals, has he not portrayed so brilliantly that he allows us to see the things that he himself could not see? What do you say to this? Do we believe either that Homer lacked any mental enjoyment and pleasure, or that any learned man lacked these things? Or if this were not the case, would Anaxagoras or Democritus himself have abandoned the farmlands they inherited, and have dedicated themselves completely to the divine joy of learning and intellectual exploration?

Therefore the augur Tiresias[630]—whom the poets always depict as having wisdom—is never portrayed as regretting his blindness. But after Homer paints Polyphemus[631] as a vicious brute, he also portrays him speaking with a ram, and praising its good fortune for having the ability to go where it desires and access the places it wants.[632] Homer's depiction was correct; the Cyclops himself was in no way more astute than the ram.

40. Is there honestly any evil in deafness? Marcus Crassus was somewhat deaf. But he experienced something more troublesome, which was that he heard himself disparaged (despite the fact that I thought the criticism to be unfair). For the most part our people do not know Greek, nor do the Greeks know Latin; thus we are deaf in their language, and they in ours. And all of us are deaf in the countless number of foreign tongues which we cannot comprehend. Here you may say, "But they do not hear the voice of a singer playing the lyre."[633] Well, neither do they hear the shrill grinding of a saw when it is being sharpened, nor the squealing of a pig when its throat is being slit, nor the crash of the thunderous ocean when they want to sleep.

And if music gives them a great deal of enjoyment, they should first keep in mind that many wise men lived very happily before music was invented. After this, they should understand that much more pleasure can be obtained from reading than from listening to music. Just as we a little while ago introduced the blind to the pleasure of

---

[630] In mythology, a blind prophet of Apollo at Thebes; son of Everes and the nymph Chariclo.
[631] The brutal Cyclops who is outwitted by Odysseus in book IX of the *Odyssey*.
[632] *Odyssey* IX.447.
[633] *Citharoedus*, a musician who sings while playing the lyre.

269

hearing, so may we introduce the deaf to the joy of seeing. For he who can speak with himself does not require discussions with anyone else.

Let everything be heaped up on one man, so that the use of both his eyes and ears is taken away from him. Let him be overwhelmed by the severest bodily pain. These hardships alone are, to begin with, enough to kill off a man. But if they are drawn out over a long period of time, and still torture him more severely than he has a justification for bearing them—then in the end, O merciful gods, what justification is there for us to persist in enduring agony?

There is indeed a sanctuary available, since death is a place of eternal shelter where one feels nothing. Theodorus said this to Lysimachus when he threatened him with death: "You've truly done something great if you've acquired the power of a blister-beetle."[634] When Perses pleaded not to be exhibited in a triumph, Paullus told him: "That matter, of course, is something within your power."[635]

We said a great deal about death on the first day, when we were probing into that subject. When we were talking about pain the day after that, we said a good amount about this topic as well. He who remembers these discussions will be in no danger of thinking either that death is abhorrent, or at least that it is something we should fear.

41. As I see it, in life we should keep to the guiding principle that the Greeks apply at their dinner parties. It says, "Let him either drink, or leave."[636] And this rule is rightly stated. Someone should either enjoy drinking congenially with others, or he should depart early, lest the sober man find himself on the receiving end of the aggression of intoxicated diners. By leaving the scene, therefore, you may avoid the abuses of fortune which you are unable to bear. Epicurus offers the same counsel; and Hieronymus echoes the idea in so many words.

If those philosophers who believe that virtue by itself is worth nothing—and who assert that what we think is morally good and praiseworthy is just emptiness embellished with trivial noises—can still maintain that the wise man is always happy, then what do you

---

[634] *Cantharis*, blister-beetle (*cantharis vesicatoria*) or Spanish fly, used in medicine and as a poison.

[635] Presumably meaning he could commit suicide instead of being exhibited as a captive. Referring to the consul Lucius Aemilius Paullus Macedonicus and Perseus of Macedon after the Battle of Pydna in 168 B.C., where Perseus was captured.

[636] *Aut bibat, aut abeat.*

think should be done by the philosophers subscribing to the views of Socrates and Plato? Some of them allege that the preeminence of the goods of the mind are so obvious that they overshadow the goods of the body and external goods. Other thinkers maintain that these things are really not goods; they locate all goods in the mind.

The dispute between these two sides was normally decided by Carneades, who was chosen as an honorary mediator. Since everything that the Peripatetics saw as goods were also seen by the Stoics as benefits, and since the Peripatetics nevertheless did not assign more worth to riches, good health, and other things of the same type than the Stoics did, he denied that there was a valid reason for a dispute between them, since what matters is the *essence* of the issue, not words. So let the philosophers of the other schools discover how they can obtain this result. For me it is gratifying that, when speaking about the wise man's perpetual ability to live rightly, they make a statement worthy of being said by philosophers.

But because tomorrow morning is the time for us to go our separate ways, let us remember the discussions we had in the past five days. I am, in fact, inclined to preserve them in writing myself. In what better way can I make use of my leisure time, however I may have acquired it? I will send a copy of these five books to my friend Brutus, who not only urged me to write about philosophy, but indeed incited me to do it. I cannot easily judge how useful my efforts will be to others. Nevertheless, for the grim sufferings and various adversities that surround me completely, no other source of relief could have been devised.

Frontispiece of the illustrated Topographia Italiae *(Frankfurt, 1688)*

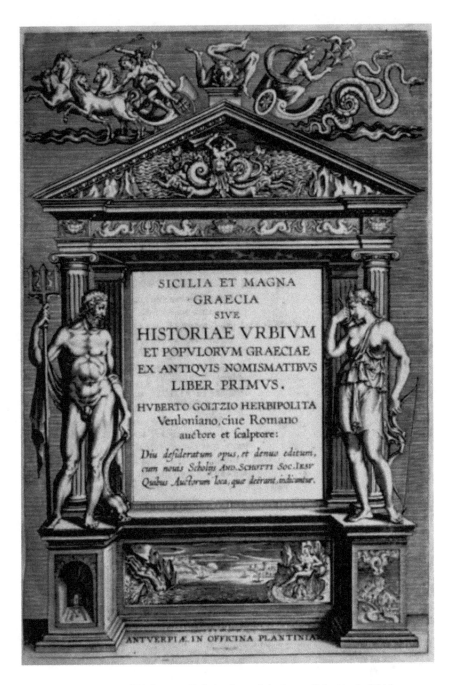

SICILIA ET MAGNA
·GRAECIA
SIVE
HISTORIAE VRBIVM
ET POPVLORVM GRAECIAE
EX ANTIQVIS NOMISMATIBVS
LIBER PRIMVS.

HVBERTO GOLTZIO HERBIPOLITA
Venloniano, ciue Romano
auctore et sculptore:

Diu desideratum opus, et denuo editum,
cum nouis Scholijs AND.SCHOTTI SOC.IESV
Quibus Auctorum loca, que deerant, indicuntur.

ANTVERPIÆ. IN OFFICINA PLANTINIA.

Title page of Hubertus Goltzius's and Andreas Schottus's 1644
numismatic survey of ancient Sicily and Magna Graecia

273

INDEX

A

Acanthoplex, 120
Accius, 64, 84, 100, 103, 111, 126, 150, 151, 160, 171, 208, 220, 246
Acheron, 36, 50, 51
Achilles, 77, 80, 83, 84, 96, 112, 114, 149, 206
Acragas, 255
Aeacus, 37, 80
Aeëtes, 153, 154, 160
aegritudo, 23, 24, 25, 144
Aelius Sextus, 41
Aeneas, 112
Aeneid, 36, 204
Aeschines, 171
Aeschylus, 15, 106, 126, 179
Aesculapius, 114
Aesopus, 115, 208
Aetolia, 33, 104
Afranius, 202, 209
Africanus, 34, 70, 88, 127, 205, 245
Agamedes, 89
Agamemnon, 15, 76, 92, 171, 191, 206
Agelastus, 156
Agenor, 228
Agrigentine Gate, 251
Agrigentum, 42
Ajax, 80, 146, 155, 176, 205, 206, 207
Akragas, 102
Albinus, 75
Albucius, 266
Alcibiades, 179, 180, 222
Alcmaeon, 146
Alexander, 122, 151, 221, 260, 262
Amphiaraus, 126
Anacharsis, 228, 260
Anacreon, 217
Anacyndaraxes, 263
Anaxagoras, 83, 155, 169, 229, 251, 269
Anaxarchus, 122
Andromacha, 166, 167
Andromache, 56, 72, 83
Anticlea, 243
Antiochus, 19, 26, 170, 234, 266
Antiochus of Ascalon, 19, 170, 234
Antipater, 266, 267
Antisthenes, 236
Apollo, 41, 57, 67, 89, 218, 269

Apologia, 66
Appius, 51, 185, 267
Aquinius, 250
Arcesilas, 266, 267
Archelaus, 229, 239
Archilaus I of Macedon, 239
Archilochus, 33
Archimedes, 62, 138, 250
Archytas, 221, 250
Argo, 55
Argos, 33, 104, 126, 167
Arion, 128
Aristippus, 23, 72, 82, 101, 154, 267
Aristo, 101, 102, 236, 238, 258
Aristomache, 248
Aristomachus, 90
Aristophanes, 193
Aristotle, 35, 42, 43, 53, 55, 63, 65, 70, 78, 99, 133, 151, 174, 237, 240, 259, 264, 266
Aristoxenus, 42, 44, 53, 57
Arpinum, 5, 131, 251, 254
Arruns, 75, 205
Artemis, 92, 112
Artemisia, 178
Asclepiades, 268
Asculum, 75
Athamas, 146
Athena, 146
Athens, 19, 33, 53, 60, 66, 78, 80, 82, 83, 86, 91, 102, 108, 159, 193, 228, 234, 237, 258, 260, 263, 264, 266
Atilius, 39, 193, 231
Atlas, 106, 133, 228
Atreus, 85, 86, 100, 208, 220, 246
Aulus Gellius, 33, 88, 128, 168

B

Bacchus, 46, 90
Bellerophon, 171
Bias, 228
Bion, 171
Biton, 89
Boeotia, 89, 92
Boii, 75
Bosporus, 55
Bug River, 78

C

Cadmus, 46
Caecilius, 39, 48, 72, 168, 215
Caius Amafinius, 34, 186
Caius Caesar, 247
Caius Catius, 34
Caius Claudius, 33
Caius Drusus, 268
Caius Fabricius, 88, 168
Caius Gracchus, 164
Caius Lucilius, 116, 156, 204
Caius Marius, 113, 122, 247
Calanus, 122
Calatinus, 39, 87
Callimachus, 71, 77
Callipho, 258, 259
Callisthenes, 151, 235
Calydon, 104
Cannae, 75
Carbo, 34
Caria, 77, 178
Carthage, 88, 167, 205, 231, 258
Cassiopeia, 228
Castor, 46
Cato, 12, 33, 34, 67, 81, 87, 165, 175, 185, 238
Catulus, 247
Caucasus, 107, 108, 122, 228, 255
Celeus, 80
Celtiberi, 128
centaur, 76, 104
Cepheus, 228
Cerberus, 36, 38, 106
Ceres, 80
Chalcedon, 42, 237
Chaldeans, 78
Chariclo, 269
Charmadas, 60
Charon, 36
Chilon, 228
Chremes, 172
Chrysippus, 86, 135, 166, 170, 178, 180, 188, 193, 207, 213, 217, 266
Chrysis, 215
Cimbri, 128, 247
Cineas, 60
Cinna, 246, 247
Cisalpine Gaul, 75
Clastidium, 205
Clazomenae, 83
Cleanthes, 86, 125, 126, 178, 179, 180, 266

Cleobis, 89
Cleombrotus, 71, 72
clepsydra, 129, 139
Clitomachus, 99, 167, 266
Clitus, 221
Clymene, 80
Clytemnestra, 92, 146
Cnaeus Aufidius, 268
Cnaeus Cornelius Scipio, 75
Cnaeus Octavius, 247
Cnaeus Pompeius, 38, 173
Cnaeus Servilius Geminus, 75
Cocytus, 36
Consolation, 63, 68, 90, 175, 179, 213
Controversiae, 109
Corinth, 43, 80, 154, 167, 197, 228, 267
Corinthian bronze, 197
Cornelius Nepos, 1, 33, 100, 125, 263
Corupedium, 82
cottabus, 79
Crantor, 90, 147, 176, 266
Crassus, 39, 70, 156, 247
Cresphontes, 90
Crete, 37, 112
Critias, 78, 79
Crito, 66, 82
Critolaus, 245, 258
Cronos, 104
Cumae, 51, 154
Cypselus, 267
Cyrenaics, 24, 154, 157, 166, 169, 178
Cyrene, 71, 72, 82, 186, 267
Cyropaedia, 263

D

Damaratus, 267
Damocles, 249
Damon, 250
Darius III, 262
De Caelo, 63
De Oratore, 247
De Philosophia, 63
De Re Publica, 58, 184, 217
De Tranquilitate Animi, 70
Decii, 125
declamatio, 35
Deianira, 104, 105
Deiphilus, 84, 85
Delphi, 41, 89
Democritus, 44, 53, 71, 122, 202, 209, 251, 264, 268, 269
Demosthenes, 37, 171, 202, 209, 264

Deucalion, 43
Diagoras, 88
Dicaearchus, 43, 44, 53, 57, 68, 217
Dinomachus, 258
Dio Cassius, 38
Diodotus, 19, 268
Diogenes, 83, 122, 168, 186, 245, 260
Diogenes Laertius, 40, 161, 180, 265, 267, 268
Diomedes, 80
Dionysius, 90, 108, 125, 126, 149, 150, 154, 248, 249, 250, 251, 262
Dioscuri, 46
Doris, 248

E

Eleusinian Mysteries, 80
Eleusis, 80, 91
Empedocles, 42, 53
Endymion, 77
Ennius, 33, 45, 46, 49, 55, 56, 65, 72, 83, 85, 92, 96, 114, 143, 153, 155, 167, 168, 169, 172, 191, 206, 217, 220, 235, 245
ennoiai, 59
Epaminondas, 33, 48, 87, 92, 125, 244
Ephesus, 33, 265
Ephyra, 37, 80
Epicharmus, 40
Epicurus, 71, 98, 101, 102, 103, 109, 117, 118, 119, 135, 154, 157, 158, 159, 160, 161, 162, 164, 165, 178, 180, 216, 236, 238, 254, 258, 259, 260, 261, 266, 267, 270
Epigoni, 126
Epinausimache, 84
Epirus, 36, 50, 72, 88
Epitaphios, 239
Erginus, 89
Erillus, 258
Erymanthian boar, 106
Erymanthus, 206
Euboea, 80
Euclid, 233
Euripides, 63, 90, 155, 170, 174, 194, 213, 217
Eurotas, 113, 262
Eurypylus, 114, 115
Eurystheus, 104
Everes, 269

F

Fabius Pictor, 33
Fannius, 200

G

Galba, 34
Ganymede, 62, 217
Gauls, 76
Gorgias, 239

H

Hades, 36, 37, 50, 51
Hamlet, 200
Hanno, 260
Hebe, 62
Hector, 83, 84, 115, 162, 191, 205, 215
Hecuba, 72, 83, 172
Hegesias, 71, 72
Hellespont, 55
hepatizon, 197
Heraclea, 60, 125, 149
Heracles, 62
Heraclides, 228
Heraclitus, 265
Herculaneum, 48
Hercules, 45, 46, 48, 52, 102, 103, 104, 105, 106, 124, 205, 206, 215, 259
Herillus, 258
Hermodorus, 265
Herodotus, 32, 81, 82, 86, 89
Hesiod, 32, 46, 80
Hesperides, 106
Hieronymus, 101, 258, 259, 270
Hindu Kush, 255
Hippodamea, 153
Hippolytus, 194
Homer, 32, 33, 46, 51, 62, 63, 69, 72, 80, 139, 149, 171, 173, 205, 206, 228, 269
Horace, 204, 266
Hortensius, 60, 97, 144
Hydra, 104, 106
hydraulus, 140
Hydraulus, 162
Hypanis River, 78
Hyrcania, 86

I

J

K

L

M

Mithridates, 231
Montaigne, 13, 20
Mulciber, 107
Musaeus, 80
Mycenae, 85, 220
Myson, 228
Mytilene, 69, 217, 228

N

Naevius, 33, 215
Naples, 73
Nasica, 41, 206
Nauplius, 80
Nearchus, 122
Nemean lion, 105, 206
Neptune, 87, 128, 218
Nessus, 104
New Academy, 19
Nicocreon, 122
Niptra, 120, 121, 243
Numa, 185

O

Odysseus, 51, 80, 120, 269
Odyssey, 33, 51, 112, 206, 243, 269
Oeneus, 104
Oenomaus, 128, 153
Oeta, 103
Oïleus, 176
Olympia, 88, 119, 220
On Duties, 1, 12, 32, 53, 250, 258
On Moral Ends, 1, 12, 13, 16, 44, 112,
    119, 170, 174, 198, 238, 253, 257,
    258, 268
Orchomenus, 89
Orcus, 56
Orestes, 146, 213
Orpheus, 80

P

Pacidianus, 204
Pacuvius, 84, 118, 120, 207, 243, 266
Palamedes, 80
Panaetius, 53, 69, 70, 185, 266
Parrhasius, 33
Parthians, 38
Patroclus, 114, 115
Pelops, 85, 86, 128, 153, 217
Perdiccas, 239
Pergamum, 206

Periander, 228, 267
Periboea, 80
Perillos, 102
Perses, 166, 270
Perseus, 88, 166, 270
Phaedo, 42, 44, 66, 72, 268
Phaedrus, 19, 58, 217
Phaedrus the Epicurean, 19
Phalaris, 102, 103, 255, 259
Pherecrates, 43
Pherecydes, 51
Phidias, 49
Philip, 241, 242
Philo of Larissa, 19, 99
Philoctetes, 64, 96, 103, 111, 118
Phintias, 250
Phlius, 228, 229, 268
Phoenicia, 159
Phrygia, 90
Phthia, 43
Plato, 19, 22, 42, 43, 44, 52, 57, 58, 59,
    60, 62, 65, 66, 67, 69, 70, 72, 79, 90,
    98, 109, 136, 159, 162, 188, 202,
    203, 209, 217, 222, 228, 230, 237,
    239, 250, 263, 265, 267, 271
Plautus, 33
Pliny, 53, 55, 60, 67, 69, 162, 197, 264
Plutarch, 71, 89, 173
Podalirius, 114
Polemo, 237, 240, 259, 267
Pollux, 46
Polyclitus, 33
Polymnestor, 84
Polyphemus, 269
Pompey, 38, 73, 126, 137, 173
Pontus, 55, 78, 228
Porta Capena, 39
Posidonius, 19, 126, 137, 266
Priam, 62, 72, 73, 77, 83, 84, 96, 163
Prometheus, 43, 106, 107, 133, 179,
    228
Ptolemy, 71, 82, 262
Ptolemy I Soter, 82
Ptolemy II Philadelphus, 71
Publius Cornelius Scipio, 41, 75, 88,
    205, 206
Publius Crassus, 70, 247
Publius Decius Mus, 75
Publius Rupilius, 200
Puteoli, 73
Pydna, 166, 270
Pyrrho, 60, 102, 258
Pyrrhus, 60, 75, 87, 96

281

CPSIA information can be obtained
at www.ICGtesting.com
Printed in the USA
LVHW081244061122
732479LV00018B/717/J